APR '86   29·00

Option
Pricing

Lexington Books/Salomon Brothers Center Series on Financial Institutions and Markets

The Deregulation of the Banking and Securities Industry
Edited by Lawrence G. Goldberg and Lawrence J. White

Exchange Risk and Exposure
Edited by Richard M. Levich and Clas G. Wihlborg

Securities Activities of Commercial Banks
Edited by Arnold W. Sametz

Mergers and Acquisitions
Edited by Michael Keenan and Lawrence J. White

Crises in the Economic and Financial Structure
Edited by Paul Wachtel

Option Pricing
Edited by Menachem Brenner

Financing and Investing in Hi-Tech
Edited by Fred B. Renwick

The Emerging Financial Industry
Edited by Arnold W. Sametz

Option Pricing

Theory and Applications

Edited by
Menachem Brenner
Hebrew University and
New York University

LexingtonBooks
D.C. Heath and Company
Lexington, Massachusetts
Toronto

Library of Congress Cataloging in Publication Data
Main entry under title:

Option pricing.

Papers presented at a conference held Jan. 18–19,
1982 and sponsored by the Salomon Brothers Center for
the Study of Financial Institutions.
1. Put and call transactions—Prices—Congresses.
I. Brenner, Menachem. II. Salomon Brothers Center for
the Study of Financial Institutions.
HG6042.067 1983   332.64′52   82-47943
ISBN 0-669-05714-2

Second printing, June 1985

Published simultaneously in Canada.

Printed in the United States of America.

International Standard Book Number: 0–669–05714–2

Library of Congress Catalog Card Number: 82–47943

Contents

               Experience in the London Market**
               Stephen Figlewski and *M. Desmond Fitzgerald*   223

               List of Contributors   237

               About the Editor   239

Preface
and Acknowledgments

On January 18–19, 1982, the Salomon Brothers Center for the Study of Financial Institutions, Graduate School of Business, New York University, sponsored a two-day conference entitled "Option Pricing: Theory and Applications." The conference participants included academics and practicing professionals whose main interest and expertise are in the area of options and commodity futures. The speakers in this two-day conference presented the current state of research in option-pricing theory and its applications. This book is the outcome of that conference.

Special thanks are due to a number of people who assisted with the planning, organization, and running of the conference. Dan Galai, Mark Rubinstein, Marti Subrahmanyam, Ed Burton, and Gary Grastineau provided very useful suggestions in planning the academic part of the conference. Paul Stevens of the American Stock Exchange provided help with publicizing it. Ligija Roze, with the help of Mary Jaffier, did a superb job in managing all the conference arrangements, mostly in my absence. Finally, Arnold Sametz, director of the center, deserves special thanks for giving me the opportunity to organize the conference.

Introduction

Menachem Brenner

Option-pricing theory is probably the major development in financial economics in the last ten years. Since the publication of "The Pricing of Options and Corporate Liabilities" by Fischer Black and Myron Scholes, the theory has been applied to the valuation of other marketable and non-marketable assets. With the advent of options trading on organized exchanges the field has become of prime interest to practitioners as well as academics. Many theoretical developments have been adopted and implemented quickly and, in some instances, new theoretical developments have been sparked by the financial market's growing interest in futures and options on financial and physical commodities.

This book is a collection of recent research in option-pricing theory and its applications. The first part of the book, which deals with the theoretical and empirical aspects of option pricing, includes two chapters that survey the main theoretical and empirical developments to date. The second part is devoted to the application of option pricing to debt securities and commodity options. In chapter 1, John C. Cox and Mark Rubinstein survey alternative option-pricing models. They start with the presentation of the Black and Scholes model, which appears to be the continuous-time limit of the binomial model suggested by William Sharpe, and continue with a comparative analysis of several models that are offered as alternatives to the Black-Scholes model. These models differ mainly in the assumption made . about the properties of a stock's underlying stochastic process. They compare by simulation the option values and the implied volatilities of six alternative models and the Black-Scholes models. While in some instances the values of the various models are very close, in other instances they differ significantly. The search for better models is still on. In the second chapter, Edwin Burton, a practitioner and theoretician, presents his view on the adequacy of the Black-Scholes approach for bond options, claiming that it will perform better for longer-term bonds, which are similar to high-dividend stocks. The term-structure approach, on the other hand, is too specific to yield more general meaningful results. If prices of assets are related to short-term interest rates, then Black-Scholes is inadequate and we need a more general approach that permits stochastic dependence between the prices and the short-term rates.

In chapter 3, Dan Galai provides a survey of empirical tests of option-pricing models. The survey opens with a discussion of the various problems associated with testing the validity of option-pricing models. Then, tests of the boundary conditions for call options are analyzed. The various approaches to validate option-pricing models, the models, and the tests of these models are described in the next three sections. A short section on models and tests for put options is also presented. The final section discusses future directions in empirical testing of option markets. The major conclusions of the survey regarding the Black-Scholes model are: (a) the model performs well for at-the-money options but consistent deviations are observed for away-from-the-money options and (b) no alternative model consistently offers better predictions.

In chapter 4, Robert Jarrow and Andrew Rudd present some empirical tests of the approximate option-valuation model that they have developed in an earlier paper. The model provides a general formula for an option when the underlying security follows an arbitrary stochastic process. Their main conclusion from testing this model is that the knowledge of variance, skewness, and kurtosis adjustments enables the investor on average to improve the Black-Scholes option value as a predictor of the option's price.

In chapter 5, Edward Blomeyer and Robert Klemkosky present tests of the Black-Scholes and Roll valuation models. The observed deviation of American call-option prices from Black-Scholes values is attributed partly to the violation of one of the basic assumptions of the model, the no-dividends assumption. Roll developed a model for American call options and this chapter compares the performance of these two valuation models. The overall conclusion of the chapter is that the Black-Scholes model is as good as Roll's more complex model even for high-dividend-yield stocks. The conclusion coincides with Burton's casual observation on the adequacy of Black-Scholes to stocks with high-dividend yield.

The first chapter in the second part of the book is by Michael Brennan and Eduardo Schwartz. They first present a bond-pricing model that relies on the assumption that there are only two independent stochastic factors that determine bond prices. In the spirit of the option-pricing model and arbitrage-pricing theory they place restrictions, implied by the above assumption, on the relative rates of return on bonds of different coupon and maturity. The resulting partial-differential equation yields bond prices and a yield curve. The rest of the chapter is concerned with estimating the parameters of the underlying stochastic process, with the ability of the model to predict bond prices, and with the efficiency of the bond market. The relationship between pricing errors and bond returns may suggest market inefficiency.

In chapter 7, Richard Brealey, Stewart Hodges, and Michael Selby deal with the risk of bank-loan portfolios. They look at the distribution of returns on a diversified-loan portfolio and at the factors that affect returns. Based on the idea that any corporate liability could be viewed as a combination of options they analyze coupon debt, in the spirit of Merton's paper, on a risky pure-discount bond. Since the distribution of returns is analytically intractable, they employ simulation to estimate the behavior of such a portfolio. The simulations show that the returns possess negative skewness and substantial leptokurtosis, that high diversification in loan portfolios is justified, and that the risk in these portfolios is sensitive to even minor changes in lending policy.

In chapter 8, James Hoag presents a study that uses the option-pricing framework to value commodity options. The analysis considers the factors that are relevant for spot and future prices and provides the stochastic processes that determine the nature of the solution for commodity-option prices. Empirical evidence on the efficiency of the market is considered by comparing the theoretical-model prices to the actual market prices and by looking for riskless arbitrage profits. The option-pricing model provides estimates that are in agreement with the prices of traded options.

In chapter 9, Stephen Figlewski and Desmond Fitzgerald analyze market premiums for cocoa- and sugar-futures contracts in London in 1980–1981. Premium values are found to be widely different from values derived from the Black valuation model for commodity options. Buying undervalued and selling overvalued options in a hedged-portfolio context appears to generate excess returns over and above the riskless rate of interest, and the risk of such returns is very low. Some possible explanations for these results are described. They conclude that the extent of model-based arbitrage trading in this market is very small.

In summary, this book provides the reader with an up-to-date report on the theoretical and empirical developments in option pricing and its applications. With the increasing interest in financial futures and commodity options, we should see an increasing wave of research on the application of the option-pricing framework to these new securities.

**Part I
Option Pricing: Theory
and Empirical Research**

1

A Survey of Alternative Option-Pricing Models

John C. Cox and
Mark Rubinstein

An *option* is a security that gives its owner the right to trade in a fixed number of shares of a specified common stock at a fixed price at any time on or before a given date. The act of making this transaction is referred to as *exercising the option*. The fixed price is termed the *striking price*, and the given date, the *expiration date*. A *call* option gives the right to buy shares; a *put* option gives the right to sell shares.

Options have been traded for centuries, but they remained relatively obscure financial instruments until the introduction of exchange-traded options in 1973. Since then, options trading has enjoyed an expansion unprecedented in U.S. securities markets. Today, in terms of share equivalents, listed-options trading is comparable to the volume of trading in all stocks on the New York Stock Exchange.

Option-pricing theory has a long and illustrious history, but it also underwent a revolutionary change in 1973. At that time, Fischer Black and Myron Scholes presented the first completely satisfactory equilibrium option-pricing model. In the same year, Robert Merton extended their model in several important ways. Later, in 1975, William Sharpe suggested an intuitively appealing way to simplify many of these developments. This work has formed the basis for the subsequent academic studies surveyed in this chapter.

Black-Scholes Option Pricing

Suppose we divide the time to expiration t of an option into n equal periods, each lasting time $h \equiv t/n$:

Assume that the stock price underlying the option follows a stationary multiplicative binomial process over each period:

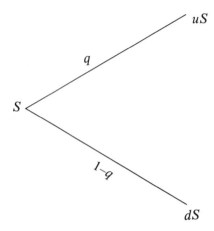

where S is the stock price at the beginning of the period and uS is the stock price at the end of the period with subjective probability q, and dS is the stock price at the end of the period with subjective probability $1-q$. By convention, we assume $u > d$ so that $u-1$ can be interpreted as the rate of return of the stock if it goes up and $d-1$ as the rate of return of the stock if it goes down.

In addition to the stock and option, we assume a riskless investment is available yielding rate of return $\hat{r}-1$ over each period. Thus, B dollars invested at the beginning of a period in this asset would be worth:

$$B \text{———} \hat{r}B$$

at the end of the period. To preclude arbitrage between the stock and cash we require $u > \hat{r} > d$.[1]

On its expiration date, the option is assumed to have a payoff that is a deterministic function of the stock price at that time. If F_n is the value of the option at expiration and S_n is the stock price at that time, then we can write the option payoff as $F_n = f(S_n)$. For example, if K is the striking price, then for a call $F_n = \max[0, S_n - K]$ and for a put $F_n = \max[0, K - S_n]$.

For $n = 3$, we can illustrate this description as shown in figure 1–1.

Suppose further we are free to trade in the stock and cash at the beginning of each period in a "perfect" market; that is, there are no transactions costs, margin requirements, taxes, special costs to short selling, or differential borrowing and lending rates. Let Δ_i be the number of shares we hold during a given period i and B_i be the dollar investment in cash during a given period i. By adjusting the amounts (Δ_i, B_i) at the beginning of each period, we can try to replicate the cash flows from an option.

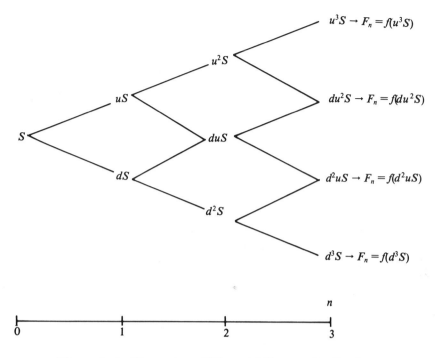

Figure 1–1. Illustration of Binomial Process for Stock

At each node i along the stock-price tree, the value of this replicating portfolio will be $F_i = S_i\Delta_i + B_i$. Over period i, this portfolio experiences returns:

$$F_i = S_i\Delta_i + B_i$$

$$F^u_{i+1} = uS_i\Delta_i + \hat{r}B_i$$

$$F^d_{i+1} = dS_i\Delta_i + \hat{r}B_i.$$

Next, in period $i + 1$, without depositing or withdrawing our own funds, we reinvest F_{i+1} by again choosing Δ_{i+1} and B_{i+1}.

If we start recursively at the end of the tree and work backwards toward the current period, at period i we will know the values of F^u_{i+1} and F^d_{i+1}. From these, using the equations in the preceding diagram, we can derive the following recursion rule:

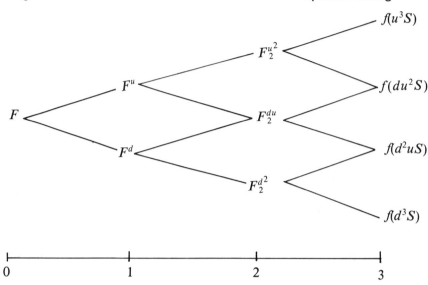

Figure 1–2. Illustration of Derived Binomial Process for Option

$$\Delta_i = \frac{F_{i+1}^u - F_{i+1}^d}{(u - d)S_i} \quad B_i = \frac{uF_{i+1}^d - dF_{i+1}^u}{(u - d)\hat{r}}$$

and using these:

$$F_i = S_i\Delta_i + B_i = \frac{pF_{i+1}^u + (1 - p)F_{i+1}^d}{\hat{r}}$$

where

$$p \equiv \frac{\hat{r} - d}{u - \hat{r}} \cdot \quad \frac{r - d}{u - d}$$

Proceeding in this way, we can trace out a corresponding tree for the value of the replicating portfolio as shown in figure 1–2.

Since the replicating portfolio experiences the same cash flows after the current date as the option, if there are to be no arbitrage opportunities, the initial investment F required to establish the replicating strategy must equal the current market price of the option.[2]

For some types of options, the initial investment in the replicating strategy has a simple analytic formulation. For example, for a European call option, the replicating strategy with n periods until expiration is:

$$\Delta = \phi[a;n,p'] \text{ and } B = -Kr^{-n}\phi[a;n,p]$$

where ϕ is the complementary binomial distribution function:

$$\phi[a;n,p] = \sum_{j=a}^{n} \frac{n!}{j!(n-j)!} p^j(1-p)^{n-j},$$

$p \equiv (\hat{r} - d)/(u - d)$, $p' \equiv (u/\hat{r})p$ and a is the smallest nonnegative integer greater than $\log(K/Sd^n)/\log(u/d)$. This means the current value of the call must be:

$$C = S\Delta + B = S\phi[a;n,p'] - Kr^{-n}\phi[a;n,p].$$

If the underlying stock pays dividends and the call is not payout-protected, then we proceed in the same manner except we construct a tree of the possible ex-dividend stock prices over time. If during each period the binomial feature of the tree is preserved, then the option value can again be solved by arbitrage reasoning. This will be the case if the stock's ex-dividend dates are known, and its dividends are either constant or a known function of at-most-time and current and past stock prices. However, except in very simple cases such as a constant- dividend yield, it will not be possible to derive an analytic solution to the value of a European call. Nonetheless, the arbitrage reasoning procedure of forming replicating portfolios and working backwards from the expiration date, will produce a current value for the option.

If the option is American so that it can be exercised early, then we may still be able to value the option by arbitrage reasoning provided its exercisable value is a known function of at-most-time and current and past stock prices. For example, at the beginning of any period i, the option may either be held for one more period or exercised with the cash inflow $g(S_i,i)$. A special case of this is a call option for which $g(S_i,i) = S_i - K$. Again, except in special cases such as a payout- protected American call, although it will not be possible to derive an analytic solution to the option value, it will still be possible to derive its value by a recursive numerical procedure. All we need to do as we work backwards along the binomial tree, is calculate:

$$F_i = \max\left[g(S_i,i), \frac{pF_{i+1}^u + (1-p)F_{i+1}^d}{\hat{r}}\right],$$

which implies the option holder will exercise the option if it is more valuable being exercised rather than held one more period.

In all these cases, the Black-Scholes option value appears in the continuous-time limit holding t fixed as $n \rightarrow \infty$ (or, equivalently, as $h \rightarrow 0$) by setting:

$$\hat{r} = r^{t/n}, \ d = u^{-1}, \ \text{and} \ u = e^{\sigma\sqrt{t/n}}$$

where, in the limit, r is identifiable with one plus the rate of interest over a year and σ with the annualized instantaneous stock volatility. Although the subjective probability of an upward move q over a single period does not enter the formula, in the derivation of the limiting result we set

$$q = \frac{1}{2} + \frac{1}{2} \left(\frac{\mu}{\sigma} \right) \sqrt{\frac{t}{n}}$$

where μ is a constant. This produces a lognormal distribution for the stock price in the continuous-time limit. In the special case of a payout-protected call option, we have the Black-Scholes formula:[3]

$$C = SN(x) - Kr^{-t}N(x - \sigma\sqrt{t}) \ \text{where} \ x \equiv \frac{\log(S/Kr^{-t})}{\sigma\sqrt{t}} + \frac{1}{2}\sigma\sqrt{t}$$

and $N(\cdot)$ is the standard normal-distribution function. Table 1–1 exhibits Black-Scholes call values under alternative levels of r, σ, K, and t. In this case, $N(x)$ is the number of shares held in the replicating portfolio and $-Kr^{-t}N(x - \sigma\sqrt{t})$ is the amount borrowed.

Summarizing this section, we are able to value an unprotected American option by arbitrage reasoning by assuming that through an option's expiration date:

1. The market for the stock, the option, and cash is perfect.
2. Present and future interest rates are known with certainty.
3. The underlying stock's ex-dividend dates are known and its dividends are either constant or, at most, a known function of time and current and past stock prices.
4. The stock price has a known variance of rate of return and has the property that only small changes can occur during very short time periods.

Table 1–1
Representative Black-Scholes Call Values

$S = 40$

| | | r = 1.03 | | | r = 1.05 | | | r = 1.07 | | |
| | | | | | Expiration Month | | | | | |
σ	K	January[a]	April	July	January	April	July	January	April	July
.2	35	5.09	5.56	6.08	5.15	5.76	6.40	5.20	5.95	6.71
	40	.97	2.04	2.77	1.00	2.17	3.00	1.04	2.30	3.24
	45	.02	.46	.98	.02	.51	1.10	.02	.56	1.23
.3	35	5.17	6.08	6.90	5.22	6.25	7.17	5.27	6.42	7.44
	40	1.43	2.95	3.97	1.46	3.07	4.19	1.49	3.20	4.40
	45	.16	1.19	2.09	.16	1.25	2.24	.17	1.33	2.39
4	35	5.34	6.74	7.85	5.39	6.89	8.09	5.44	7.05	8.34
	40	1.89	3.86	5.16	1.92	3.98	5.37	1.95	4.10	5.58
	45	.41	2.02	3.27	.42	2.10	3.43	.43	2.18	3.59

Note: No adjustment is made for dividends.

[a]The January options have one month to expiration, the April options have four months, and the July seven months; r and σ are expressed in annual terms.

Alternative Option-Pricing Formulas

Although widely used among option traders, the Black-Scholes formula is often reported to produce model values that differ in systematic ways from market prices. An example might be the overpricing of out-of-the-money near-maturity calls relative to at-the-money middle-maturity calls on the same underlying stock.

These reports have stimulated interest in alternative option-pricing formulas. While several assumptions underlying the Black-Scholes analysis have been questioned, emphasis has focused on assumption 4: the properties of the stochastic process followed by the underlying stock.

The stock-price movements that led to the Black-Scholes formula had three important properties: (a) the possible percentage changes in the stock price over any period did not depend on the level of the stock price at the beginning of the period; (b) over a very small interval of time, the size of the change in stock prices was also *small*; roughly speaking, although we were certain a change would occur, not much could happen before we could do something about it; and (c) over a single period, only *two* stock-price outcomes were possible.

We will now ask what happens to our option-pricing approach if

1. (a) is false but (b) and (c) are true,
2. (b) is false but (a) and (c) are true,   p / 7
3. (c) is false but (a) and (b) are true,   p. 20
4. (b) and (c) are false but (a) is true.   p 21

*Alternative 1: Stock-Price Movements with Volatility
Dependent on the Level of the Stock Price*

Constant-Elasticity-of-Variance Formula: As we mentioned, we could certainly have allowed the u and d movements of our binomial process to differ *predictably* from period to period. This would be relevant, for example, if a firm's investment policy were changing systematically over time. As an extreme illustration, suppose a firm that now holds only government bonds announced that at time τ in the future it will sell the bonds and use the proceeds to enter the stock market and buy some of the shares of another firm with step sizes u' and d'. Then, for our firm, $u = d = \hat{r}$ before time τ, and $u = u'$ and $d = d'$ after time τ.

This line of argument suggests an even more fundamental generalization. Suppose that we allowed the step sizes to depend on the beginning-of-the-period stock price, as well as the date. Once we specify this dependence, giving the step sizes and probabilities for every possible stock price and time, we again will have said everything necessary to determine the probability distribution of the stock price at any future date.

More explicitly, suppose we now represent the up-and-down movements of our binomial process as $u(S,t)$ and $d(S,t)$ to indicate their dependence on the stock price and time. Similarly, we represent the probability of an up movement by $q(S,t)$. For example, suppose we let:

$$u(S,t) = 1 + \frac{1}{2\sqrt{S}}, \ d(S,t) = 1 - \frac{1}{2\sqrt{S}}, \text{ and } q(S,t) = \frac{1}{2}$$

Figure 1–3 illustrates the path the stock would then follow over two periods if its initial value were 100.

In this example, u and d depend only on the beginning stock price in each period and not separately on time. Although it is still possible to value an option by an arbitrage analysis, the distribution of stock-price changes in each period is no longer independent of changes in previous periods. In particular, an up movement followed by a down movement no longer yields the same final stock price as a down movement followed by an up movement.

Suppose, now, we require the absolute magnitude of an up or down move in any period to be the same. That is:

$$u(S,t) - 1 = 1 - d(S,t).$$

Let $\mu(S,t)$ and $\sigma(S,t)$ denote the limiting instantaneous mean and volatility of the stock rate of return at time t when the stock price is S. If we then set

$$u(S,t) = 1 + \sigma(S,t)\sqrt{t/n} \text{ and } q = \frac{1}{2} + \frac{1}{2}\left[\frac{\mu(S,t)}{\sigma(S,t)}\right]\sqrt{t/n},$$

we can show that, as $n \rightarrow \infty$, the mean and variance of the binomial process approach the correct limiting values. If $\sigma(S,t) = \sigma$, independent of S and t, we could again derive the Black-Scholes formula, as a check on our generalization.

This gives us a general procedure, well suited for computational purposes, for valuing options when the variance of the stock rate of return depends on the price of the underlying stock, or on time as well. For certain types of dependence, we can find an explicit expression for the value of European calls that will be analogous to the Black-Scholes formula. An important illustration of this occurs when the instantaneous volatility $\sigma(S,t)$ has the form:

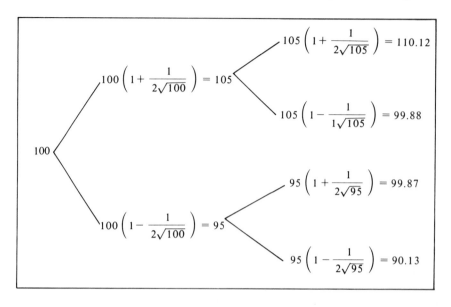

Figure 1–3. Illustration of Square-Root Process

$$\sigma(S,t) = \dot{\sigma} S^{\rho},$$

where $0 \leq \rho < 1$. Observe this implies $\partial \sigma / \partial S < 0$.

This family of processes has the property that the elasticity of the variance is constant,[4] and they can be labeled in this way as *constant elasticity of variance diffusions*. The Black-Scholes case corresponds to $\rho = 1$. For these processes, if ρ is less than 1, the variance of the rate of return, $\sigma^2(S,t)$, will vary inversely with the stock price, a feature that several studies have found to be characteristic of actual stock-price movements.

For the constant-elasticity-of-variances processes, the value of a payout-protected American call can be represented by an explicit formula. Let $(n-1)! \equiv \int_0^\infty e^{-v} v^{n-1} dv$ represent the gamma function. Here n can have any positive real values greater than or equal to one. If n is an integer, then this function simplifies to $(n-1)! = (n-1)(n-2) \cdots 2 \cdot 1$. Now define the gamma density function:

$$g(n,z) \equiv \frac{e^{-z} z^{n-1}}{(n-1)!}$$

and complementary gamma distribution function:

$$G(n, w) \equiv \int_w^\infty g(n,z)\,dz.$$

These functions are used widely in statistics and are well tabulated. We can now state the continuous-time limiting valuation formula as the *constant-elasticity-of-variance-option-pricing-formula*.[5]

$$C = S \sum_{n=1}^\infty g(n,x)G(n + \lambda,y) - Kr^{-t} \sum_{n=1}^\infty g(n + \lambda,x)G(n,y)$$

where

$$\lambda \equiv \frac{1}{2(1 - \rho)}$$

$$x \equiv \frac{2\lambda \log r}{\hat{\sigma}^2(r^{t/\lambda} - 1)} S^{1/\lambda} r^{t/\lambda}$$

$$y \equiv \frac{2\lambda \log r}{\hat{\sigma}^2(r^{t/\lambda} - 1)} K^{1/\lambda}$$

Compound-Option Formula: Are there good economic reasons for believing that the variance of stock rate of return will vary inversely with the stock price? One rationalization lies through the capital structure of the underlying firm. Suppose we assume the *value V* of the firm, rather than the stock, follows a multiplicative binomial process. If the firm has m shares of stock and B dollars in bonds, then $V = mS + B$. To keep this as simple as possible, suppose the bonds are all pure discount debt maturing at date T with face value B. Then the stock itself may be likened to a call option on the value of the firm with striking price B and time to expiration T. A call option on the stock is then an option on an option, which we term a *compound option*. From this perspective, since the stock rate of return is nonstationary, we would expect a modified formula for the value of the call that takes account of the influence of the capital structure of the firm on the stock-return distribution.

We can think of the call as valued through a two-stage binomial process. First, the value of the firm V determines the stock price S at each point in time prior to the maturity of the bonds. With two periods remaining:

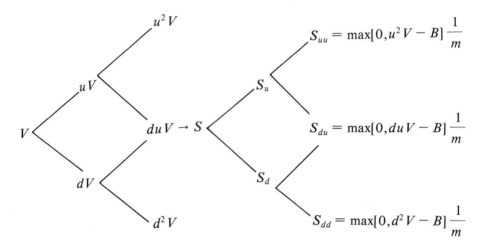

$$S_{uu} = \max[0, u^2 V - B]\frac{1}{m}$$

$$S_{du} = \max[0, du V - B]\frac{1}{m}$$

$$S_{dd} = \max[0, d^2 V - B]\frac{1}{m}$$

To eliminate profitable riskless arbitrage between the stock and debt of the firm:

$$S_d = [pS_{du} + (1 - p)S_{dd}]/\hat{r}, \quad S_u = [pS_{uu} + (1 - p)S_{ud}]/\hat{r},$$

and $S = [pS_u + (1 - p)S_d]/\hat{r}$

where $p \equiv (\hat{r} - d)/(u - d)$.

Now, suppose we want to value a call option on the stock with one period to go (for example, it expires one period before the bond matures). Representing its striking price by K,

$$C_u = \max[0, S_u - K]$$

$$C$$

$$C_d = \max[0, S_d - K]$$

Since the call can only have two possible values at the end of the period, as before we can set up a riskless hedge with the stock. This implies:

$$C = [pC_u + (1 - p)C_d]/\hat{r}.$$

However, this result is different from our original binomial model developed because $S_u \neq uS$ and $S_d \neq dS$. Instead, the distribution of the stock price is more complicated, but can nevertheless be deduced from the stationary binomial distribution of the value of the firm. In particular, by successive substitutions, we can relate the call value C directly to V, B, K, u, d, and $\hat{r}$. Thus, the call value is related to V and B, which determine the capital structure of the firm. More generally, the number of periods until the expiration of the call and the number of periods until the maturity of the bonds also enter the relationship.

With this motivation, we simply will state the resulting continuous-time limiting valuation formula.[6] Letting:

V be the current value of the firm,

B the face value of the bonds,

K the striking price of the call,

T the time to maturity of the bonds,

t the time to expiration of the call ($t \leq T$),

σ_v the volatility of the *value of the firm*,

r one plus the default-free interest rate, and

m the number of outstanding shares.

The current value of the call is the sum of three terms.

Compound-option-pricing-formula:

$$mC = VN_2(x,y;\sqrt{t/T}) - Br^{-T}N_2(x - \sigma_v\sqrt{t}, y - \sigma_v\sqrt{T};$$

$$\sqrt{t/T}) - mKr^t\, N\,(x - \sigma_v\sqrt{t})$$

where $x \equiv \dfrac{\log(V/\bar{V}r^{-t})}{\sigma_v\sqrt{t}} + \dfrac{1}{2}\sigma_v\sqrt{t}, \;\; y \equiv \dfrac{\log(V/Br^{-T})}{\sigma_v\sqrt{T}} + \dfrac{1}{2}\sigma_v\sqrt{T}$

and $\bar{V}$ satisfies $\bar{V}N(z) - Br^{-(T-t)}N(z - \sigma_v\sqrt{T-t}) - mK = 0$

where $z \equiv \dfrac{\log(\bar{V}/Br^{-(T-t)})}{\sigma_v\sqrt{T-t}} + \dfrac{1}{2}\sigma_v\sqrt{T-t}$

$N_2(z_1,z_2;\rho)$ is the probability that, for two random variables having a *bivariate* standard normal distribution with correlation coefficient ρ, the first variable takes on a value less than or equal to z_1 and the second variable takes on a value less than or equal to z_2. $N(z)$ is, as before, the univariate standard normal-distribution function.

By breaking this formula into components, its seeming complication is easily unraveled. From its definition, $\bar{V}$ is the value of the firm on the expiration date of the call for which the stock price at that date equals the striking price. $\bar{V}$ is then the value of the firm for which we are indifferent between exercising or not exercising the call. Therefore, if $V > \bar{V}$, the call is currently in-the-money. Similarly, if $V > B$, the debt is also "in-the-money." When both $V > \bar{V}$ and $V > B$, then as $\sigma \to 0$, $mC \to V - Br^{-T} - mKr^{-t}$. $V - Br^{-T}(\equiv mS)$ is the value of the stock when the firm is certain not to default. If the call is certain to finish in-the-money, then S minus the present value Kr^{-t} of its striking price is the value of the call. To consider the possibility of default and the call finishing out-of-the-money, these three terms—V, Br^{-T}, and mKr^{-t}—are each weighted by a probability.

The compound-option formula generalizes the Black-Scholes formula to consider the effects of firm capital structure on the volatility of its stock. Instead of regarding the stock volatility as fixed, the formula moves one step backward and regards the firm-value volatility as fixed. The Black-Scholes formula emerges as a special case if either $B = 0$ or $T = \infty$. In either case, the firm effectively has no debt and $V = mS$.

Finally, with σ continuing to denote the instantaneous volatility of the firm's stock rate of return, it can be shown that:

$$\sigma = N(y)\,\frac{V}{mS}\,\sigma_v > 0.$$

This in turn implies $\partial\sigma/\partial S \leq 0$, so that the stock volatility varies inversely with the stock price. As the stock price rises, the market value debt-equity ratio of the firm falls causing the volatility of the stock to fall. In contrast to the constant-elasticity-of-variance formula, which is also consistent with this observation, the compound-option formula takes explicit account of this mechanism.

Displaced-Diffusion Formula: Another rationale for a functional relationship between variance of stock rate of return and stock price is contained in the displaced diffusion-option-pricing model.[7] Suppose a firm holds only two assets—one of which is risky and the other riskless. The value of the risky asset is assumed to follow a multiplicative binomial process with movements u and d and the riskless asset grows at the rate $\hat{r}$. If the firm has no debt then

$V = mS$. Let α be the proportion of the total firm value currently invested in the risky asset and $(1 - \alpha)$ in the riskless asset.

With two periods remaining in the life of a call option, if R is the current value of the risky asset; then (see figure 1–4). Again, $S_u \neq uS$ and $S_d \neq dS$, and the stock volatility will be stochastic. For example, if the value of the firm rises quickly it will be primarily because of the contribution of the risky component. This will shift the portfolio composition toward the risky component, and, since its own volatility is assumed constant, this will end up increasing the volatility of the stock. On the other hand, if the value of the firm falls or rises more slowly than $\hat{r}$, then the volatility of the value of the firm will fall. Thus, in contrast to the constant-elasticity-of-variance and compound-option models, the stock volatility and stock price will tend to move in the same direction.

In the continuous-time limit, the displaced-diffusion formula becomes the *displaced-diffusion option-pricing formula*:

$$C = \alpha SN(x) - [Kr^{-t} - (1 - \alpha)S]N(x - \alpha_R\sqrt{t})$$

$$\text{where } x \equiv \frac{\log[\alpha S/(Kr^{-t} - (1 - \alpha)S)]}{\sigma_R\sqrt{t}} + \frac{1}{2}\alpha_R\sqrt{t}$$

where α_R is the instantaneous volatility of the rate of return of the risky component of the firm's assets.

Alternative 2: Jump Stock-Price Movements

Turning now to the second alternative,[8] there are indeed situations where the stock price can have a large change over a very small time period, yet our arbitrage-type valuation arguments will still apply. These situations, as in the Black-Scholes case, are obtained as limiting cases of a binomial process. Previously, as h became small, each of the step sizes, u and d, also became small, and each of the probabilities, q and $1 - q$, became close to one-half. Had we instead assumed u and d were both fixed as h became small, then the stock price over the time to expiration would either have exploded to infinity or vanished to zero with certainty.

However, this was not the only alternative. Suppose, instead, that as h becomes small, one of the step sizes (say, for the upward move) remains constant, but the probability q that it will occur becomes very small. At the same time, the size of the other move becomes very small, but its probability

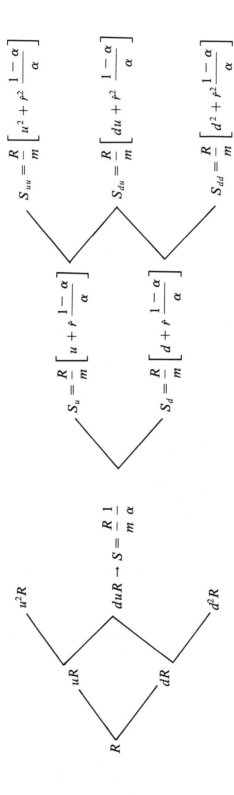

Figure 1–4. Illustration of Displaced-Diffusion Stock Process

becomes very close to one. Such a situation need not be explosive or vanishing.

As an illustration, suppose, in place of our former correspondence for u, d, and q, we instead set:

$$u = u, d = e^{\zeta(t/n)}, \text{ and } q = \lambda(t/n).$$

This correspondence captures the essence of a *pure jump process* in which each successive stock price is almost always close to the previous price $(S \rightarrow dS)$, but occasionally, with low but continuing probability, significantly different $(S \rightarrow uS)$. Observe that as $n \rightarrow \infty$, the probability of change by d becomes larger and larger, while the probability of a change by u approaches zero.

Since this situation is included as a special case of our original binomial analysis, we can find the corresponding option price by taking the appropriate limits of the binomial formula. Let us define:

$$\Psi[x;y] = \sum_{i=x}^{\infty} \frac{e^{-y} y^i}{i!}$$

as the complementary Poisson distribution function with argument x and parameter y. The limiting-option-pricing formula for the above specification[9] of u, d, and q turns out to be the *jump-process option-pricing formula*:

$$C = S\Psi[x;y] - Kr^{-t}\Psi[x;y/u]$$

where

$$y \equiv \frac{(\log r - \zeta)ut}{u - 1}$$

and x is the smallest nonnegative integer greater than or equal to

$$\frac{\log(K/S) - \zeta t}{\log u}$$

a very similar formula applies if d stays constant while $u - 1$ becomes small. Of course, q must also become large to prevent the stock price from vanishing with certainty.

Alternative 3: Multinomial Stock-Price Movements

Suppose that the period-by-period stock-price movements follow a trinomial instead of a binomial process, as we have thus far assumed. The simplest example would be one where the stock price either went up, stayed the same, or went down. Each period we would then have three possible outcomes:

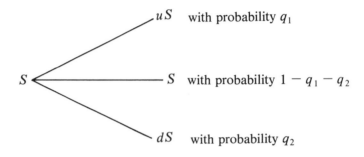

uS with probability q_1

S with probability $1 - q_1 - q_2$

dS with probability q_2

Now we can no longer create a riskless portfolio with a hedge, since a hedge ratio that would equate the returns under two outcomes could not in the third. Thus we could not exactly replicate the payoff to an option with a controlled portfolio of stock and cash. We no longer have a way of linking the option price and the stock price that does not depend on investors' attitudes toward risk or on the characteristics of other assets. Now the equilibrium option price will, in general, depend on these variables, as well as on those appearing previously.

We might now suspect that binomial stock-price movements must be in some sense necessary, as well as sufficient, to derive option-pricing formulas based solely on arbitrage considerations. To value an option by arbitrage methods, there must exist a portfolio of other assets that exactly replicates in every circumstance the payoff received by an optimally exercised option. Our basic proposition is the following: Suppose, as we have, that markets are perfect, that changes in the interest rate are never random, and that changes in the stock price are always random. In a model with *discrete* periods, a necessary and sufficient condition for options of all striking prices and times to expiration to be valued by arbitrage using only stock and cash in the portfolio is that in each period:

1. The stock price can change from its beginning-of-period value to only two ex-dividend values at the end of the period, and
2. The dividends and the size of each of the two possible changes are presently known functions depending on (a) current and past stock prices, (b) current and past values of random variables whose changes in each

period are perfectly correlated with the change in the stock price, and (c) calendar time.

The sufficiency of the condition can be established by a straightforward generalization of alternatives 1 and 2. Its necessity is implied by the discussion at the beginning of alternative 3.

On the other hand, there are discrete-period multiple-state processes that will converge as the length of the periods becomes smaller and smaller to the same limit as a given two-state process meeting the above conditions. For instance, suppose that in the three-state example given above we let:

$$u = e^{\sigma\sqrt{2t/n}}, \qquad d = 1/u, \qquad q_1 = 1/4 + 1/4 \cdot (\mu/\sigma)\sqrt{2\,t/n},$$

and

$$q_2 = 1/4 - 1/4 \cdot (\mu/\sigma)\sqrt{2\,t/n}$$

It can be verified that as $n \to \infty$ (that is, $h \to 0$), this process will converge to the same lognormal process that we obtained as the limit of a multiplicative binomial process. Since the resulting descriptions of stock-price movements would be the same in the continuous-time limit, it seems reasonable to think that the corresponding option values would also be the same, even though over discrete periods one value will depend on preferences and the other will not. Intuitively, it seems that as the length of the period becomes small (that is, as $h \to 0$), this dependence must also become small more rapidly than h. This is essentially true, although we will not attempt to justify it properly.

Alternative 4: Diffusion-Jump Stock-Price Movements

The type of stock-price movements in alternative 2 captures the phenomenon of a discontinuous jump in the stock price, as might be caused by the sudden and unexpected arrival of important information. Such jumps may be important, and the ability to represent them for option pricing may be very useful. At the same time, stock-price movements may be better described by multinomial instead of binomial movements. For example, if a jump occurs, we would want the resulting price change to be itself random rather than constant. We might also want to combine this type of behavior with the type discussed earlier, so that we would have rare and possibly large changes superimposed on very frequent small changes.

This brings us to alternative 4.[10] Now, for the first time, we will not be able to value all options by arbitrage methods, even in the continuous-time

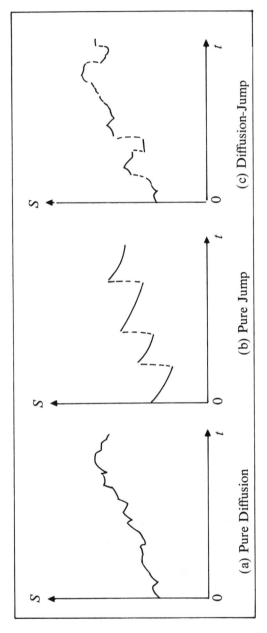

Figure 1–5. Alternative Stock-Price Movements

limit. This is caused both by the combination of continuous and discontinuous changes and by the random nature of the discontinuous changes. This stands in sharp contrast to the earlier cases, where either the changes became continuous in the continuous-time limit or else there was only a deterministic discontinuous change.

It might be useful to pause and depict the alternative types of stock-price movements we are considering. Figure 1–5 contrasts the types of stock-price behavior governing alternatives 1, 2, and 4, respectively. Although (a) is jagged (for example, nondifferentiable), it is nonetheless continuous throughout. In (b) and (c), the dashed vertical lines indicate discontinuities. Observe that in (b) the jumps are of the same relative (to S) magnitude and all in the same direction, while this is not true for (c). Moreover, unlike (b), between jumps, the movement in (c) follows an uncertain path.

In certain cases, despite the impossibility of constructing riskless arbitrage positions, we can still derive an option-valuation formula that does not depend on preferences. Suppose that there is a very large number of securities available, so that each security will make up only a very small fraction of a well-diversified portfolio. Suppose, also, that the rare events that cause sudden discontinuous changes in the price of a stock affect only that stock or, at most, the stock of a few other firms (such as the other party in a litigation or in a merger). The risk of these sudden changes will be diversifiable, and the market will consequently pay no risk premium over the riskless rate for bearing this risk. The equilibrium-expected rate of return on the stock, and on an option, would thus not be affected by the presence of this diversifiable jump risk.

Although these arguments are only intuitive, they can be completely justified. They give us a way to link the equilibrium price of an option with the price of the underlying stock. Let us recall our original valuation arguments. There we constructed a portfolio containing a long position in Δ shares of stock and the amount B in bonds to replicate the returns of a call. We then argued that in equilibrium the current value of the stock-bond portfolio must equal the current value of the call. Suppose that in the present case we create a similar portfolio and choose the number of shares of stock to again replicate the call for the small continual movements. The portfolio would, in equilibrium, replicate the call if a jump did not occur but not if one did occur. But when a jump did occur, the risk would be completely diversifiable, so, in equilibrium, the expected return (but not necessarily the realized return) must be the riskless rate times the amount invested.

This linkage again gives us a valuation equation that must be satisfied by the equilibrium-option price. Notice that even though the diversifiability of the jump risk meant that attitudes toward risk and the characteristics of other assets will not matter, this is still not an arbitrage theory in the same sense as before. One could again realize sure profits if market prices deviated from formula values—but only by holding a portfolio that was not only continually adjusted but also well diversified.

A specific pricing formula is available for one particularly interesting case. Suppose that the stock price at the end of the period can take on these values with the corresponding possibilities:

Ending Value	*Probability*
uS	$q[1 - \lambda(t/n)]$
dS	$(1 - q)[1 - \lambda(t/n)]$
uzS	$q\lambda(t/n)$
dzS	$(1 - q)\lambda(t/n)$

where $\log z$ is a normally distributed random variable with mean $-\frac{1}{2}\delta^2$ and variance δ^2. This implies z itself is lognormally distributed with an expected value of one.[11]

Let us now fix t and let n approach infinity and specify u, d, and q in the same way we did for the Black-Scholes formula.[12] We would then obtain a continuous-time, continuous-state lognormal process upon which are superimposed infrequent jumps that are themselves lognormally distributed. The parameter λ determines the frequency of the jumps. When the jumps are perfectly diversifiable, we can employ the procedure outlined above to price the call in terms of the underlying stock. The resulting formula for the value of a call is the *diffusion-jump process option-pricing formula*:

$$C = \sum_{i=0}^{\infty} \frac{e^{-\lambda t}(\lambda t)^i}{i!} C_i\left(S, t, K, \sqrt{\hat{\sigma}^2 + \delta^2 \frac{i}{t}}, r\right)$$

where C_i is the Black-Scholes value of a call with time to expiration t and striking price K on a stock with current price S and volatility:

$$\sigma_i = \sqrt{\hat{\sigma}^2 + \delta^2 \frac{i}{t}}.$$

Table 1–2 shows how diffusion-jump call values depend on the importance of the jump component of their underlying stock-price movement. This component is measured by (1) the percentage γ of the total stock volatility σ^2 explained by the jump, and (2) the expected number of jumps per year λ. To facilitate comparison with the corresponding Black-Scholes values (middle panel of table 1–1), the parameters of the diffusion-jump stock price process have been chosen so that the total volatility over the time to expiration of the option is the same in both formulas ($\sigma^2 t = \hat{\sigma}^2 t + \lambda\delta^2 t$).

Table 1–2
Representative Diffusion-Jump Call Values

$S = 40$ $\sigma = .3$ $r = 1.05$

γ	K	$\lambda = 1$ January[a]	$\lambda = 1$ April	$\lambda = 1$ July	$\lambda = 3$ January	$\lambda = 3$ April	$\lambda = 3$ July	$\lambda = 5$ January	$\lambda = 5$ April	$\lambda = 5$ July
.2	35	5.23	6.25	7.16	5.22	6.25	7.17	5.22	6.25	7.17
	40	1.43	3.05	4.17	1.45	3.06	4.18	1.45	3.07	4.18
	45	.17	1.24	2.22	.17	1.25	2.23	.17	1.25	2.23
.5	35	5.24	6.23	7.14	5.24	6.25	7.16	5.23	6.25	7.16
	40	1.36	2.98	4.11	1.41	3.04	4.16	1.42	3.05	4.17
	45	.17	1.20	2.17	.17	1.23	2.21	.17	1.24	2.22
.8	35	5.25	6.22	7.12	5.25	6.24	7.15	5.24	6.25	7.16
	40	1.30	2.92	4.06	1.37	3.01	4.14	1.40	3.03	4.16
	45	.18	1.16	2.12	.18	1.22	2.19	.18	1.23	2.12

Note: No adjustment is made for cash dividends. $\sigma^2 \equiv \hat\sigma^2 + \delta^2$ is the total volatility squared of the continuous and jump components. $\gamma \equiv \lambda\delta^2/\sigma^2$ is then the percentage of the total volatility squared due to the jump component. Given σ, γ, and λ, the remaining variables $\hat\sigma$ and δ are then chosen to satisfy these equalities.

[a]The January options have one month to expiration, the April options have four months, and the July have seven months; r and σ are expressed in annual terms.

For the diffusion-jump model, since the stock volatility is stationary over time, this correspondence will not depend on the time to expiration.

For a given λ and σ, as the magnitude of a typical jump increases, γ increases, and the call departs further from its corresponding Black-Scholes value. Similarly, for a given γ, as λ increases, the expected frequency of the jump increases, and the jump component looks more like a diffusion. As a result, the call value begins to approximate its corresponding Black-Scholes value. In brief, a comparison of the middle panel of table 1–1 shows that when $\gamma = .2$ and $\lambda = 5$, there is almost no difference between diffusion-jump and Black-Scholes call values. However, as the jump component becomes more significant in terms of γ and λ, some interesting differences arise.

Comparative-Option Values

Table 1–3 gives an indication of the comparative properties of alternative option-pricing formulas. All call values are based on an underlying current stock price of $50 and a discrete annualized rate of interest of 7 percent. The remaining parameters in each formula were chosen to yield an at-the-money ($50 striking price), middle-maturity (120 days to expiration) call value of $3.97. For example, for the *Black-Scholes formula*, this implied an annualized instantaneous volatility of stock rate of return of 30 percent. In all cases, no cash dividends were assumed paid prior to expiration.

In addition to the current stock price, interest rate, striking price, and time to expiration the *displaced-diffusion formula* requires two parameters: the current proportion α of the assets of the firm invested in risky assets and the instantaneous volatility of the rate of return on these assets. In one case, α has been set equal to .5 and in another to 1.5. In the latter case, the firm can be interpreted as financing additional investments in risky assets by borrowing.[13] To produce an at-the-money, middle-maturity call value of $3.97, it was necessary to set the annualized instantaneous volatility of stock rate of return equal to 61 percent when $\alpha = .5$ and equal to 19.93 percent when $\alpha = 1.5$.

In the *compound-option formula*, in addition to the current stock price, riskless interest rate, striking price, and time to expiration, it is necessary to specify the time to maturity T of the firm's pure discount debt, the debt-to-equity ratio (B/mS) where the debt is measured by its face value, and the current instantaneous volatility of stock rate of return. To allow the compound-option formula to produce noticeably different values than the Black-Scholes formula, T was set equal to three years and B/mS equal to .8. Again to produce an at-the-money, middle-maturity call value of $3.97, it was necessary to choose a current annualized instantaneous stock[14] volatility of 29.85 percent.

Table 1-3
Comparative-Option Values

$S = 50$ $r = 1.07$ $\sigma = .3$

Time to Expiration (in days)

Displaced diffusion ($\alpha = .5$)

Striking Price	10	40	120	200	270
40	10.07	10.30	11.02	11.78	12.43
45	5.09	5.59	6.93	8.04	8.89
50	1.05	2.19	3.97	5.27	6.23
55	.04	.62	2.14	3.38	4.33
60	—	.14	1.10	2.14	3.00

Pure jump ($\alpha = .3$, $\lambda = 1$)

Striking Price	10	40	120	200	270
40	10.07	10.30	10.88	11.47	11.95
45	5.08	5.33	5.99	7.47	8.88
50	.43	1.59	3.97	5.58	6.55
55	.30	1.12	2.71	3.69	4.22
60	.18	.65	1.44	2.14	3.17

Diffusion-jump ($\lambda = 1$, $\gamma = .8$)

Striking Price	10	40	120	200	270
40	10.09	10.39	11.26	12.17	12.94
45	5.14	5.67	7.13	8.37	9.34
50	.92	2.06	3.97	5.39	6.46
55	.07	.54	2.00	3.30	4.32
60	.04	.19	.98	1.97	2.82

Black-Scholes

Striking Price	10	40	120	200	270
40	10.07	10.31	11.14	12.03	12.79
45	5.10	5.63	7.06	8.26	9.19
50	1.04	2.16	3.97	5.31	6.32
55	.03	.54	1.98	3.21	4.17
60	—	.09	.88	1.84	2.66

True formula

?

Displaced diffusion ($\alpha = 1.5$)

Striking Price	10	40	120	200	270
40	10.07	10.32	11.19	12.12	12.90
45	5.10	5.65	7.11	8.34	9.29
50	1.03	2.16	3.97	5.33	6.35
55	.03	.51	1.93	3.16	4.13
60	—	.07	.82	1.74	2.55

Compound option ($T = 3$, $\dfrac{B}{mS} = .8$)

Striking Price	10	40	120	200	270
40	10.07	10.32	11.20	12.15	12.95
45	5.10	5.65	7.12	8.36	9.32
50	1.03	2.16	3.97	5.33	6.36
55	.03	.50	1.91	3.14	4.11
60	—	.07	.79	1.71	2.52

Absolute diffusion

Striking Price	10	40	120	200	270
40	10.07	10.33	11.28	12.28	13.11
45	5.10	5.69	7.20	8.45	9.42
50	1.04	2.16	3.97	5.32	6.34
55	.02	.47	1.83	3.01	3.95
60	—	.05	.68	1.51	2.26

The *absolute-diffusion formula* is the simplest case, other than the Black-Scholes formula, of a constant elasticity of variance model. Since it presumes the stock rate of return is normally distributed, the formula requires the same inputs as the Black-Scholes formula, except the discrete volatility of the stock rate of return replaces the instantaneous volatility of the stock rate of return replaces the instantaneous volatility. To yield an at-the-money, middle-maturity call value of $3.97, the discrete volatility was set equal to 30 percent.

The *pure-pump formula*, in addition to the current stock price, interest rate, striking price, and time to expiration, requires the instantaneous stock volatility σ, the expected number of jumps per year λ, and the downward drift of the constant component of stock return. Setting $\sigma = 30$ percent, and $\lambda = 1$, necessitated a drift of -25.1 percent.

The *diffusion-jump formula* (with zero drift of the continuous component), in addition to the current stock price, interest rate, striking price, and time to expiration, requires the total instantaneous stock volatility σ, the proportion γ of σ^2 attributable to the jump component, and the expected number of jumps per year λ. Setting $\lambda = 1$ and $\gamma = .8$, necessitated setting $\sigma = 31.8$ percent to produce the $3.97 value for the at-the-money, middle maturity call.

To provide an easier visual comparison, a more useful way to compare the formula values in tables 1–3 is given in table 1–4. For each value in table 1–3, table 1–4 reports its Black-Scholes implied volatility divided by .3. For example, the 120-day call with a striking price of 55 is worth $1.98 according to the Black-Scholes formula and $2.71 according to the pure-jump formula. The Black-Scholes implied volatility for this option given a market price of $1.98 is, of course, .3. However, the Black-Scholes implied volatility would be .366 if the market price were instead $2.71. Dividing each of these by .3 yields the respective entries 1.00 and 1.22 in table 1–4.

We can use table 1–4 to make loose qualitative statements about the values of options produced by alternative formulas *relative to the values of those same options according to the Black-Scholes formula.*[15] To do this we will ask two types of questions:

1. Given a fixed striking price, how does the time to expiration affect the relative value of a call?
2. Given a fixed time to expiration, how does the striking price affect the relative value of a call?

For example, given a fixed striking price, reducing the time to expiration has little effect on the relative values of compound options, while it causes out- and in-the-money pure-jump relative values to increase and at-the-money

Table 1–4
Comparative Implied Volatilities

$S = 50 \qquad r = 1.07 \qquad \sigma = .3$

Time to Expiration (in days)

Black-Scholes

Striking Price	10	40	120	200	270
40	1.00	1.00	1.00	1.00	1.00
45	1.00	1.00	1.00	1.00	1.00
50	1.00	1.00	1.00	1.00	1.00
55	1.00	1.00	1.00	1.00	1.00
60	1.00	1.00	1.00	1.00	1.00

Displaced diffusion ($\alpha = 1.5$)

Striking Price	10	40	120	200	270
40	1.01	1.04	1.04	1.04	1.05
45	1.02	1.02	1.02	1.02	1.03
50	1.00	1.00	1.00	1.00	1.01
55	.98	.98	.99	.99	.99
60	.97	.97	.97	.97	.98

True formula

(?)

Compound option ($T = 3$, $\dfrac{B}{mS} = .8$)

Striking Price	10	40	120	200	270
40	1.02	1.05	1.05	1.06	1.06
45	1.02	1.02	1.03	1.03	1.03
50	1.00	1.00	1.00	1.00	1.00
55	.98	.98	.98	.98	.99
60	.96	.96	.96	.97	.97

Absolute diffusion

Striking Price	10	40	120	200	270
40	1.07	1.12	1.12	1.12	1.12
45	1.05	1.05	1.05	1.06	1.06
50	1.00	1.00	1.00	1.00	1.00
55	.95	.95	.95	.96	.96
60	.92	.91	.91	.91	.91

Displaced diffusion ($\alpha = .5$)

Striking Price	10	40	120	200	270
40	.99	.89	.87	.86	.85
45	.96	.96	.94	.93	.92
50	1.02	1.01	1.00	.99	.98
55	1.06	1.06	1.05	1.04	1.03
60	1.13	1.10	1.09	1.08	1.07

Pure jump ($\sigma = .3$, $\lambda = 1$)

Striking Price	10	40	120	200	270
40	.98	.58	.41	.35	.32
45	.55	.34	.24	.75	.92
50	.38	.71	1.00	1.06	1.05
55	1.71	1.37	1.22	1.11	1.01
60	*	1.64	1.22	1.08	1.11

Diffusion-jump ($\lambda = 1$, $\gamma = .8$)

Striking Price	10	40	120	200	270
40	*	1.32	1.10	1.07	1.06
45	1.28	1.04	1.03	1.03	1.04
50	.87	.95	1.00	1.02	1.03
55	1.18	1.00	1.01	1.02	1.03
60	1.78	1.17	1.04	1.03	1.04

*Extremely high values.

pure-jump relative values to decrease. Given a fixed time to expiration, reducing the striking price causes $\alpha = 1.5$ displaced-diffusion relative values to increase and $\alpha = .5$ displaced-diffusion relative values to decrease. Notice also that the relative values of the $\alpha = 1.5$ displaced-diffusion and the compound-option models are almost identical. This is what one would expect if corporate leverage—but not the chance of default—has a significant influence on option prices.

Some Loose Ends

What aspects of our theory of option pricing should leave us most uncomfortable? We assumed *zero transaction costs* in our arbitrage-portfolio revision strategy to arrive at exact option-pricing formulas. Here the frequency of transacting may mean that the exact formulas are very sensitive to the imposition of even small trading costs. Although we do not think this is a serious difficulty, a definitive conclusion awaits formal analysis. This is merely a symptom of a general indictment of modern financial theory. One of the most serious criticisms of this broader theory, of which option pricing is a part, is its failure to give adequate treatment to transaction costs. In essence, positive transaction costs impose some risk on neutral hedgers who must adopt finite holding periods. If these costs are not too high and the hedgers not too risk-averse, then our exact formulas will still prove useful.

Our theory may also be vulnerable to a second set of assumptions—interest rates that are perfectly predictable, and stock-price movements and dividend policies that meet the conditions given in the section that discusses Black-Scholes option pricing. Without these assumptions, our arbitrage operations break down and the derivation of exact option-pricing formulas seems to require additional assumptions about investor preferences and the joint probability distribution of returns of all securities in the economy.[16] In this case, option pricing ceases to be a separable field and merges with the general theory of finance. This is not to say these preference-based models are not interesting. Indeed, they may hold the key to future progress in theoretical-options research. First, they may be less sensitive to the assumption of zero-transaction costs. Second, they may permit considerably more realistic modeling of interest rate and stock-price movements.

For example, despite our assumptions, jumps in the stock prices are likely to be correlated with the market as a whole. In that case, we are forced to use restrictions on investor preferences to derive option-pricing results. Research along these lines is in progress and may produce a superior explanation of actual option prices.

To take another example, consider stock prices generated in the following way: Given the past stock volatility, at each date the change in that volatility is first drawn from a suitable fixed distribution, and then the next stock-price realization is drawn from a lognormal distribution with the updated volatility. This model of random stock volatility, currently under investigation, promises to provide a better (but more complex) explanation of option prices than any currently developed approach. However, the additional source of risk cannot be hedged away, so that it is necessary to resort to preference-based models to derive a procedure for valuing options.

For practical purposes, preference-based models are also necessary to cope with stock-price movements arising from multiple jumps. Of course, if the number of possible jumps is finite, an extension of our binomial-arbitrage argument indicates it will still be possible to write down some formulas based on arbitrage independent of preferences. However, the arbitrage operation will now require a delicate simultaneous balancing of as many securities (for example, the stock and several of its associated options) as there are jumps. The resulting formulas are inelegant, and the prospect of enforcing them through arbitrage unappetizing. Arbitrage with just the stock and a single call is difficult enough!

Notes

1. It is a simple generalization to allow u, $\hat{r}$, and d to be deterministic functions of time.

2. This is explained in more detail in Rubinstein and Leland (1981). For technical details, see Cox, Ross, and Rubinstein (1979).

3. The original derivation of this formula appears in Black and Scholes (1973).

4. In particular, $(\partial\sigma/\partial S)(S/\sigma) = \rho$.

5. Simplified formulas for two special cases, $\rho = 1/2$ (square-root process) and $\rho = 0$ (absolute process) can be found in Cox and Ross (1976).

6. See Geske (1979).

7. This model was developed by Rubinstein (1981).

8. This alternative was first developed by Cox and Ross (1975).

9. Of course, we continue to set $\hat{r} = r^{t/n}$.

10. This alternative was first developed by Merton (1976).

11. We are assuming here that the expected rate of return of the stock, given that a jump has occurred, is zero. See Merton (1976) for a more general formula that allows for an arbitrary expected rate of return.

12. In particular, $d = 1/u$ and $u = e^{\hat{\sigma}\sqrt{t/n}}$. $\hat{\sigma}$ is the volatility of the diffusion component and σ will continue to represent the overall-stock volatility, considering both diffusion and jump components. Of course, we continue to set $\hat{r} = r^{t/n}$.

13. Technically, α cannot be greater than one in the displaced diffusion model because the firm would then consist of assets that could fall in value arbitrarily close to zero and a fixed obligation of riskless debt.

14. As originally developed, the compound-option formula requires as inputs the current *value of the firm* V, and the instantaneous volatility of the rate of growth of the value of the firm σ_V. Instead one can input the current stock price S and the current instantaneous volatility of the stock rate of return σ and then solve numerically the following two simultaneous equations for V and α_V:

$$mS = VN(y) - Br^{-T}N(y - \sigma_v\sqrt{T})$$

$$\alpha = N(y)\frac{V}{mS}\sigma_v$$

where

$$y \equiv \frac{\log(V/Br^{-T})}{\sigma_v} + 1/2\ \sigma_v.$$

For empirically realistic parameter values, a multivariate Newton-Raphson search converges quickly to the solution.

15. Here we use the fact that, other things equal, the higher the value of an option, the higher will be its implied volatility.

16. For an example of such a preference-based theory, which nonetheless produces the Black-Scholes formula, see Rubinstein (1976).

References

Black, F., and Scholes, M. "The Pricing of Options and Corporate Liabilities." *Journal of Political Economy* 81 (1973): 637–659.

Cox, J.C., and Ross, S.A. "The Valuation of Options for Alternative Stochastic Processes." *Journal of Financial Economics* 3 (1976): 145–166.

———. "The Pricing of Options for Jump Processes." Mimeographed. University of Pennsylvania, 1975.

Cox, J.C.; Ross, S.A.; and Rubinstein, M. "Option Pricing: A Simplified Approach." *Journal of Financial Economics* 7 (1979): 229–263.

Geske, R. "The Valuation of Compound Options." *Journal of Financial Economics* 7 (1979): 63–81.

Merton, R.C. "Option Pricing When Underlying Stock Returns are Discontinuous." *Journal of Financial Economics* 3 (1976): 125–144.

Rubinstein, M. "The Valuation of Uncertain Income Streams and the Pricing of Options." *Bell Journal of Economics* 7 (1976): 407–425.

_____. "Displaced Diffusion Option Pricing." Mimeographed. University of California, Berkeley, Institute of Business and Economic Research, Research Program in Finance, 1981.

Rubinstein, M., and Leland, H. "Replicating Options with Positions in Stock and Cash." *Financial Analysts Journal* 37 (1981): 63–72.

2 Observations on the Theory of Option Pricing on Debt Instruments

Edwin T. Burton

The early derivations of stock-option pricing formulas ignored dividend payments.[1] Later, the Black-Scholes approach was extended to include dividend payments in a way that seemed very natural. It turned out that call prices were nonincreasing functions of the level of constant and certain dividend payments. The analytic results assumed that the riskless instantaneous interest rate did not influence dividend payments typically because interest rates were assumed certain and constant over time. Presumably an option on a preferred stock would be amenable to this type of analysis.

Consider an issue of preferred stock of a company whose common stock is owned exclusively by the government. Let us suppose the government guarantees the dividend payments and let us further assume that the government itself is without risk. The preferred stock with a fixed and constant dividend policy is a default-free bond with an infinite maturity. How would a call option on such a security be priced if that option has a fixed maturity and a fixed exercise price? How would a change in the level of the instantaneous interest rate affect the price of the option?

If we were to ask a Black-Scholes theorist about the pricing of an option on a stock with a constant dividend (we might choose to leave out the fact that the stock is a preferred issue and that the dividends are guaranteed by the government—a utility common stock is not, in practice, far removed from the type of security that I have in mind), we would probably be given the following theorems, among others:

1. (B-S) The price of a call option is a *nonincreasing* function of the level of *dividend* payments; and
2. (B-S) The price of a call option is a *nondecreasing* function of the level of the instantaneous *rate of interest*.

These theorems have a practical side in that several stocks that have listed options on American option exchanges also have high and relatively fixed dividends and rather intimate relationships with various levels of government. Black-Scholes dividend-adjusted models seem, at least casually, to fit the observed option prices on these stocks.

More recently, a body of literature has developed that focuses upon the determinants of the term structure of interest rates. Interestingly enough, this literature is based upon a Black-Scholes analytical argument presented by Merton (1973) that derives, under certain assumptions, a yield curve for default-free bonds. Since our preferred stock example is essentially a default-free bond with an infinite maturity, it would be interesting to ask what qualitative proposition would follow from this *term-structure* analysis. The following conclusions seem to be inherent in the term-structure approach:[2]

1. (C) The price of a call option is a *nondecreasing* function of the coupon (read *dividend*) payments; and
2. (C) The price of a call option is a *nonincreasing* function of the level of the instantaneous *rate of interest.*

We could reconcile the Black-Scholes theorems and the term-structure theorems if the price of a call option were independent of the dividend payments and the level of the instantaneous rate of interest. If not, the two approaches lead to precisely opposite conclusions. No doubt in polar cases it is easy to see why these conclusions are so dissimilar, but, in practice, debt and equity blur often in the same security—certainty is near certainty, and absolute is approximately absolute.

There are many securities that could be conceptualized as hybrids of a risky common stock and riskless default-free bond—virtually all corporate-debt instruments and virtually all common-stock instruments with a fixed short-run dividend policy. Is the Black-Scholes approach the right way to think about these securities or is the term-structure approach the better way?

In what follows, I shall review informally the Black-Scholes approach and what I shall call the term-structure approach to option pricing, in an attempt to clarify what is at issue. Later in the chapter I will touch on what I see as the critical issues involved in the term-structure way of looking at these matters.

The Black-Scholes Approach

The original Black and Scholes research published in 1973 has been extended, assumptions weakened, and applications broadened. Let me stay within the original version without observing for the moment the extensions and modifications. We shall assume that the rate of interest is certain and unchanging, that stock prices are lognormally distributed and continuous functions of time .The lognormal distributions will be assumed time invariant with given means and variances.

Black and Scholes constructed a portfolio under the above assumptions that involves positions in stock and its associated call options. The portfolio was selected and adjusted every instant in its proportions so that the portfolio would be risk free .This construction of a riskless portfolio is the key to the entire derivation. The reason for its significance is that the argument that a risk-free portfolio earns the risk-free rate is an argument that is independent of individual preferences toward risk. Hence, this *arbitrage* argument of Black-Scholes was preference independent and therefore the option-pricing formula that followed was preference independent.

The so-called Black-Scholes option-pricing-model formula was not new. It turned out that it was essentially the option price that would have resulted if one merely assumed an option's price should equal its mathematical expected value (assuming that the expected return to the stock was the rate of interest). What was new was that the result was (a) independent of preferences, and (b) independent of the expected return of the stock price.

Anyhow, once the risk-free portfolio was shown to earn the risk-free rate, the mathematics took over and it was shown that a specific formula for the option price as a function of the stock price (and other things) must result. The resulting formula and its modifications and extensions have been very powerfully supported by the empirical data (excepting the extension to put options where, in my opinion, the empirical validation is very weak). What discrepancies exist between the Black-Scholes formula and the data are well known and have been the continuing subject of research. That research notwithstanding, the Black-Scholes edifice is powerful indeed. Let us conclude this summary by reiterating the assumptions that constructed this powerful edifice:

1. The rate of interest is a known certain function of time. That is, there is absolutely no ambiguity regarding what short-term interest rate[3] will prevail at any future time. It is assumed that expectations of those rates will prove to be correct.
2. The price of the underlying stock satisfies time-invariant lognormality. The time invariance is not crucial. That the stock-price stochastic distribution be independent of present and future rates of interest is absolutely crucial to the analysis.
3. The stock price is a continuous function of time. This assumption has been weakened to permit discrete jumps now and then (in fact infinitely often). However the prices of the stock must be integratable in the mathematical sense. (This rules out trading halts when the price of the stock is undefined over finite periods of time involving positive measures.)

Black-Scholes and the Default-Free Bond Option

A glance at the three critical assumptions of the Black-Scholes analysis quickly reveals problems for analyzing options on default-free bonds in such a framework. The stochastic characteristics of bond prices cannot safely be assumed to be independent of current and future short-term interest rates. It is difficult enough to assume, as do modified Black-Scholes arguments, that the American Telephone and Telegraph Company's stock-price behavior is independent of present and all future interest rates. The idea that a long-term government bond's future price behavior is consistent with essentially any future course of short-term interest rates seems ridiculous.

Forgetting default-free bonds for a moment, return to the consideration of dividend-yielding stocks. Is it reasonable to assume that the stochastic price distribution of a dividend-yielding stock is independent of a known and certain future course of interest rates? Black-Scholes assumes this and yet observed call-option prices on dividend-yielding stocks are very well approximated (at least as well as dividendless stocks) by dividend-adjusted Black-Scholes formulas. This is puzzling and we shall return to it later.

Term-Structure Analysis

Interest-Rate Certainty

From our discussion in the previous section, it is natural to explore the possibility that the price behavior of a bond might depend crucially upon the current and future short-term interest rates. If future short-term interest rates are certain and known, then a very uninteresting theory of the term structure of interest rates emerges .Suppose that $r(t)$ is given as in figure 2–1.

According to the function $r(t)$ of figure 2–1, if today is t_0 with r_0 the prevailing short-term interest rate, then it is assumed that all market participants know now at t_0 that at some future date, T, interest rate r_T will prevail. When time T arrives it turns out that r_T is the prevailing interest rate.

Under these assumptions, it is a simple matter to note that this theory exhibits the property that it really makes no difference whether an investor rolls over short-term bonds or purchases a long-term bond. Equilibrium bond prices will equalize the rates of return over any finite interval (in the absence of transaction costs). This theory has the uninteresting conclusion that an investor's rate of return to default-free bonds over any period of time depends only upon the total amounts owned but does not depend upon the differing maturities held.[4]

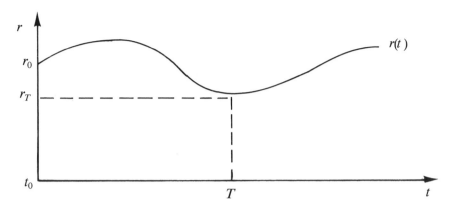

Figure 2-1. Future Short-Term Interest Rates Known with Certainty

No one, I suspect, is willing to settle for this theory of the term structure. It is, however, the only term-structure theory consistent with the Black and Scholes assumption of short-term interest-rate behavior. Obviously the option theory associated with this theory of bond prices is trivial and uninteresting.

Instead of assuming that expectations turn out to be correct, we could assume that market participants learn over time and that expectations depend in some way upon past and present interest rates. The term structure that would emerge from this view would be mechanical and artificial and would carry the paradox that people are always certain about things, that, in general, always prove their expectations to be incorrect.

Interest-Rate Uncertainty

Recently, researchers have concentrated on a term-structure theory that assumes that the future course of interest rates is uncertain and that future interest rates are generated by some known stochastic process.[5] Examining figure 2-2, we see that what is known at time, t_0, is the prevailing short-term rate, r_0. $r_1(t)$ and $r_2(t)$ are two of an infinite number of measurable functions that might describe future rates. Which $r(t)$ will emerge is unknown but is assigned a specific probability.

Discount-Bond Analysis

Suppose that we think only of bonds that pay one dollar at maturity but have no coupon-interest payments.[6] Various researchers have derived the term

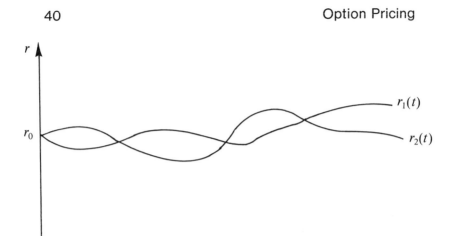

Figure 2–2. An Example of Two Interest Rate Functions That May Prevail
in the Future

structure of interest rates by an application of the Black and Scholes
arbitrage technique. Typically, future short-term interest rates are described
by either a geometric or mean-reverting Wiener process in these derivations.[7]
The technique involves constructing a hedged portfolio of two bonds with
different maturities (it is important to assume that there exists at least one
other security that is instantaneously risk free). The hedged portfolio is
constructed to be riskless and thus must earn the instantaneously risk-free
rate of return. This argument permits a derivation of the yield curve and
hence the term structure of interest rates. There is one important problem
with the derivation, however. It requires an explicit assumption on individual
preferences.[8] The intertemporal preference assumption that tends to "work
best" in these derivations is that individuals attempt to maximize:

$$\int_t^T x(t) \ \log c(t) \, dt$$

where $x(t)$ is an arbitrary continuous function and $c(t)$ is consumption of
goods and services as a function of time. Even though the arbitrage argument
of Black and Scholes is preference independent, the term structure that
results is *not preference independent*.

Options on Default-Free Bonds via
the Term-Structure Approach

Option-pricing theory imbedded in the term structure assumes that one of the securities is an option on a bond of maturity T. It is assumed that the option will expire before the bond matures. The Black-Scholes hedging construction is used to derive simultaneously the term structure of interest rates as well as the pricing behavior of the option. Again, specific preference assumptions are required to derive the results. These results typically imply the following propositions:[9]

1. The price of a call option is a nondecreasing function of the coupon on the underlying bond.
2. The price of a call option is a nonincreasing function of the instantaneous rate of interest and of the average rate of interest over time.

While there are a number of other propositions in term-structure analysis, these two cited above are by far the most interesting, since they are in direct opposition to the stock-option conclusions contained in the Black and Scholes framework. Consider the first conclusion in a slightly stronger form—the higher the bond's coupon the higher the price of the option. The term-structure framework implies that *higher coupons must imply higher bond prices* assuming no change in the pattern of present and future short-term interest rates. It should be no surprise then that call prices increase with coupons since bond prices increase as well.

The second proposition yields a similar interpretation. Increasing present and future short-term interest rates should lower all bond prices with fixed coupons. Hence, lower call prices should obtain. The result, then, becomes proposition 2 above.

In short, the option theory contained in these propositions is really little more than the statement that call prices are nondecreasing functions of the price of their underlying assets. It is difficult to see how any meaningful option propositions taken from term-structure analysis escape this problem. The structure is elegant but rigid.

Conclusions

1. The term-structure approach to default-free bond-option pricing suffers the theoretical weaknesses of being forced to make rather specific

preference assumptions. As compared to the Black-Scholes arbitrage argument for the determination of stock-option prices, this aspect of the term-structure approach robs it of any real generality. (This criticism applies with equal force to the term-structure derivation.)

2. The effort to yield meaningful qualitative propositions about default-free bond-option pricing is made almost impossible by the rigidity imposed by the term-structure framework. The only real conclusion that can be reached involves the propositions that call prices are nondecreasing functions of their underlying asset prices—not a very remarkable conclusion since it follows trivially from the definition of a call option in any context.

3. To the extent that the price of an asset is related in a meaningful way to the determination of short-term interest rates, the problem of option pricing cannot be satisfactorily treated by the Black-Scholes stock-option analysis.

A Final Note

At the beginning of this chapter I made the observation that Black-Scholes prices appear to fit the data on high-dividend stock options reasonably well. I am unaware of any research that tests this implied proposition—that is, the proposition that Black-Scholes option prices fit the data for high-dividend stocks at least as well as for nondividend-paying stocks. Nevertheless, my own casual observations lead me to my current belief.

It is well to ask the question: Why, if interrelationships between instantaneous interest rates and the term structure of bonds are of such importance, does the Black-Scholes model work well for high-dividend stocks that appear to be crude proxies for infinite-maturity default-free bonds? My guess is that the life of the option is short in relation to the life of the asset and that term-structure considerations may not be very important in this case. If this is anywhere near the mark, it would imply that a Black-Scholes model might perform reasonably well in forecasting option prices on a thirty-year treasury bond, less well for Government National Mortgage Association bonds, and poorly on three-month treasury bills.

Finally, the term-structure derivations utilized for bond-option pricing theory simply may be too rigid a framework to yield meaningful option-theoretical results. It seems to me that a more general approach that permits stochastic dependence between asset prices and short-term interest rates can be utilized for a general theory of option pricing for a broad class of assets that could nevertheless admit of some interesting qualitative propositions.

Notes

1. There is no attempt here to survey this vast literature. No attempt is made to give credit to specific authors for specific contributions. This discussion is intended merely as a general commentary on the issues that have arisen in the option-theoretical literature.

2. Throughout this chapter, I use the phrase *term-structure approach* to describe models derived by methods developed by Merton (1971). See also Dothan (1978), Rendleman and Bartter (1980), and Richard (1978).

3. I use the term *instantaneous interest rate* and *short-term interest rate* interchangeably throughout this chapter.

4. See Richard (1978), pp. 35–43.

5. See Dothan (1978) as an example of this type of analysis.

6. See Dothan (1978) or Richard (1978) as examples of this theoretical approach. Assuming a fixed coupon payment would in no material way alter the analysis in these articles. The absence of a coupon payment is assumed for simplicity, I gather.

7. Courtadon (1982), pp. 4 and 29 define each of these processes.

8. If a preference assumption is made prior to an arbitrage derivation , then it is true, as Cox and Ross (1976), Merton (1971), and others have argued, that the resulting theorem may still be preference independent .But , this is not the case with term-structure derivations under discussion. While the Black-Scholes hedge argument does not require preference specification, the resulting equations determining the term structure are absolutely dependent upon the specific individual preferences that are assumed. This puts the term-structure derivations on a very subjective footing that is absent from the Black and Scholes stock-option derivation .

9. See, for example, Courtadon (1982), p. 88.

References

Black F., and Scholes, M. "The Pricing of Options and Corporate Liabilities." *Journal of Political Economy* 81 (1973): 637–659.

Courtadon, Georges. "The Pricing of Options on Default-Free Bonds." *Journal of Financial and Quantitative Analysis* 17 (1982): 75–100.

Cox, J.C., and Ross, S.A. "The Valuation of Options for Alternative Stochastic Processes," *Journal of Financial Economics* 3 (1976): 145–166.

Cox, J.C.; Ingersoll, J.; and Ross, S.A. "A Theory of the Term Structure of

Interest Rates." Mimeographed. Graduate School of Business, Stanford University, 1978.

Dothan, U. "On the Term Structure of Interest Rates." *Journal of Financial Economics* 6 (1978): 59–69.

Merton, R.C., "Optimum Consumption and Portfolio Rules in a Continuous-Time Model." *Journal of Economic Theory* 3(1971): 373–413.

Rendleman, Jr., R.J., and Bartter, B.J. "The Pricing of Option on Debt Securities." *Journal of Financial and Quantitative Analysis* (1980): 11–24.

Richard, Scott F. "An Arbitrage Model of the Term Structure of Interest Rates." *Journal of Financial Economics* 6 (1978):33–57.

3 A Survey of Empirical Tests of Option-Pricing Models

Dan Galai

A decade has passed since the first empirical test of the option-valuation equilibrium model of Black and Scholes (B-S) was published.[1] During the decade, the B-S model was extended and modified by assuming weaker conditions and different stochastic processes for the prices of the underlying assets. While the theoretical advances were significant and noticeable, empirical research met strong obstacles. Nevertheless, in the last few years, there has been an impressive accumulation of studies, as the reference list shows, and the end of a decade is an appropriate time to summarize the state of the empirical research pertaining to the tests of model validity and market efficiency.

Can we agree with Rubinstein's claim (1981, p. 2) that "theoretical ingenuity has long since outrun definitive empirical knowledge . . . The state of our empirical knowledge is in considerable disarray"? The answer is yes and no. While tests in the area of options are not the most efficient, accurate, and conclusive, they have paved the way to better understanding not only of the behavior of option prices but also of stock prices. What empirical research on options has revealed is, first of all, that empirical research on stock markets may have suffered from many problems that were ignored in the past. For example, the question of the stationarity of the distribution of stock-price changes as well as the problems associated with the market microstructure were reexamined in the option literature.[2] Second, the studies helped to demonstrate the importance of data accuracy, showing that even slightly inaccurate data can substantially affect results. This discovery led to the compilation of an outstanding data set, the "Berkeley Option Data Base."[3] Third, while the tests in almost any empirical study are joint tests, this issue was stressed in the option area more than in any other area in finance. Fourth, research on options showed that fine adjustment of data on the one hand, and of hypotheses on the other, is more than today's statistical tools can handle. There are problems, for example, in parametric inference on the stationarity of distributions over time. In addition, the applicability of statistical tools is very limited in cases of deviations from normality.

All of these problems, it should be emphasized, are not unique to research on options. Despite the obstacles and qualifications, several major results emerge from the studies:

1. The B-S model well approximates market prices for at-the-money options with medium to long time-to-maturity, though unexplained deviations from model predictions are still observed for these options.
2. There are significant relative deviations between market prices and model prices for deep-in and deep-out-of-the-money options.
3. No other alternative model offers a consistently better explanation for the actual behavior of option prices over time than the B-S model.
4. Despite the deviations from model predictions, the markets for options seem to be quite efficient in the sense of not allowing a trader to make consistently above-normal profits on an after-commission and after-tax basis.

The various problems associated with testing the validity of an option-pricing model will be discussed in the next section of this chapter. Most of the discussion will concern testing the validity of the B-S model for pricing of call options. In the subsequent section we discuss the tests of the distribution-free boundary conditions for pricing call options. If these conditions cannot be validated empirically, then there is no chance of validating a more specific and restrictive pricing model. The various approaches to validating option-pricing models are described next. The models for pricing calls are presented briefly in the following section, and the tests of the pricing models are analyzed after that. Most of the discussion will concern testing the validity of the B-S model for pricing European call options. In the subsequent section the major conclusions of the tests are summarized followed by a section containing a brief presentation of pricing models for put options and the empirical tests of these models. The final section will discuss future directions in empirical testing of option markets and pricing models. The discussion will assume that the reader is familiar with the basic terminology of options and with the B-S pricing model.

The Problems of Testing Model Validity and Market Efficiency

This section is devoted to the general methodology of empirical-model verification with special attention given to option-pricing models. Before proceeding with the discussion, a few terms should be defined and explained:

1. *Efficient market*—A market (or a set of markets) will be termed *efficient* if no single trader can consistently make above normal, risk-adjusted profits on an after-transaction cost and after-tax basis. In our context, the

efficiency of the option markets will be questioned, given the prices of the underlying stocks.

2. *Synchronous markets*—Synchronous markets are markets in which trading in related assets take place simultaneously and quoted prices reflect this simultaneity. Synchronization, therefore, has two facets: trading synchronization and data synchronization. The former stands for parallel trading in two related securities. This is not a necessary condition for market efficiency, though it may be required for recording arbitrage profits. Trading synchronization is not sufficient for proving market synchronization since data recording may be nonsynchronized. The technology for registration of trades must be such that the data accurately present the timing of the transaction and the time the information is made available to market participants. Nonsynchronous markets, in this chapter, will be markets where quoted prices reflect transactions that took place at different times. More specifically, if data on a class of options and the underlying stocks are used and the price quotes are not taken at the same time, based on parallel trading, the markets will appear to be nonsynchronous, though they may still be efficient.

3. *Above-normal profits*—For a completely riskless strategy, above-normal profits mean profits in excess of the risk-free rate of interest (say, on a government bond with the same maturity as the strategy). Uncertain yield is considered above normal if after adjusting for risk it yields in excess of the expected return. The important point is that the expected return for a given level of risk is also determined by a model, usually the capital-asset-pricing model (CAPM) or, recently, by the arbitrage-pricing model (APM).

4. *Hedge return*—Hedge return is the return from a strategy of buying (selling) an option and selling (buying) a number of shares so that over a short time interval it is expected to be riskless.

5. *Spread return*—Spread return is the return from a strategy of buying one option and selling a number of units of a related option. *Related option* refers to options on the same underlying stock with differing exercise prices and/or differing maturities.

6. *Ex-post tests*—Based on information at time t, a trading strategy is devised and, by assumption, a position is established based on these same prices. The position will be liquidated one period later at $t + 1$ at prices that are theoretically unknown at time t.

7. *Ex-ante tests*—Based on information at time t, a trading strategy is devised, but the position is established at time $t + 1$ at prices that are unknown at time t. The position will be liquidated at prices available at $t + 2$. It will be argued below[4] that an ex-ante test is suitable for testing market efficiency.

Options are derivative assets whose stochastic value is generated by changes in the value of the underlying stock. Option-valuation models, therefore, derive their values from the prices of the underlying stock. For the same reason, measurement of efficiency of the option market may depend on the synchronous price of the stock. How the level of the stock price is determined is immaterial for option-valuation models, but the knowledge of the process generating stock prices is necessary for option-valuation models. It must be admitted at the outset that our knowledge of the "true" distribution of stock prices is rather limited. Many studies have shown the existence of empirical deviations from the common assumptions of lognormal distribution, and the stationarity of the distributions over time is also very questionable. There is no strong evidence in favor of a single alternative process, say, the constant elasticity of variance.[5]

Should the B-S model or the Cox model be rejected due to these deviations from the basic assumptions of the models? According to Milton Friedman, model validity is tested not by its assumptions' approximation of reality, but, rather, by its ability to predict future events better than any competing model. The critical test is the empirical one, and in statistical-inference terminology, the model can either be rejected in favor of another model or not rejected (and the latter is not synonymous with acceptance).

If the option-pricing model (OPM) fails to predict future prices, is it invalid? Not necessarily. It may well be the case that the markets are inefficient or nonsynchronous, though the model itself is correct. If by using a specific OPM above-normal profits can be generated consistently, and these risk-adjusted profits are higher than those generated by any alternative approach, this evidence can be interpreted as supporting the model.

The major problems concern joint tests of the model validity, market efficiency (or market synchronization), and data accuracy. Initially, it will be assumed that data are accurate and that estimates of input parameters are unbiased, with minimal errors. Based on the above definitions the following statements can be made:

1. If markets are efficient and synchronous and the model is correct, we would expect the model to predict future prices well, given the stocks' prices.
2. If markets are efficient and synchronized, no OPM can offer a way to make above-normal profits. The test for market efficiency must be an ex-ante test. Moreover, following a wrong model in constructing neutral hedge positions will yield risky returns averaging a normal return for the given risk (though below what is "normal" by the wrong model).
3. If markets are nonsynchronized and the model is correct, the model should be able to produce, on paper, above-normal profits. These profits

Table 3–1
Joint Hypotheses and Expected Results

Model is Correct	Option Market is Efficient	Markets are Synchronous	Expected Results
Yes	Yes	Yes	Good predictions of options prices given stock prices.
Yes	Yes	No	"Paper," ex-post profits, but no abnormal profits can be expected ex ante.
Yes	No	Yes	Ex-ante above-normal profits are expected. No alternative model is expected to yield more.
Yes	No	No	Both paper and realized profits are expected.
No	Yes	Yes	Less-than- (risk-adjusted) expected profits, though normal.
No	Yes	No	Less-than- (risk-adjusted) expected profits, may be ex-post profits.
No	No	Yes	Potential for above-normal profits, but an alternative model may yield more.
No	No	No	Bad predictions of options prices, an alternative model may show higher profits, ex post and ex ante.

can be recorded for both ex-post and ex-ante tests only if the option market is inefficient.

The expected results for the different permutations of the joint hypotheses are summarized in table 3–1. In general, if above-normal profits are revealed for an ex-ante test, it is an indication of market inefficiency. Above-normal profits for the ex-post test may indicate either market inefficiency or that markets are nonsynchronous. It is necessary that markets are synchronized and efficient to obtain good prediction of option prices. All the above depends, as was mentioned, on the assumption that the data are accurate, and estimates and adjustment of returns for risk are perfect.

The statistical inference based on empirical studies may be further complicated by trading practices. For example, the discreteness of trading with minimum price changes (one-eighth for stocks and one-sixteenth for options) may affect the results, especially for thinly traded securities or low-priced securities. Another source of problems in tests involving options is the adjustment of stock prices on the ex-dividend day for future dividend payments. Because the terms of the options do not change with cash dividends, it may be optimal to exercise options before an ex-dividend day to acquire the right on the dividend. No known analytical model can handle the problems of American options valuation when uncertain future dividends may be paid to the underlying stock.

Another potential distortion may stem from the existence of transaction costs and taxes. The operational OPMs ignore transaction costs and taxes. Even if efficiency is measured from the point of view of the more efficient trader, such as a market maker, the problem of *frictions* in the markets can be serious.[6] The commissions that a market maker has to pay are very small, but he may face transaction costs in the form of bid-ask spreads.

Tests of the Boundary Conditions

All analytical models of options must comply with a set of rules that exclude arbitrage opportunities. These rules define a set of boundary conditions.[7] If, for a given data set violations of the boundary conditions are found, these violations will reappear when the specific pricing model is tested with the same data. The market cannot be shown to be inefficient to weak conditions and, at the same time, efficient for compatible but stronger assumptions.

Galai (1978, p. 194) argues that ex-post tests of arbitrage profits based on boundary conditions can only indicate whether the relevant markets are not synchronized, or whether they are not continuously in equilibrium. To test for market inefficiency; that is, revealing and exploiting above-normal profits by means of arbitrage, an ex-ante test should be carried out. When a dealer observes a deviation from a boundary condition, he must place orders in, say, two different markets to exploit what seems to be a profit opportunity. There is no real guarantee that the prices at the next available transaction will still be favorable for the arbitrageur. Two empirical tests, one ex-post, the other ex-ante were performed to test the synchronization and efficiency hypotheses.

For an American-dividend-unprotected-call option the lower boundary condition is:[8]

$$C(V,\tau,K,D) \geq \text{Max}\left\{0, \underset{i}{\text{Max}}\left[V - Ke^{-r\tau_i} - \sum_{j<i}D_{t_j}e^{-r\tau_j}\right],\right.$$

$$\left. V - Ke^{-r\tau} - \sum_{i=1}^{n}D_{t_i}e^{-r\tau_i}\right\} \qquad (3.1)$$

where $C(.)$ is the value of the unprotected American call that can be exercised within τ periods ($\tau = T - t$, where T is the maturity date and t is the current date); V is the value of the underlying stock, K is the striking price and D_{t_i} is a known dividend to be paid in τ_i periods ($\tau_i = t_i - t$, where t_i is the date of dividend payment). The empirical test of the lower boundary conditions was performed on data on daily closing prices of the Chicago Board Options Exchange (CBOE) options during the exchange's first six months of operation (April 1973 to October 1973).

The major results of Galai's study can be summarized as follows:

1. The closer the option is to maturity, the greater the number of observed violations, the frequency of which is an increasing function of the stock price (given the exercise price).
2. The hypothesis that the stock and options markets are sufficiently synchronized, that simultaneous closing prices are within the theoretical boundaries, is rejected.[9] The frequent deviations could not have been explained by either the assumption of perfect knowledge of the firm's dividend policy or by possible inaccuracy of data. Tests that were run on hourly data yielded similar results.
3. The ex-ante test showed that positive profits could have been exploited, on the average, by a market participant who followed the arbitrage trading rules. The magnitude of profits, however, was small relative to the dispersion of the yields.[10]

Another general condition applying to call options is the convexity rule. Merton (1973a) shows that the European call price is a declining convex function of the striking price. In Galai (1979) the convexity condition is also proved for CBOE options and is subjected to an empirical test. During April to October 1973, on the basis of approximately one-thousand relevant observations, twenty four violations of the convexity revealed that deviations occurred when closing prices were considered, while during the day prices behaved as expected. The lesson is, therefore, that closing prices may mislead the researchers, and if this is true for general boundary conditions it may be even more so for any specific-pricing model.

An additional explanation of the deviations is that transaction costs must also be considered. Phillips and Smith (1980) show that the transaction cost involved in exploiting any deviation from the boundary conditions is between thirty five to forty dollars. Hence, it may be said that if the most efficient traders in the stock and option markets are also subject to transaction costs, the empirical results are not inconsistent with market synchronization and efficiency. But, as discussed above, pricing models should take transaction costs explicitly into account.

Before presenting the empirical results for tests where a pricing model is involved, it should be reemphasized that if the null hypothesis of market efficiency (or synchronization) is rejected, based on testing the boundary conditions, it must also be rejected when a pricing model is used on the same data base. The market cannot be shown to be inefficient (or nonsynchronous) for weak conditions, and, at the same time, efficient for compatible but stronger assumptions.

Approaches to Validating Option-Pricing Models

The complexity of testing model validity was outlined in an earlier section of this chapter, followed by a section examining evidence pertaining to market synchronization. This section deals with different approaches to testing model validity.

A survey of the literature reveals four major approaches for testing models' validity. These approaches will be outlined briefly in this section, while the empirical results will be described later.

The first approach for testing pricing models is by means of simulations and quasi-simulations of deviations from the basic assumptions of the models. According to this approach the sensitivity of the model prices to empirical deviations from the assumptions is tested. Actually, simulations cannot be used for a direct test of model validity; they should be used for examining the robustness of the given model to varying conditions. For example, Bhattacharya (1980) uses the actual distribution of stock prices rather than the assumed lognormal distribution.

The second approach is based on direct comparison of model prices to actual prices. According to this approach, the estimated parameters of the model and the actual observations of stock prices are placed in the pricing model to generate expected option prices. In the second stage the model prices are compared to the actual, realized option prices. The tests are intended to show whether model prices are unbiased estimators of actual prices or whether there are consistent deviations that can be exploited for better prediction or for making above-normal profits. The major disadvantage of this approach is that the statistical characteristics of the time series of model prices or the deviations between them and actual prices are nonstationary. The risk characteristics change with time to maturity and with changes in stock prices.

The third approach, initially suggested by Black and Scholes (1972), is based on creating neutral hedge positions and testing the behavior of the returns from the investment. The idea is to create, with options and their underlying stocks, a position that, if the model is correct, should be riskless. By so doing the problem of risk-adjustment for investment in options is eliminated.

The fourth approach is based on imputing the standard deviations from actual option prices by using a pricing model. It is assumed that all parameters, except for the risk measure of the underlying stock, are known and that markets are efficient and synchronous. By equating the actual price to the model price, the standard deviation can be imputed as the only unknown in the equation. The behavior of the implied standard deviation is then investigated to determine the validity of the assumed model.

The majority of recent empirical papers use either the third or fourth approaches, and most of the discussion that follows will be devoted to them. The survey will follow the aforementioned classification to facilitate comparison.

The Suggested Models for Pricing Call Options

Since the beginning of the sixties, considerable effort has been invested in deriving pricing models for options.[11] Yet only with the publication of the Black-Scholes model in 1972–1973 did the pricing of options become consistent with modern financial theory. The model has attractive features and is easy to apply.

The Black-Scholes pricing model gives the price of a European call option that would be obtained in a perfect capital market when no dividends are expected to be paid on the underlying stock during the life of the option. The inputs to the model consist of four observable variables: the price of the underlying stock (V); the exercise price (K); the time to maturity (τ); and the riskless interest rate (r), and one variable that is not observable, the variance of the stock's distribution of rates of return (σ^2). The model price C is

$$C = VN(d_1) - Ke^{-r\tau}N(d_2) \qquad (3.2)$$

where

$$d_1 = \frac{\ln(V/K) + (r + \sigma^2/2)\tau}{\sigma\sqrt{\tau}}$$

and

$$d_2 = d_1 - \sigma\sqrt{\tau}$$

and $N(.)$ is the cumulative standard normal distribution.

The assumptions needed to derive the model[12] are: (1) there is a perfect capital market characterized by an absence of taxes and commissions, free access to all available information, and divisibility of all financial assets (in addition, borrowing and short selling as well as free use of all proceeds are permitted to all investors); (2) the short-term interest rate and the variance rate of return are known and constant; and (3) the stock price is lognormally distributed at the end of any finite interval.

Cox,[13] rather than assuming the variance of a stock's rate of return to be constant and independent of the stock price, assumes the price *elasticity* of the variance to be constant. Hence, the variance, in Cox's model, is a function of the stock price and the B-S model is a special case where the elasticity is zero. This assumption is based on empirical evidence that the variance of the rate of return is inversely related to stock price (for example, Black (1976) and Beckers (1980)). The model, which yields higher (lower) prices than B-S prices for out-of-the-money (in-the-money) options, was subjected to empirical testing by MacBeth and Merville (1980) and Rubinstein (1981).

Cox and Ross (1976) and Merton (1976) introduced a jump process for stock prices to replace the B-S assumption of a pure diffusion process. Our statistical tools, however, are not refined enough to yield reliable estimates of a jump process, especially if a combinal diffusion-jump process is assumed. Only Rubinstein (1981) offers some indirect evidence on the validity of the jump process.

Geske (1979) regards an option on common stock as an option on an option. If the assumptions of B-S apply to the firm's equity, the value of the call option can be calculated as a compound option. The major empirical problem in testing the model is that the assumption that the firm has a pure discount debt with a fixed maturity does not hold in reality. The required data on the capital structure of the firm is rarely available. Hence, despite the fact that the compound-option model is more general than the B-S model (and the latter is a special case of the former), it has not yet been subjected directly to empirical testing.

While Geske considered the effect of the capital structure of the firm on the validity of its equity, Rubinstein (1980) considers the effect of the assets structure on the validity. Again, the problems researchers may face are, first, data availability on the assets' structure and, second, the unrealistic assumption concerning the simplicity of the assets' composition.

Madansky (1977) offers an empirical model of option prices (see also Gastineau (1979)). The model uses an empirical stock-price distribution rather than the lognormal distribution and also assumes that the variance is proportional to the square of the stock price. The Gastineau-Madansky model requires input data similar to that required by the B-S model and can be adjusted for dividend, interest rates, and commission charges. It is a probability model that gives the estimated option value as a discounted expected future value of the option by means of numerical integration.

Tests and Results of Call-Option-Pricing Models

The initial tests presented in the following paragraphs are based on simulations. The data used may be based on actual observations of stock prices, but this is not necessarily the case. The simulations, which test the robustness of a given model, are useful in interpreting the results of the empirically based tests. Later in this section direct tests are discussed, followed by a presentation of the results of the hedge-return tests. The final subsection contains tests based on the implied standard deviation.

Results of Simulations

It is a fact that the assumptions of the B-S model do not hold perfectly in reality. The question, therefore, is how robust the model is and how sensitive the results will be when deviations from the basic assumptions are observed.

Merton (1976b) shows through simulation of the effects of specification errors on the B-S option prices. Although he assumes that the true distribution of stock prices is a mixed jump and diffusion process, he nevertheless uses the B-S model (with its lognormality assumption). His conclusion is that "the effect of specification error in the underlying stock returns on option prices will generally be rather small. . . . However, there are some important exceptions: short-maturity options or options on stocks with low total variance rates can have significant discrepancies. . . . In addition, deep out-of-the-money options can have very large percentage errors" (p. 345).

Boyle and Ananthanarayanan (1977) examine the implications of using an estimate of the variance in option-valuation models. They show the bias in the average option value to be rather small, even for relatively small samples of a stock's rates of return. However, the dispersion of the distribution of option prices may be quite significant.

Another study that uses simulation to check the robustness of the B-S model is Bhattacharya (1980). To eliminate the problem of measurement errors he uses model prices for options. These values, coupled with the actual distribution of stock prices, are used in creating neutral hedge positions. If the "mathematical structure of the formula"[14] is correct, according to Bhattacharya, the average hedge return will be insignificantly different from zero. Significant excess hedge returns may be attributed to the deviation of the actual distribution of stock prices from the assumed stationary, lognormally distribution, and "would be considered as evidence in support of the hypothesis that when observed stock prices are used as input, the B-S formula exhibits pricing biases" (p. 1085).

It should be emphasized that Bhattacharya does not use actual option prices in his study and employs actual data solely on stock returns. The major result of the study is that options near-in-the-money and near-out-of-the-money with maturities of five days or less are frequently statistically

significant where at-the-money one-day-to-maturity options provide statistically and operationally significant excess returns. This leads Bhattacharya to
conclude that "the B-S formula exhibits no operationally significant
mispricing, except for at-the-money options with one day to maturity" (p.
1094). Bhattacharya also performs similar tests using uniform and Poisson
distributions rather than the empirical one. Again he finds that the "errors"
decrease in absolute terms and in significance level as the time to maturity
increases.

Actually Bhattacharya does not test the validity of the model but rather
its robustness. The title of his paper is therefore misleading. His study is a
continuation of the other simulation studies already discussed, with the
advantage of using the hedge-return approach rather than direct comparison.

Two additional studies use simulation to measure the effect of trading
practices. Bookstaber (1981) simulates the impact on option prices of
nonsimultaneity of stock and option quotations. He finds the problem of
mispricing due to nonsimultaneity to be significant when there are less than
twenty option trades during the day. The problem is less serious for at-the-
money and out-of-the-money options. Boyle and Emanuel (1980) simulate
the effect of the discreteness of trading on the hedge returns and find it to be
rather small in absolute terms. This issue will be further discussed with the
presentation of the tests using the hedge-return approach.

To sum up, the various simulations show that while the B-S model can
give a wrong price for the option if some of the underlying assumptions of the
model are violated, the derivations are usually rather small and on average
insignificant. The deviations usually decrease as time to maturity increases
and as the degree the stock is in-the-money rises.

Direct Comparisons

Trippi (1977) conducts a simple test: he buys all the options in his sample
(30 August 1974 to 14 March 1975) that are undervalued by more than 15
percent against the B-S price, and sells short those that are overpriced by at
least 15 percent. The weekly rates of return are calculated for all the option
positions and are averaged. Based on the result of an 11.4 percent weekly
average, Trippi concludes that the Chicago Board Option Exchange (CBOE)
was inefficient during the sample period.

The major problem with this study, however, is that the returns are not
risk adjusted; considering the high level of risk in options trading, this is a
serious drawback. In addition, the test was conducted as an ex-post test,
while efficiency requires an ex-ante test.

In their initial paper, MacBeth and Merville (1979) analyze the standardized difference between the actual and B-S model call prices[15]

$$\frac{C_t^A - C_t^M}{C_t^M}.$$

For a sample of daily closing prices for six stocks from 31 December 1975 to 31 December 1976, they observe this statistic to be an increasing function of the extent to which the option is in- or out-of-the-money,

$$\frac{V_t' - K_e^{-r\tau}}{Ke^{-r\tau}}.$$

For options that are deep-in-the-money the difference between observed market prices and model prices appeared to be constant and positive. The difference was negative for deep-out-of-the-money options. Regression results of $C^A - C^M$ against the degree the option is in-the-money, and against the time to maturity, confirm the impressions gained from inspecting the individual scatter diagrams.

The authors conclude that if the B-S model correctly prices at-the-money options with medium to far maturities (such as, with at least ninety days to maturity), then the B-S model underestimates (overestimates) market prices for in-the-money (out-of-the-money) options. The extent of the mispricing decreased as the time to expiration decreased.

MacBeth and Merville assume all along market efficiency and attribute the deviations of the model price from the actual price to the weakness of the model, especially to its assumption of a constant variance of the stock's rate of return.[16] Therefore, in their second paper (1980) they confront the B-S model with the Cox model of constant elasticity of variance, assuming that the latter should reduce the mispricing of B-S prices observed in the first paper. They repeat the 1979 tests and conclude that "the stochastic-process-generating stock prices can best be considered . . . as a constant elasticity of variance process" (1980, p. 299).

In his discussion of the MacBeth and Merville paper (1980) Manaster (1980) points out that the empirical superiority of the Cox model over the B-S model is not surprising at all: "Given that the Cox model includes B-S models as a special case, it is clear that the Cox model must explain observed option prices at least as well as the B-S model" (p. 301). He suggests that an ex-ante trading strategy should be perfomed to decide which model is superior. Remembering table 3–1, the reader is cautioned that proving the superiority of one model over an alternate one is complicated by the joint hypotheses' nature of the tests.

Thorp and Gelbaum (1980) also believe, for empirical and theoretical considerations, that the constant elasticity of variance is a better model than the B-S one. But, contrary to the findings of MacBeth and Merville, Thorp and Gelbaum claim that their experience in trading CBOE options while applying the B-S model is that this model tends to underprice the out-of-the-money options. The same phenomenon is also stated by Black (1975). In a cross-section study with more recent data for 1979, they find only small deviations of the B-S model prices from the actual prices. The differences in results between the two studies may stem from changes in the tax rules that occurred in September 1976; changes in the average volatility of the market; better adjustment for the potential early exercise of the CBOE options in the latter study; and/or changes in the procedure for estimating the variance of the rate of return. MacBeth and Merville use the average implied standard deviation for at-the-money options and hence their prices are relative to the average (assuming that at-the-money options are efficiently priced). Thorp and Gelbaum use the historical stock volatilities.

The findings that the parameters of either the B-S or Cox model are nonstationary over time are confirmed by MacBeth (1981) who repeated his earlier work with Merville using 1978 data. For 1978 he finds periods when the B-S model gives good prediction for market prices and periods when the model misprices options in a manner opposite to the mispricing observed for 1976.

In a recent paper Blomeyer and Klemkosky (1982) use the MacBeth and Merville technique of plotting the relative deviation of the model price from the market price against the degree the option is in-the-money to compare the B-S model to the Roll model.[17] The Roll model, which gives the price of the dividend-unprotected American call option, is more general than the B-S model and hence is expected to give more accurate predictions of market prices. Transaction data for CBOE options written on eighteen stocks, for one trading day per month from July 1977 to June 1978, are employed. Based on 9108 observations of option prices they draw the conclusion that the two pricing models have virtually identical pricing-bias characteristics. The results are contrary to the MacBeth and Merville (1979) findings, but consistent with Thorp and Gelbaum (1980); both models undervalue, relative to the market, the out-of-the-money options and price fairly well the at- and in-the-money options.

A subsample of the Blomeyer and Klemkosky study is employed by Blomeyer and Resnick (1982) to test the Geske model of compound option against the B-S model. The Geske model allows for nonstationary variance of the stock's rate of return, and the changing variance is related to changes in the capital structure of the firm. For five stocks they estimate, on a monthly basis, the firms' capital structure and the implied change in variance for the equities. The data for the firms' capital structure are rather crude and require several simplifying assumptions. The results of Blomeyer and Resnick, based on the MacBeth and Merville approach, show that prices based on the Geske model overvalue out-of-the-money calls and undervalue the in-the-money options. The bias of Geske model prices is nearly opposite to what is shown for B-S model prices. While neither model is without bias, the B-S model appears to be less biased than the Geske model.

The tests in this subsection, while limited in their scope and burdened with statistical problems, bring out three important results:

1. The B-S model prices do not consistently give good predictions of market prices, especially for out-of-the-money, near-maturity options.
2. The parameters of the B-S model, especially the variance of the stock's rate of return, are probably nonstationary.
3. Alternative models for pricing options, such as those suggested by Cox, Roll, or Geske, while more general than the B-S model, did not yield consistently better predictions of actual prices than B-S prices. The B-S model, with its relatively simple structure, may be as good a proxy for actual prices as any alternative model, especially for at-the-money options. The nonstationarity problem may affect all the suggested models.

Results Based on Risk-Adjusted Returns

The aforementioned tests suffer from a serious deficiency they all ignore the risk associated with an option position. For example, the stochastic nature of $C_t^A - C_t^M$ in MacBeth and Merville's study may change from day to day and across the underlying stocks. Moreover, the uncertainty is also a function of the extent to which the option is in-the-money. Hence the appropriateness of using a regression technique may be questionable.

It is one of the basic tenets of modern finance theory that investment evaluation should include consideration of the risk associated with the return on the investment. It is not an easy task, especially when contingent assets are considered. Since the distribution of the rates of return from an investment in an option is not expected to be symmetrical and stationary over time, simple measures of risk, such as standard deviation of the distribution, are not suitable.

In their empirical paper, Black and Scholes (1972) offer a way to adjust for the changing risk of a position in an option. Since the stochastic process of option prices is generated from, and thus dependent on, the stochastic process of the underlying stock prices, Black and Scholes suggest offseting the former uncertainty with the latter. This can be done by creating a neutral hedge position composed of buying (selling) one option and, at the same time, selling (buying) a fraction of the underlying stock. This fraction, the *hedge ratio*, is determined in such a way as to cancel, over a very short time period, the risk of the option position with that of the equity position. If C_v is the partial derivative of the call option price with respect to the stock price, then for a very short time interval, Δt, the investment in an option (on one share), while short selling a fraction C_v of the share, should be riskless. It is therefore expected that for small Δt,

$$\Delta C - C_v \Delta V = (C - C_v V) r \Delta t \tag{3.3}$$

where the Δ is the change operator. The left-hand side of the expression is the return on the portfolio, and the right-hand side is riskless opportunity cost on the investment in the portfolio.

The procedure for creating the hedge position on day t is:

1. Compute the model price C_t^M and compare it with the actual price C_t^A.
2. If $C_t^M < C_t^A$ the option is considered to be overvalued; it should be sold and C_v units of the underlying share should be bought. For the B-S model, the hedge ratio, C_v, is equal to $N(d_1)$.[18]
3. If $C_t^M > C_t^A$, act to buy the call and sell short C_v units of V.
4. The hedge position will be held over a time interval, and assumed to be liquidated on $t + 1$.

The ex-post hedge return based on the B-S model is thus,[19]

$$R_{H,t+1} = (C_{t+1}^A - C_t^A) - N(d_{1t})(V_{t+1} - V_t) \tag{3.4}$$

for the undervalued call option and

$$R_{H,t+1} = N(d_{1t})(V_{t+1} - V_t) - (C_{t+1}^A - C_t^A)$$

for overvalued call options. The hedge return minus the opportunity cost on the investment will give the excess-dollar return for the hedged position.

Black and Scholes (1972) calculated the excess-dollar return for options traded during the period May 1966 to July 1969 on the over-the-counter (OTC) market. By comparing their model prices with the actual ones at the issuing date of an option, they could classify options into two groups—those the market *overvalued* compared with the model and those it *undervalued*. The initial position in the underlying stock was adjusted on a daily basis to maintain the neutral hedge. On theoretical grounds they expected the excess return to have zero systemmatic risk.

The major finding of the Black and Schole's study was that by using past data to estimate the variance, the model overpriced options on high-variance securities and underpriced options on low-variance securities. This may indicate that traders underestimated variances for volatile stocks and overestimated them for stocks with low volatility. By also using ex-ante estimates of the variance based on data for the life of the option they concluded that "if the model has an accurate estimate of the variance it works very well" (p. 416). In addition, they observed nonstationarity in the variance. The results may indicate market inefficiency. But, the profits from selling options on low-variance securities and buying options on high-variance securities completely disappeared when transaction costs were considered.

A secondary market in options was virtually nonexistent in the OTC market. Thus, while stock prices in Black and Schole's study were actual daily closing prices, the option prices they used in their tests were imputed for the model. As a result their average excess-hedge return mainly reflected the difference between the option's actual price and the model price on the initial day. Because model prices instead of actual prices were used after the initial day, the relative changes in the underlying stock quite closely matched those imputed for the option during the life of the option, and the excess-dollar return for these days was very close to zero. This procedure is also expected to have affected the regression results.

In Galai (1977) the option positions are adjusted on a daily basis, and actual option prices are used. The data employed are the daily closing prices of all options traded during the first months of the CBOE, from 26 April 1973 to 30 November 1973.[20] The total number of observations on option prices is 16,327. The ex-post test is performed under the assumption that trading at the closing price on day t, based on a trading rule that has been decided by using the same price, is possible.

The average hedge dollar return over 202 option classes, traded during the initial period of the CBOE, was approximately $9.8 per option day. For 71 options out of 202 the average of the time-series hedge return was significantly different from zero (at 5 percent). The results are thus consistent with the results shown for the boundary conditions in Galai (1978); ex-post, the hedge strategy effectively located deviations from the model price, generating substantial "book profit." During the sample period the average hedge returns were stable across maturities. Regressing the hedge returns on the market index yielded estimates of beta that were, in most cases, not significantly different from zero, while the estimates of the intercept (that is, the return adjusted for risk) were all significant (at 1 percent). The results were quite robust with respect to various estimates of the riskless interest rates and the variance of the rate of return. The latter was estimated in different ways from time series of past rates of return. By imposing a 1-percent transaction cost on changing the daily investment, almost all the hedge returns were eliminated.

The effect of dividend payment on the valuation of CBOE options was tested by classifying stocks in four groups according to their dividend yields and repeating the regression analysis for each group. The results clearly indicate that the ability of the unadjusted B-S model to locate over- or undervalued options declined as the dividend yield increased. The model performed better when applied to situations in which the basic assumptions of the model were better maintained, such as without-dividend payment. This conclusion was supported by the results obtained when the tests were limited to the trading days after the last expected ex-dividend day for any option. Finally, a simple adjustment for dividends was introduced to the B-S model by subtracting the present value of the expected dividends during the life of the option from the price of the underlying stock—and using this adjusted price in the model. The hedge returns were substantially higher, by 50 percent on the average, after introducing the dividend adjustment. The dividend correction increased the ability of the hedging strategy to locate profitable opportunities.

Galai's study emphasized that to test market efficiency, an ex-ante test simulating the trading opportunities for the trader should be performed. The procedure used was similar to the one used in the ex-post tests, except that in the ex-ante test the execution of trading is delayed by one trading day. On day t it is decided whether the option is over- or undervalued and the hedge ratio is calculated; the hedge is established on day $t + 1$ and liquidated on $t + 2$. The ex-ante hedge return is

$$R_{H,t+2} = \begin{cases} (C_{t+2}^{A} - C_{t+1}^{A}) - N(d_{1t})(V_{t+2} - V_{t+1}) \text{ if } C_t^{A} < C_t^{M} \\ \\ N(d_{1t})(V_{t+2} - V_{t+1}) - (C_{t+2}^{A} - C_{t+1}^{A}) \text{ if } C_t^{A} \geq C_t^{M} \end{cases}$$

The average of the hedge returns fell from \$9.8 to \$5.0 per option per day for the ex-ante test. In addition, the dispersion of the returns increased substantially, and, hence, the number of averages that are significantly different from zero declined from seventy-one to twelve. The average ex-ante hedge return declined with the dividend yield from \$7.3 per contract for the low-dividend-yield portfolio to \$2.4 for the high-dividend yield portfolio.

The evidence of the ex-ante test shows that profit opportunities might still have existed in the CBOE for the market to exploit. These profits were lower and perhaps riskier than those that seemed possible at first glance. Profits may be completely eliminated if bid-ask prices are considered, as suggested by Phillips and Smith (1980).

The results reported above were also confirmed when spreading strategy was tested. Spreading strategy consists of a long position in one option and a short position in another option on the same underlying stock. Galai's study shows that the average spreading return for all options was $8.4 for ex-post spreading for July 1973 maturity against October 1973 maturity, and only $4.8 for the ex-ante strategy. The spreading tests suggest that ex-post prices of similar options that differ by maturity alone were not fully synchronized.

While the B-S model assumes continuous trading, in practice, trading is discrete, with the exchanges open for business for a limited time period each day. Can this deviation from a basic assumption affect the results? Galai (1983) shows that the results obtained for the ex-post and ex-ante hedge returns are not due to the discreteness of trading. The major component in the hedge return is the change in the deviation between the model and market prices, while the opportunity cost and the discrete daily adjustment are marginal.[21]

Chiras and Manaster (1978) calculate the spread returns for positions that indicate high profit potential. They use the B-S model with an adjustment for the expected dividends,[22] and the weighted implied standard deviation (WISD) as an estimator of the standard deviation. A spread position is established for those options that deviate by 10 percent from the market price; that is,

$$\frac{C^M - C^A}{C^A} > 10 \text{ percent.}$$

The volume of each option in the portfolio is determined by its hedge ratio. All option positions are maintained over one month. During twenty-two holding periods, from June 1973 to April 1975, 118 positions were formed and 93 of them were found to show *paper profits*. The average gain per position was $9.96 per month, or 9.7 percent (assuming a 100-percent margin requirement in writing options).

Chiras and Manaster claim that the results indicate market inefficiency. However, they are careful to note the ex-post nature of their tests and the potential problem of nonsimultaneity of option prices. Bookstaber (1981) uses the data of Chiras and Manaster to check the effects of potential nonsimultaneity in their data. His conclusion is that there is strong support of the concern "that the observed profits were due to the noncontemporaneous data, and are not achievable in practice" (p. 155). In addition, Phillips and Smith (1980) show that by introducing transaction costs, especially those contained in the bid-ask spread, the profits of Chiras and Manaster are eliminated.

Blomeyer and Klemkosky (1982) test the validity of Roll's model for pricing the unprotected call option. They investigate to what extent the observed deviation of the B-S model prices from actual prices are due to the fact that the model ignores the early exercise opportunity of the unprotected

American call. The data used in the study are transactions data for eighteen stocks and their CBOE options for one trading day per month during the period July 1977 to June 1978. Blomeyer and Klemkosky follow Galai's testing procedure, repeating the ex-post performance test for both the B-S and Roll models and comparing the average percentage-excess hedge returns generated by each model. The hedge positions are adjusted for each new option transaction price, and the returns are calculated over the intervals between successive transactions. The averages reported for each underlying stock and for each trading day are also aggregated for three groups according to their dividend yields.

It is expected that since the Roll model allows for the early exercise of CBOE options, it should outperform the Black-Scholes model for options written on high-dividend-yield stocks. The results do not support the expectations, according to Blomeyer and Klemkosky. They claim that the ex-post results suggest that the Roll model is not superior to the B-S model in its ability to identify overvalued and undervalued call options.

While no significant differences are found between the results based on the Roll model and those based on the B-S model, the ex-post excess-hedge returns are significantly different from zero (at 5-percent significance level) for both models over most trading days and underlying securities. To test for market efficiency an ex-ante hedging strategy is constructed: a position is established based on the prices of the option and the stock approximately five to fifteen minutes after a substantial deviation between the model and market prices is observed. The position is held over one month and then is assumed to be liquidated. The returns are also adjusted for transaction costs for relatively efficient traders as suggested by Phillips and Smith (1980). On a before-transaction--cost and opportunity-cost basis they find the two models to produce significant positive returns, but these average profits disappear after the adjustments are made. From average excess monthly returns over all days and securities of 1.2 to 1.6 percent,[23] the excess return fell to -1.1 to -1.0 percent after adjusting for transaction costs. The results thus support market efficiency. Blomeyer and Klemkosky also conclude that the B-S model is an acceptable pricing alternative to the mathematically complex Roll model.

When analyzing Blomeyer's and Klemkosky's results it should be noted that they use the average percentage-excess return, which they get by dividing the excess-dollar return by the absolute investment, $C - C_v V$. One problem may arise due to the size the investment can take; in some cases it may get very close to zero and the rate of return will be very high. One extreme value can significantly affect the average and its standard deviation. Another problem may result from using the weighted implied standard deviation (WISD) based on the B-S model. If the Roll model is correct, the B-S model prices will give an underestimation of the American call prices, and therefore, the B-S implied standard deviation will be overstated. Using these WISD's in the Roll model will bias the prices upward. This problem will be especially serious for the high-dividend-yield stocks.

Testing the Implied Standard Deviation

One of the basic assumptions of the B-S model is that the standard deviation of the stock's rate of return is known and constant.[24] If the model is correct and option and stock markets are efficient and synchronous, by equating the model price to the actual market price the standard deviation implied by the option price can be imputed. It is expected, therefore, that the implied standard deviation (ISD) be stationary over time, across maturities and striking prices. The ISD is also expected, given the assumptions of the model, to be equal to the time-series standard deviation. Deviations from expectations may be due to markets' inefficiency or lack of synchronization among related markets, or to the model being misspecified.

The estimation of the standard deviation of the stock's rate of return by the ISD was initially suggested by Latané and Rendleman (1976). They calculate the ISD's for all options written on a particular stock and use the weighted average[25] of the ISDs (WISD) as estimators of return variability. Lantané's and Rendleman's data set contain weekly closing option and stock prices on twenty-four firms during the period 5 October 1973 to 28 June 1974. The weekly hedge returns are calculated separately for over- and undervalued options for various criteria for option selection and hedge-ratios determination. The criteria are the individual option's ISD, the underlying stock's WISD, and the ex-post time-series standard deviation. The strategy, based upon the historical series of rates of reutrn, is considered to be a naive strategy against which the returns generated from the use of the WISDs can be compared. Under the assumption that the WISD is the proper measure of the standard deviation, Latané and Rendleman expect absolute higher returns for strategies employing WISDs. They find all the portfolios employing WISDs to produce significant (at 5 percent) mean excess returns, which are also consistently higher than those using the ex-post standard deviations. Latané and Rendleman conclude that "the WISD based upon the Black and Scholes model is useful, not only in determining proper hedged positions, but also in identifying relatively over- and under-priced options" (p. 375).

From comparing the WISDs to the time-series standard deviations they conclude that options were generally overpriced in terms of the Black and Scholes model during the sample period. While the WISDs for a given stock are not perfectly stable, they find a strong tendency for the cross-section estimators to move together over time. This led Latané and Rendleman to conclude that while the model can be used effectively to determine whether individual options are properly priced, "the model may not fully capture the process determining option prices in the actual market" (p. 375).

Schmalensee and Trippi (1978) assume the validity of the B-S model and impute the standard deviation from weekly observations over the period April 1974 to May 1975 for six widely traded stocks and their options. Based on previous studies that claimed that the B-S model worked poorly for deep-in-the-money and deep-out-of-the-money options, they eliminate these options from their sample. The purpose of their study is to investigate "the determinants of changes over time in the market's collective expectations of common stock volatility" (p. 130).

Schmalensee and Trippi use an arithmatic average of ISDs, based on closing prices, as an estimator of the standard deviation and check the behavior of the changes in the average over time. They find the changes in volatility to contain nonwhite-noise elements, which would indicate market inefficiency, given the validity of the B-S model. But, because actual volatilities change over time, as do the average ISDs, the B-S model may be inappropriate.

Similar to the results of Latané and Rendleman, they also find some market-based effects that influenced the change in volatility across stocks. Surprisingly, a weak relationship is found between changes in the average ISDs and the ex-post time-series standard deviations. Also surprising is the strong impact of the direction of change of the stock prices on the changes in the ISDs. Increases in the price of a stock that are accompanied by lower volatilities are also reported by Black (1976). These results are not consistent with the B-S model framework, nevertheless, the B-S model can be useful in predicting such ex-ante changes.

Beckers (1980) notes that there is a basic inconsistency in using the B-S model to obtain predictions of a presumably nonstationary variance. However, the results of Latané and Rendleman and Schmalensee and Trippi indicate that the B-S model is still valuable in predicting future volatilities. It may be the case that the model is not very sensitive to violations of the nonstationarity assumption. Beckers extends the above studies by considering alternative weighted schemes of the volatility estimator and by using a dividend-adjusted model. For a sample of CBOE options during the period 13 October 1975 to 23 January 1976, Beckers finds the ISD derived from an at-the-money option to be a better predictor of the actual time-series standard deviation over the life of the option than a weighted ISD. He also finds the ISDs to be extremely volatile over time and suggests using an intertemporal arithmatic average. While the instability of the ISD may indicate market inefficiency, Beckers attributed it to the trading mechanism and especially to the lack of market synchronization. Expanding the sample over the period May 1975 to July 1977 and using five-day arithmatic averages of ISDs,

Beckers reconfirms his earlier findings. In the regression analysis he finds that past time-series standard deviations add to the explanation of the ex-ante time-series standard deviation above and beyond what is explained by the ISD. This, again, may indicate market inefficiency in using available data; it may also indicate model misspecification or data problems. Some support to the latter is received from analyzing a sample of transaction data that show that closing pricing may seriously distort the ISD calculations.

While all the estimated ISDs are point estimation usually based on closing prices for shares and options, little is known about their distribution properties. Brenner and Galai (1981) examine some properties of the ISDs based on transactions data[26] on five stocks for ninety-eight trading days starting from 3 June 1977 to 21 October 1977. It appears that there are significant deviations of the ISDs based on the last transaction for the day (LISD) from the daily average ISD (AISD). Longer maturity options exhibited a tendency to higher AISDs than short maturities, which implies that options with a long life were overpriced relative to short maturity options. There were also significant differences of AISDs across striking prices. Moreover, the distributions of AISDs over time were not stationary. Thus, the results are consistent with findings of other researchers, and lead to the rejection of the joint hypotheses that the B-S model is valid—that the stocks and options markets are efficient and synchronous, and that the estimation procedures are correct.

Rubinstein (1981) uses the ISDs to test a number of alternative models: the displaced-diffusion model of Rubinstein, the pure-jump model of Cox and Ross, the diffusion-jump model of Merton, the compound-option model of Geske, and the constant-elasticity-of-variance model of Cox. He argues that with good data base the problem of data accuracy can be solved, and he believes that markets are not systematically inefficient. Hence, the deviation of observed-option prices from the B-S model prices must be due to model misspecification. By examining the ISDs across maturities and striking prices, Rubinstein tries to distinguish which pricing formula seems to explain better the observed biases from B-S values. The null hypothesis is that the B-S formula produces unbiased values and hence ISDs should be constant for various options on the same underlying stock.

For any matched pair of options, the probability, under the null hypothesis, is one-half that the option with shorter life should have the higher implied volatility. The same probability is expected for matched pairs based on the ratio of the stock price to the striking price, V/K. The tests are nonparametric where the relative frequency of the ratio of ISDs for each class is examined.

Rubinstein uses transactions data from the Berkeley Option Data Base, for the period 23 August 1976 to 31 August 1978. After a thorough process of cleaning the data and eliminating "troublesome" observations, he is left

with 19,094 matched pairs for time-to-maturity classes and 12,239 for the
V/K comparisons. For each matched pair the ratio of the implied standard
deviation is recorded.

One important result is that out-of-the-money options with shorter
maturities had higher ISDs, which means that they were relatively overpriced. This is the only result that is unchanged over the whole sample
period. Other results depended on time, and they changed when measured
during the first subperiod (23 August 1976 to 21 October 1977) or the
second subperiod (24 October 1977 to 31 August 1978). For at-the-money
options, during the first subperiod, the longer the time to expiration, the
higher was the relative ISD. However, for the second subperiod, the longer
the time to expiration the lower was the relative ISD. In addition, in-the-
money options tended to be overpriced during the first subperiod, but
underpriced in the second subperiod. These results lead Rubinstein to
conclude that "no one model seems to capture them all. Even during the first
period alone, the models that pick up the time to expiration biases are disjoint
from those that pick up the striking price biases." Rubinstein confirms
MacBeth's and Merville's (1979) findings that ISDs tended to rise with
decreasing striking prices for 1976 data, and this bias continued until about
October 1977. However, toward the end of 1977 and during 1978, this bias
was reversed, as is also documented by MacBeth (1981). So, while the
striking-price biases from B-S values are significant and tend to go in the
same direction for most stocks at any point in time, the direction of the bias
changes from period to period. Rubinstein's conclusion is that a composite
model should be built, and in addition, the bias observed in any period should
be correlated with the level of some macroeconomic variables, such as the
level of stock-market prices and volatilities and the level of interest rates.

Conclusions for Testing Call-Option Models

The amount of work devoted to empirical testing of call options is rather
impressive. While various approaches have been applied to different data
sets and time periods, some common results appear to be dominating the
studies.

First, with respect to *model validity*, the major conclusions are:

1. The Black-Scholes performs relatively well, especially for at-the-money
   options. Deviations from model prices are consistently observed for deep-
   in and deep-out-of-the money options.
2. No alternative model consistently offers better predictions of market
   prices than the B-S model. There is some evidence to prefer the constant
   elasticity of variance model, but it is not conclusive.

3. The major problem faced by the B-S model, or any other model suggested so far, is the nonstationarity of the risk estimator of the underlying stock. The nature of the nonstationarity is not clear yet. Nevertheless, for short time periods, say of days, the B-S model may give good predictions of market prices and reveal under- and overvalued options.
4. Trading mechanism and market synchronization may have affected the results of the tests. However, by using more detailed and accurate data, the major results were reconfirmed.
5. No one model accounts for transaction costs and taxes, which may affect the prices of traded options.

Second, the evidence so far is also consistent with rejecting the null hypothesis of *market synchronization*. The significant ex-post hedge returns reported by a few of the studies may indicate the lack of either trading synchronization or data synchronization. This conclusion is also reached from testing the boundary conditions.

Third, the results with respect to option market efficiency are not conclusive. While ex-ante hedge returns are usually found to be significant and hence indicate market inefficiency, they are completely eliminated after the proper adjustments for transaction costs for the most efficient trader are introduced. All agree that an outsider to the exchange cannot consistently make above-normal profits. A market maker who is affected by the bid-ask spread, and who incurs opportunity costs, may also find it difficult to generate above-normal net excess profits.

Tests of Put Option-Pricing Models

Valuation of Put Options

Most attention in the literature has focused on call options, while relatively very little has been written about put options. Historically, this phenomenon can be explained by the relatively small volume of put trading. In addition, for European options the value of the put is a simple function of the call price and other observable variables. Hence, if a pricing model is available for a European call, it can easily be adjusted for a European put. The *put-call parity*, which expresses the relationship in a "frictionless" option market between a European put and a European call with similar terms, is given by:[27]

$$P = C - V + Ke^{-r\tau} \qquad (3.5)$$

where P is the put price, V is the price of the underlying stock, while K is the striking price, r is the riskless interest rate, and τ is the time period remaining to maturity. If the stock pays dividends during the life of the options, and the options are not dividend-protected, then in equation 3.5 the price of the underlying stock, V, will be adjusted by subtracting from it the present value of the dividend stream.[28]

Merton (1973b) shows that equation 3.5 is invalid for an American put, since it may be profitable to exercise the put before maturity. Hence, the value of the American put will be higher than the value of a European put with similar terms. Simulated evidence on the importance of early exercise of the put option is supplied by Merton, Scholes, and Gladstein (1982). They show the bias between the correct put price (which considers the value of early exercise) and the parity put price to be moving between 4 to 14 percent for at-the-money options over the period 1963 to 1976. The bias is largest in periods of high interest rates. They conclude that the parity model is not an appropriate put-pricing model. They also show that "a significant fraction of all put options exercised will be exericised prior to the expiration date" (p. 16). About 44 percent of all at-the-money puts would have been exercised before maturity according to the simulated results.

Merton (1973a) derives the partial differential equations for the dividend-unprotected American put price. No closed-form solution is available for this problem, and numerical methods should be applied. Brennan and Schwartz (1977) use a finite-differences method to solve the model, while Parkinson (1977) applies a numerical-integration approach to the pricing problem. Both do it for a set of assumptions consistent with the B-S framework.

Testing the Put-Call Parity

Stoll (1969) tested the put-call parity model by transforming equation (3.5) into a least-squares regression model of the relative form.[29]

$$\frac{C}{V} = \alpha + \beta \left(\frac{P}{V} \right) + \gamma \left(\frac{r}{1+r} \right) \qquad (3.6)$$

and the absolute form:

$$C = \alpha + \beta P + \gamma \left(\frac{r}{1+r} \right) V.$$

Stoll's data set included weekly submissions during 1967 to the Securities and Exchange Commission by the Put and Call Brokers and Dealers

Association of representative prices for ten companies with relatively great amounts of activity. In his regression analysis Stoll found deviations from expectations; the intercept was higher and the slope lower than expected.

Gould and Galai (1974) follow Merton's (1973b) adjustment of the put-call parity conditions for American options. In addition, they introduce tax and transaction-cost considerations in forming the put-call parity conditions. It is shown that the condition is not dependent on the tax rate, but transaction-costs increase the upper boundary and reduce the lower boundary of the difference $C - P$.

Gould and Galai claim that regression technique is not an appropriate methodology for testing the existence of arbitrage profits. If, in the absence of transaction costs, the boundary condition for at-the-money options is:

$$\frac{C - P}{V} \leq \frac{r}{1 + r} \tag{3.7}$$

then any deviation revealed in the market may indicate market inefficiency. The regression technique is based on averaging, while for market inefficiency only outliers are of interest. Using Stoll's data set, expanded to include 1968 and 1969, they show a rather surprising number of violations of equation 3.7 that represent potential profit opportunities. These apparent returns would disappear for a nonmember of the exchange who has to incur the transaction costs. These results are supported by the analysis of an additional data set on actual transactions in straddles and calls. Gould and Galai conclude that "the findings . . . are that transaction's costs appear to play a nontrivial role in the explanation of observed premiums on puts and calls, at least in the period 1967–1969" (p. 122). Even after transaction costs, it seems that a member of the New York Stock Exchange (NYSE) could have filtered the high-profit opportunities. The market, thus, was somewhat inefficient from the point of view of the members of the exchange.

Trading in standardized puts on registered option exchanges commenced on June 1977, four years after trading in call options on the exchanges began. Since these options are not adjusted for the dividend payments, the put-call parity should be restated for the registered exchanges. Klemkosky and Resnick (1979) derive the parity conditions and subject them to empirical testing based on data on CBOE puts. The put-call relationship is described by boundaries within which the difference $C - P$ should be found to eliminate arbitrage possibilities. The upper boundary:

$$C - P \leq V - Ke^{-r\tau} - \sum_{i=1}^{n} D_{t_i} e^{-r\tau_i} \tag{3.8}$$

is tested in Klemkosky's and Resnick's paper. This condition assumes away the possibility of early exercising the call option.

Transactions data for one day each month during the period July 1977 to June 1978 for fifteen stocks and their options were employed in testing inequality 3.8. This data set made it possible to construct a nearly simultaneous position in the call, the put, and the underlying stock. Only 1 position was constructed each day per option class, and altogether 606 positions were considered. After eliminating 66 positions due to violating the sufficient condition for no premature exercising of the call option, they found 234 profitable hedges. After introducing transaction costs of twenty dollars for a member of the exchange and sixty dollars for the nonmember investor, it was found that paper profits were still available for the former but almost completely eliminated for the latter.[30] Similar to Gould and Galai, most of the deviations from parity were due to the low- to middle-price stocks. With the exceptions of short-term options, Klemkosky and Resnick did not reveal any significant relationship between time to maturity and the proportion of deviations from the parity conditions.

Klemkosky and Resnick also employed least-squares regression based on the terms in inequality 3.8. The results for the full sample "show simultaneous put and call prices to be thoroughly consistent with the put-call parity" (p. 1153). Running the regressions on the profitable hedges and unprofitable hedges separately, led them to conclude that overpriced calls and overpriced puts were the dominant factors in their respective hedges. This conclusion, however, is trivial and true by definition.

In Klemkosky and Resnick (1980) the previous work was extended by performing an ex-ante analysis of the boundary conditions. Hedges were constructed five and fifteen minutes after they had been initially identified as having an ex-post return in excess of twenty per hedge. They found that the majority of the five- and fifteen-minute lagged observations[31] would be economically profitable ex ante. However, the overall tendency for the ex-ante profitability was to be less than the ex-post profitability. By also including the average bid-ask spread in each position, they conclude that "price correction appears to take place rapidly enough on the registered option exchanges to eliminate most if not all of the economic profits for an aribtraging member firm" (p. 372).

In both studies of Klemkosky and Resnick, short conversions, consisting of the purchase of a call, a short position in the underlying stock, and lending at the riskless rate of interest to replicate the cash flow of a put were also tested. However, for the American put no perfect short hedge can be established since for the put a possible, rational premature exercise is not determinable at inception. The results of these tests, under the assumption of no early exercise of the put (except as can initially be determined) were usually consistent with the long conversion results as summarized above. For the ex-ante analysis, positive net returns were earned on average from short conversions. Since these conversions are not riskless the positive returns may be regarded as a compensation for the risk associated with the investment.

The importance of the tests of the put-call parity condition is similar to that of testing the boundary condition for the call option; any rational valuation model must be consistent with the weaker boundary conditions. If violations are revealed for boundary conditions, they should be expected to reappear—and usually by larger magnitude in specific tests of valuation models. Hence the same adjustments that are suggested for the general conditions should also apply to the models.

Testing Put–Valuation Models

Brennan and Schwartz (1977) test their American put-valuation model on fifty-five observations on actual OTC put options during the period May 1966 to May 1969. These options were dividend protected, though not perfectly.[32] Since the assumptions employed in their model are consistent with those of the B-S model, they suggest the use of ISDs derived from calls with the same terms for the put valuation. As a benchmark, they also calculate the B-S values as though the puts were European. All the calculations are repeated for variance restrictions based on ex-post and ex-ante time series of the stocks' rates of return. The differences in values between the Brennan-Schwartz numerical-solution prices and the B-S model prices are rather small, and both overestimated market prices by 25 to 40 percent. "Based on this evidence it is easy to reject the hypothesis that puts and calls are priced consistently and in accordance with this model, and our results confirm the findings of Gould and Galai of frequent violations of put-call parity" (p. 455). They also conclude that the Black-Scholes model is a reasonable one for six-month dividend-protected American puts since the right to early exercise is not of great economic value.

Brennan and Schwartz also analyze the exercise strategy of the put in the sample and find that put-option buyers were reluctant to exercise their options prior to maturity even though the model indicated that it was optimal to do so. They attribute this phenomenon to the tax system, which may have penalized for early realization of profits. Finally, they perform an analysis of hedge positions with the puts and the underlying stock to find, as can already by expected, that the puts were undervalued in the market.

Farkas and Hoskin (1979) test the Parkinson model with data on puts traded on the CBOE. The data set consist of weekly closing prices for stocks and options from 3 June 1977 to 24 December 1977. The variance estimation is based on historical time series. By comparing the model prices to the actual prices for 365 puts, they find the median percentage differences between model prices and actual prices to be -7.4, and the interquartile range from -27.6 to 2.0 percent. They also find the model to work better for at-the-money and in-the-money options than for out-of-the-money puts. The median of the absolute percentage errors was 19.2 percent for the latter. Farkas and Hoskin find no significant relationship between the accuracy of the prediction and time to expiration.

Conclusions for Testing Put-Option Markets

The major conclusion of all studies is that there are significant deviations of put values from their expected values. The tendency of puts is to be undervalued in the OTC market relative to calls and the underlying stocks. For the CBOE Klemkosky and Resnick claim the puts to be relatively undervalued, while Farkas and Hoskin indicate that the puts are overvalued.

It may also very well be the case that the tests reflect the lack of market synchronization. But the persistence of significant deviations over a long time period needs a better explanation; none of the tests offers one yet. In a sense, it is useless to test the validity of a model before market synchronization and efficiency are established and before explaining the violations of the boundary conditions for puts. Much research needs to be done on pricing puts and on the behavior of the markets for puts.

Future Research Directions

This chapter has emphasized a major problem with the empirical test. That problem is the joint-hypotheses nature of the tests used: market synchronization, market efficiency, model validity, and quality of data and estimates are jointly tested. Future research should try to decompose the problem and analyze each component separately. This cannot be done without improving the statistical tools available at present.

There are problems in measuring ex-ante efficiency. For an arbitrage condition it is almost an impossibility to establish, on an ex-ante basis, a perfect, riskless arbitrage position. When an arbitrage situation exists, orders must be placed for the various assets contained in the position and the transaction prices usually cannot be guaranteed in advance.[33] For risky positions the adjustment procedure for risk is not accepted universally. The capital-asset-pricing-model is under attack these days, and the arbitrage-pricing model is not yet fully established and commonly accepted, and its adjustment procedure is not yet employed on a wide scale of problems.

I do believe that ex-ante efficiency tests should be carried out on the floor of the exchange by monitoring, on real time, the opportunities available to market participants. Stored data may mislead, even when refined transaction data are used. The problem of timing the transaction—when it was agreed upon, when stamped by the board broker, and when actually appearing on the screens—is not fully solved even when using transaction data.[34] Stored data rarely can reveal whether a transaction was consumated at the bid or ask prices or somewhere in between. These differences, especially for options, can be significant.[35] By monitoring the trades, signals for trading can be located and the transformation procedure of turning the signals into profitable investments can be studied.

While we may lose information, it may be recommended that some of the tests can be carried out on subsamples, clean of problems and distortions, subsamples not plagued by problems that may bias the results. For example, the B-S model does not adjust for dividends but registered options are not dividend protected. If the B-S model is to be tested, it should be done on low-dividend-yield stocks or on options for which no dividends are expected before maturity.[36] Another example is for tests trying to minimize the problem of market synchronization. These tests should rely on options with high volumes of trading. It should be expected that model prices for IBM at-the-money options will better approximate market prices. Nevertheless—even for a stock like IBM—with transactions data, it was found in Brenner and Galai (1981) that the parameters of the distribution of the stock's rate of return are nonstationary and the changes are cross-sectionally correlated.

This leads us to one of the major areas of future research, that of nonstationarity. It seems that all models failed due to changes in their basic parameters. These changes may be due to macroeconomic variables. The nature of the nonstationarity should be studied, and it is expected that better predictions of market prices for options can be achieved. More importantly, such studies will teach us more on the behavior of the underlying assets, which are usually of greater economic importance.

Notes

1. See Black and Scholes (1972, 1973).
2. See, for example, Brenner and Galai (1981) and Phillips and Smith (1980).
3. See Bhattacharya and Rubinstein (1978).
4. Following Galai (1977).
5. See MacBeth and Merville (1979, 1980).
6. See more on this issue in Phillips and Smith (1980).

7. See Merton (1973).

8. See Galai (1978, p. 191) and Merton (1973a).

9. For example, during October 1973, there were 987 observations on closing prices of the options maturing in October, of which 704 were cases where $V > K$. Of these, 287 violated the boundary conditions and the average deviation $\varepsilon = V - Ke^{-r\tau} - \Sigma_{i=1}^{n} D_{t_i} e^{-r\tau_i} - C$ was equal to \$37.8 for the ex-post test.

10. For the ex-ante test the average of ε fell to \$18.8 per one option with a standard deviation of \$45.7.

11. For additional details pertaining to each of the models, the reader is referred to Cox and Rubinstein (chapter 1, this book) to Cox and Rubinstein (1983), or to the original papers.

12. The assumptions are those appearing in Black and Scholes (1973). Other authors showed that some of these assumptions may be relaxed or eliminated at the cost of adding other assumptions.

13. See also Cox and Ross (1976) and Cox and Rubinstein (chapter 1, this book).

14. Bhattacharya (1980), p. 1081, and especially p. 1085.

15. Superscrips A and M denote actual and model prices, respectively.

16. They also raise the possibility that their results may be affected by the potential early exercise of the dividend-unprotected call option.

17. Their paper concentrates on ex-post and ex-ante tests of hedge returns. The tests and the results are discussed in the following subsections.

18. $N(d_1)$ is defined in equation 3.2.

19. This is the right-hand-side of equation 3.3.

20. The same data set was used for testing the boundary conditions as is reported in Galai (1978) and is summarized in the section entitled, "tests of the Boundary Conditions."

21. See also Boyle and Emanuel (1980).

22. The adjustment is based on Merton's (1973a) derivation of option valuation for continuous dividends.

23. The 1.2 percent is found for a 5-percent filter and 1.6 percent is for the 10-percent filter, where the filter measures the percentage deviation of the model price from the actual price when the trading strategy is devised.

24. Merton (1973a) shows how the B-S model should be adjusted when the standard deviation changes in a deterministic way. Patell and Wolfson (1979) test the reflection of anticipated information content of financial-accounting disclosures on call-option prices by using the adjusted model suggested by Merton. Their results are consistent with the model allowing for changing deviations.

25. The weights are the partial derivatives of the B-S model with respect to the standard deviation.

26. The data were taken from the Berkeley Option Data Base (see Bhattacharya and Rubinstein (1978)).

27. Stoll (1969) offered the first formal proof of this relationship.

28. Assuming that the dividends and their timings are perfectly known in advance.

29. The tests employing data for OTC options are for at-the-money options and the put-call parity condition is adjusted accordingly by equating K to V.

30. Phillips and Smith (1980) claim that the bid-ask effect seems to approximate fifty dollars per position, even for a market marker, and thus most of the paper profits will disappear.

31. The sample contains 139 five-minute-lagged observations and 137 fifteen-minute-lagged observations.

32. See Merton (1973a).

33. See Galai (1977) for a further discussion of this issue, which is more of a paradox of the impossibility to test for market efficiency with arbitrage-riskless positions.

34. See Rubinstein (1981) and Cox and Rubinstein (1983) for a discussion of this issue.

35. See Phillips and Smith (1980).

36. The last suggestion may limit the sample to short-maturity options only. See Galai (1978) on the effect of such procedure on the results.

References

Beckers, S. "The Constant Elasticity of Variance Model and Its Implications for Option Pricing." *Journal of Finance* 35 (1980): 661–673.

———. "Standard Deviations Implied in Option Prices as Predictors of Future Stock Price Variability." *Journal of Banking and Finance* 5 (1981): 363–381.

Bhattacharya, M. "Empirical Properties of the Black-Scholes Formula under Ideal Conditions." *Journal of Financial and Quantitative Analysis* 15 (1980): 1081–1105.

Bhattacharya, M., and Rubinstein, M. "Berkeley Options Data Base." Mimeographed. University of California, Berkeley, 1978.

Black, F. "Studies of Stock Prices Volatility Changes." Proceedings of the American Statistical Association (1976), pp. 177–181.

———. "Facts and Fantasy in the Use of Options." *Financial Analysts Journal* 31 (1975): 36–72.

Black, F. and Scholes, M. "The Pricing of Options and Corporate

Liabilities." *Journal of Political Economy* 81 (1973): 637–659.

———. "The Valuation of Option Contracts and a Test of Market Efficiency." *Journal of Finance* 27 (1972): 399–417.

Blomeyer, E.C., and Klemkosky, R.C. "Tests of Market Efficiency for American Call Options," in *Option Pricing Theory and Applications*, Brenner, M., (ed.) Lexington, Mass.: D.C. Heath and Co., Lexington Books (1983).

Blomeyer, E.C., and Resnick, B.G. "An Empirical Investigation of the Compound Option Pricing Model." Unpublished Manuscript. 1982.

Bookstaber, R.M. "Observed Option Mispricing and the Nonsimultaneity of Stock and Option Quotations." *Journal of Business* 54 (1981): 141–155.

Boyle, P.P., and Ananthanarayanan, A.C. "The Impact of Variance Estimation in Option Valuation Models," *Journal of Financial Economics* 5 (1977): 375–387.

Boyle, P.P., and Emanuel. D. "Discretely Adjusted Option Hedges." *Journal of Financial Economics* 8 (1980): 259–282.

Brennan, M. J., and Schwartz, E.S. "The Valuation of American Put Options," *Journal of Finance* 32 (1977): 449–464.

Brenner, M. and Galai, D. "The Properties of the Estimated Risk of Common Stocks Implied by Options Prices." Mimeographed. University of California, Berkeley, 1981.

Chiras, D.P., and Manaster, S. "The Information Content of Option Prices and a Test of Market Efficiency," *Journal of Financial Economics* 6 (1978): 213–234.

Cox, C.J. "Notes on Option Pricing I: Constant Elasticity of Variance Diffusions." Mimeographed. Stanford University, 1975.

Cox, C.J., and Ross, S.A. "A Survey of Some New Results in Financial Option Pricing Theory," *Journal of Finance* 31, (1976): 383–402.

———. "The Valuation of Options for Alternative Stochastic Processes," *Journal of Financial Economics* (1976b).

Cox, J., and Rubinstein, M. *"Options Markets.* Englewood Cliffs, N.J.: Prentice-Hall, 1983, forthcoming.

Finnerty, J.E. "The CBOE and Market Efficiency," *Journal of Financial and Quantitative Anaysis* 13 (1978): 29–38.

Farkas, K.L., and Hoskin, R.E. "Testing a Valuation Model for American Puts," *Financial Management* 8 (1979): 51–56.

Fuller, R.J. "Factors Which Influence Listed Call Option Prices." *Review of Business and Economic Research* 13 (1977–1978).

Galai, D. "The Components of the Return from Hedging Options Against Stocks," *Journal of Business* 56 (1983).

_____. "A Convexity Test for Traded Options." *Quarterly Review of Business and Economics* 19 (1979): 83–90.

_____. "Empirical Tests of Boundary Conditions for CBOE Options." *Journal of Financial Economics*, 6 (1978): 187–211.

_____. "Tests of Market Efficiency of the Chicago Board Options Exchange." *Journal of Business* 50 (1977): 167–197.

_____. Pricing of Options and the Efficiency of the Chicago Board Options Exchange," Unpublished Ph.D. dissertation, University of Chicago, 1975.

Gastineau, G. "*The Stock Options Manual*, 2nd ed. New York: McGraw-Hill, 1979.

Geske, R. "The Valuation of Compound Options." *Journal of Financial Economics* 7 (1979): 63–81.

Gombola M.J., Roenfeldt, R.L., and Cooley, P.L. "Spreading Strategies in CBOE Options: Evidence on Market Performance." *Journal of Financial Research* 1 (1978): 35–44.

Gould, J., and Galai, D. "Transactions Costs and the Relationship Between Put and Call Prices." *Journal of Financial Economics* 1, (1974): 105–129.

Klemkosky, R.C., and Resnick, B.G. "An Ex-Ante Analysis of Put-Call Parity." *Journal of Financial Economics* 8 (1980): 363–378.

_____. "Put-Call Parity and Market Efficiency." *Journal of Finance* 34 (1979): 1141–1155.

Latané, H.A., and Rendleman, R.J. "Standard Deviations of Stock Price Ratios Implied in Option Prices." *Journal of Finance* 31 (1976): 369–381.

MacBeth, J.D. "Further Results on Constant Elasticity of Variance Call Option Model." Mimeographed. University of Texas, 1981.

MacBeth, J.D., and Merville, L.J. "Tests of Black-Scholes and Cox Call Option Valuation Models." *Journal of Finance* 35 (1980): 285–303.

_____. "An Empirical Examination of the Black-Scholes Call Option Pricing Model." *Journal of Finance* 34 (1979): 1173–1186.

Madansky, A. "Some Comparisons of the Case of Empirical and Lognormal Distributions in Option Evaluation." Proceedings of the Seminar on the Analysis of Securities Prices, Chicago: Center for Research in Securities Prices, University of Chicago (1977): 155–168.

Manaster, S. "Discussion." *Journal of Finance* 35 (1980): 301–303.

Merton, R. "Option Pricing When Underlying Stock Returns are Discontinuous." *Journal of Financial Economics* 3 (1976a): 125–144.

_____. "The Impact of Option Pricing of Specification Error in the Underlying Stock Price Returns." *Journal of Finance* 31 (1976b): 333–350.

_____. "Theory of Rational Option Pricing." *Bell Journal of Economics and Management Science* 4(1973a): 141–183.

_____. "The Relationship Between Put and Call Option Prices: Comment." *Journal of Finance* 20 (1973b): 183–184.

Merton, R.C., Scholes, M.S., and Gladstein, M.L. "The Returns and Risks of Alternative Put-Option Portfolio Investment Strategies." *Journal of Business* 55, (1982): 1–55.

Parkinson, M. "Option Pricing: The American Put." *Journal of Business* 49 (1977): 21–36.

Patell, J.M., and Wolfson, M.A. "Anticipated Information Releases Reflected in Call Option Prices." *Journal of Accounting Research* 1 (1979): 117–140.

Phillips, S.M., and Smith C.W. "Trading Costs for Listed Options: The Implications for Market Efficiency." *Journal of Financial Economics* 8 (1980): 179–201.

Roll, R. "An Analytic Valuation Formula for Unprotected American Call Options on Stocks with Known Dividends." *Journal of Financial Economics* 5 (1977): 251–258.

Rubinstein, M. "A Survey of Alternative Option Pricing Models." in *Option Pricing: Theory and Applications*, Brenner, M., (ed.) Lexington, Mass.: D.C. Heath and Co., Lexington Books (1983).

_____. "Displaced Diffusion Option Pricing," Mimeographed. University of California, Berkeley, 1980.

_____. "Nonparametric Tests of Alternative Option Pricing Models Using All Reported Trades and Quotes on the 30 Most Active CBOE Option Classes from August 23, 1976 through August 3, 1978," Mimeographed. University of California, Berkeley, 1981.

Schmalensee, R., and Trippi, R.R. "Common Stock Volatility Expectations Implied by Option Premia," *Journal of Finance* 32 (1978): 129–147.

Stoll, H.R. "The Relationship Between Put and Call Option Prices: Reply," *Journal of Finance* 28 (1973): 185–187.

_____. "The Relationship Between Put and Call Option Prices," *Journal of Finance* 24 (1969): 801–822.

Thorp, E., and Gelbaum, D. "Option Models: Black-Scholes or Cox-Ross?" Unpublished manuscript. 1980.

Trippi, R. "A Test of Option Market Efficiency Using a Random-Walk Valuation Model." *Journal of Economics and Business* 29 (1977): 93–98.

4

Tests of an Approximate Option-Valuation Formula

Robert Jarrow and
Andrew Rudd

Several option-valuation formulas have appeared in the literature during the last decade or so.[1] Typically, the starting point for these valuation models is to assume a particular stochastic process for the underlying security. This assumption frequently is crucial to the subsequent derivation and the form of the ultimate valuation formula. From a practical point of view, an investor first has to decide which assumed stochastic process is closest to the true process and then hope that any differences between the assumed and true distributions are not critical for option valuation.

For example, it is generally accepted that stock prices are close to being lognormally distributed, but with fatter tails. Provided the impact of the fatter tails does not materially affect the option price, the Black-Scholes formula (which assumes lognormality with a constant variance of the underlying security) may be a satisfactory method of valuing listed options.

Unfortunately, it is an open question just how important the observed departures from lognormality are for listed option valuation.[2] More generally, it is far from clear how the specification of the underlying security's distribution manifests itself in the resulting option price. Of course, in theory one could compute the option value for all distributions of interest. However, the computation of option values for certain specifications of the underlying security distribution may be exceedingly complicated, even using advanced numerical techniques.

The ambiguity between the specification of the underlying process and resulting option price is important because there exists a large class of valuation problems where the underlying distribution is itself a convolution of other distributions and hence may not be amenable to simple computational procedures. For example, consider the valuation of an option on a portfolio or index where the component securities are assumed to be distributed lognormally with constant variance. Only in special (and fairly unrealistic) cases will the index itself be distributed lognormally so that the Black-Scholes formula may be applied. In all other cases, the index will not be lognormally distributed and there is little guidance as to whether the Black-Scholes formula, for instance, is an accurate method for valuing options.

Another example is the valuation of an option on a stock whose distribution is convoluted from the distributions of the real assets held by the corporation (Rubinstein 1980). As a final example, consider the valuation of Government National Mortgage Association (GNMA) options. The contract is specified in terms of the price of a $100,000 face-value GNMA pass through, although the important underlying processes are those driving the (forward) interest rates. Hence, realistic assumptions for the interest-rate process are unlikely to result in tractable distributions for the price process. In these problems, partial information concerning the underlying distribution may be known (for instance, its moments may be tabulated) but the distribution function itself may be so complex as to prevent analytical manipulation or direct integration.

In an earlier paper (Jarrow and Rudd 1983) we developed an option-valuation approach that explicitly provided the impact of the underlying distribution, summarized by its moments, on the option price. The approach approximates the underlying distribution with an alternate (more tractable) distribution. This approach, similar to the familiar Taylor series expansion for an analytic function, is called a *generalized Edgeworth series expansion*. It has the desirable property that the coefficients in the expansion are simple functions of the moments of the true and approximating distributions.

In the following section we review the application of the Edgeworth series expansion to the problem of option valuation. In the special case where the approximating distribution is the lognormal, the (approximate) option price is found to be the Black-Scholes price plus an adjustment for each of the terms in the expansion. Previously we specified three adjustments that depend, respectively, on the differences between the variance, skewness, and kurtosis of the true underlying and the approximating lognormal distribution. The remaining adjustments are lumped together in an error term.

The presence of the error term in the Edgeworth expansion indicates that our results are only approximate. Intuition suggests that for practical purposes the first four moments of the underlying distribution should capture the majority of its influence on the option price. Of course, the ultimate test is to determine empirically how well the model performs on market data. Later in this chapter we will describe an empirical test that investigates whether all three adjustments are necessary or whether a simpler representation is sufficient. The implications of this test are twofold: (for the investor) knowledge of the adjustment terms provides information as to whether the Black-Scholes formula over- or undervalues the option and, (from an academic perspective) the adjustments provide information on whether systematic biases in the Black-Scholes formula arise due to departures from lognormally of the underlying security distribution. The final section summarizes this chapter and suggests directions for further research.

The Approximate-Valuation Model

The first step is to approximate a given probability distribution, $F(s)$, called the *true distribution*, with an alternative distribution, $A(s)$, called the *approximating distribution*.[3] The following notation will be employed:

$$\alpha_j(F) = \int_{-\infty}^{\infty} s^j f(s)\,ds, \qquad \mu_j(F) = \int_{-\infty}^{\infty} (s - \alpha_1(F))^j f(s)\,ds \quad (4.1)$$

where $i^2 = -1$, $\alpha_j(F)$ is the *j*th moment of distribution F, and $\mu_j(F)$ is the *j*th central moment of distribution F. We assume that $\alpha_j(F)$ exists for $j \leq n$.

Given $\alpha_n(F)$ exists, the first $n - 1$ cumulants (or semi-invariants) $\kappa_j(F)$ from $j = 1, \ldots, n - 1$ also exist (see Kendall and Stuart 1977). For reference, the first four cumulants are:

$$\kappa_1(F) = \alpha_1(F) \qquad\qquad\qquad (4.2)$$
$$\kappa_2(F) = \mu_2(F)$$
$$\kappa_3(F) = \mu_3(F)$$
$$\kappa_4(F) = \mu_4(F) - 3\mu_2(F)^2$$

The first cumulant is the mean, the second the variance, the third a measure of skewness, and the fourth a measure of kurtosis.

Analogous notation will be employed for the moments and cumulants of A; such as, $\alpha_j(A)$, $\mu_j(A)$, and $\kappa_j(A)$. It is assumed that both $\alpha_j(A)$ and $d^j A(s)/ds^j$ exist for $j \leq m$ (where m can differ from n).

The following series expansion for $f(s)$ in terms of $a(s)$ is proven in Jarrow and Rudd (1983), given $n, m \geq 5$:

$$f(s) = a(s) + \frac{(\kappa_2(F) - \kappa_2(A))}{2!}\frac{d^2 a(s)}{ds^2} - \frac{(\kappa_3(F) - \kappa_3(A))}{3!}\frac{d^3 a(s)}{ds^3}$$

$$+ \frac{((\kappa_4(F) - \kappa_4(A)) + 3(\kappa_2(F) - \kappa_2(A))^2)\,da^4(s)}{4!}\frac{}{ds^4} + \varepsilon(s) \qquad (4.3)$$

where $\kappa_1(A) \equiv \kappa_1(F)$.

By construction, the first moment of the approximating distribution is set equal to the first moment of the true distribution. The difference between $f(s)$ and $a(s)$ is then expressable as a series expansion involving the higher-order cumulants of both distributions and the derivatives of $a(s)$. The first term adjusts $a(s)$ to reflect any differences in variance between $f(s)$ and $a(s)$. The weighting factor is the second derivative of $a(s)$. The second term adjusts $a(s)$ to account for the difference in skewness between $f(s)$ and $a(s)$. The weighting factor is the third derivative. Similarly the fourth term compensates for the difference in kurtosis and variance between the two distributions with a weighting factor of the fourth derivative.[4] Depending on the existence of the higher moments, this expansion could be continued.

Our approach to obtain an approximate option-valuation formula is now straightfoward. Using $f(s)$ as the true distribution of the stock price at maturity, the expected value at maturity of a payout-protected option on that stock can be obtained.[5] The generalized Edgeworth series expansion then gives us an approximate expected value for the option at maturity in terms of the approximating distribution $a(s)$. To obtain the value of the option prior to maturity, we need to restrict the model such that a risk-neutrality valuation argument is valid. This reduces the class of stochastic processes acceptable for approximation (see Jarrow and Rudd 1981 for details).

Consider a payout-protected call option with striking price K and maturity date t, where its underlying stock's value at time 0 (today) is denoted S_0. The distribution of the stock price at the maturity of the option, S_t, given the current price, S_0, will be denoted by $Pr[S_t \leq s \mid S_0] \equiv F(s)$ and represents the true underlying distribution for the stock price over $[0,t]$. Let the risk-free rate r be constant over $[0,t]$. Consequently, under the risk-neutrality argument, the true value for the call option, $C(F)$, is (using the boundary condition at maturity):

$$C(F) = e^{-rt} \int_{-\infty}^{\infty} \max[0, S_t - K] dF(S_t) \qquad (4.4)$$

where $\alpha_1(F) \equiv S_0 e^{rt}$.

From the generalized Edgeworth series expansion (equation 4.3), we can rewrite the valuation formula as:

$$C(F) = C(A) + e^{-rt} \frac{(\kappa_2(F) - \kappa_2(A))}{2} \int_{-\infty}^{\infty} \max[0, S_t - K] \frac{d^2 a(S_t)}{dS_t^2} dS_t$$

$$- e^{-rt} \frac{(\kappa_3(F) - \kappa_3(A))}{3!} \int_{-\infty}^{\infty} \max[0, S_t - K] \frac{d^3 a(S_t)}{dS_t^3} dS_t \qquad (4.5)$$

$$+ e^{-rt} \frac{((\kappa_4(F) - \kappa_4(A)) + 3(\kappa_2(F) - \kappa_2(A)^2)}{4!} \int_{\infty}^{\infty} \max[0, S_t - K]$$

$$\cdot \frac{d^4 a(S_t)}{dS_t^4} \, dS_t + \varepsilon(K)$$

where $\alpha_1(A) \equiv e^{+rt} S_0$ and $C(A) \equiv e^{-rt} \int_{-\infty}^{\infty} \max[0, S_t - K] a(S_t) dS_t$.

Expression 4.5 approximates the option's true value with a formula, $C(A)$, based on the distribution $a(s)$ and corresponding adjustment terms. It is valid for any distribution $a(s)$ satisfying the assumptions behind the generalized Edgeworth series expansion. Given its widespread use in academics and professional trading, an obvious candidate for the approximating distribution, $a(s)$, is the lognormal distribution. In this case $C(A)$ will correspond to Black-Scholes (1973) formula and expression 4.5 will give the adjustment terms between the true option value, $C(F)$, and Black-Scholes formula, $C(A)$ arising from the departures from lognormality between the true and the lognormal distribution.

In this case, the expression for the approximate option price is:

$$C(F) = C(A) + e^{-rt} \frac{(\kappa_2(F) - k_2(A))}{2!} a(K) \qquad (4.6)$$

$$- e^{-rt} \frac{(\kappa_3(F) - k_3(A))}{3!} \frac{da(K)}{dS_t}$$

$$+ e^{-rt} \frac{((\kappa_4(F) - \kappa_4(A)) + 3(\kappa_2(F) - \kappa_2(A))^2)}{4!} \frac{d^2 a(K)}{dS_t^2} + \varepsilon(K)$$

where $C(A) = S_0 N(d) - Ke^{-rt} N(d - \sigma\sqrt{t})$,

$$d = \left[\log (S_0/Ke^{-rt}) + \frac{\sigma^2 t}{2} \right] / \sigma\sqrt{t},$$

and $N(\cdot) = $ cumulative standard normal.

A simple, "Bayesian" explanation of the formula is as follows: The investor's prior belief for the process of a particular optionable stock is that it follows Brownian motion with a constant variance. Hence (assuming the other requirements hold), the investor's anticipation is that the option price will be given by the Black-Scholes formula, $C(A)$. Further research, however, may suggest that the underlying process shows some degree of serial dependence so that the variance of the stock price at expiration will be $\kappa_2(F)$ rather than $\kappa_2(A)$. Expression 4.6 shows that, ceteris paribus, the impact of this departure from lognormality is $e^{-rt}(\kappa_2(F) - \kappa_2(A))a(K)/2$.

Similarly, we can also determine the effect of differing skewness and kurtosis between the lognormal and true distribution. Of course, there is no reason to stop with the fourth moment; all differing moments theoretically will have some impact on the true option price. However, computational considerations and the problems of estimation suggest that the effects of moments higher than the fourth be lumped into the error term, $\varepsilon(K)$.

Empirical Tests

We are primarily concerned as to whether the approximation technique, equation 4.6., is a useful device for investors. Our aim is to show that 4.6 provides information about whether the Black-Scholes formula over- or undervalues listed options. In other words, are there biases in the Black-Scholes model that can be attributed to departures from lognormality of the underlying security distribution?

It is well known that there are considerable problems in estimating skewness and kurtosis in common stock. These moments typically exhibit instability from one period to another. Hence a subsidiary goal is to determine if all three adjustments are required or whether the variance adjustment, for example, captures the majority of any bias in the Black-Scholes formula.

Data

To minimize computational costs, we selected the universe of all companies with exchange-traded options that did not split their stock from January 1974 to April 1982. There are 122 stocks meeting these criteria, which are displayed in table 4–1 together with the exchange and rotation cycle of the options.

All options were then assigned to a particular cell in a grid categorized by two dimensions: time-to-maturity and exercise price. Because of estimation difficulties with long-term options, we restrict at each date of analysis options

Table 4–1
Companies with Options and No Splits in Period January 1974 to April 1982

Underlying Stocks	Exchange
December-March-June Rotation	
Anheuser Busch Coc Inc	Philadelphia
Asarco Inc	Amex
Avco Corp	Philadelphia
Beatrice Foods Co	Amex
Becton Dickinson & Co	Philadelphia
Browning Ferris Inds	Amex
Brunswick Corp	Chicago
Champion Intl Corp	Chicago
Chase Manhattan Corp	Amex
Coastal Corp	Chicago
Coastal Corp	Amex
Computer Sciences Corp	Chicago
Corning Glass Wks	Chicago
Data Gen Corp	Pacific
Evans Prods Co	Chicago
Fuqua Inds Inc	Philadelphia
General Elec Co	Chicago
General Mtrs Corp	Chicago
General Tel & Electro	Amex
Gillette Co	Amex
Hercules Inc	Amex
International Tel & Tel	Chicago
K Mart Corp	Chicago
LTV Corp	Amex
Lear Siegler Inc	Philadelphia
Lockheed Corp	Pacific
McDonalds Corp	Chicago
Middle South Utils Inc	Chicago
Mohawk Data Sciences	Pacific
NCR Corp	Chicago
NLT Corp	Amex
Newmont Mng Corp	Philadelphia
Pfizer Inc	Amex
RCA Corp	Chicago
Safeway Stores Inc	Chicago
Trans World Corp	Pacific
U S Air Inc	Pacific
Whittaker Corp	Amex
January-April-July Rotation	
Allied Corp	Philadelphia
Allis Chalmers Corp	Philadelphia
American Cyanamid Co	Amex
American Express Co	Chicago
American Express Co	Amex
American Home Prods CP	Amex
American Tel & Teleg Co	Chicago
Avon Prods Inc	Chicago

Bethlehem Stl Corp	Chicago
Citicorp	Chicago
City Investing Co	Philadelphia
Clorox Co	Philadelphia
Communications Satelli	Philadelphia
Continental Telecom In	Amex
Duke Power Co	Philadelphia
Eastman Kodak Co	Chicago
Federal Natl Mtg Assn	Chicago
GAF Corp	Philadelphia
Goodyear Tire & Rubr	Amex
Greyhound Corp	Amex
Gulf Oil Corp	Amex
International Harvestr	Chicago
International Paper Co	Chicago
Lilly Eli & Co	Amex
Merck & Co Inc	Chicago
Merrill Lynch & Co Inc	Chicago
Merrill Lynch & Co Inc	Amex
Minnestoa Mng & Mfg Co	Chicago
Monsanto Co	Chicago
Motorola Inc	Amex
Northwest Airls Inc	Chicago
Phelps Dodge Corp	Amex
Pitney Bowes Inc	Amex
Pogo Producing Co	Pacific
Polaroid Corp	Chicago
Polaroid Corp	Pacific
Procter & Gamble Co	Amex
Scott Paper Co	Philadelphia
Sperry Corp	Chicago
TRW Inc	Amex
Texaco Inc	Amex
Texas Instrs Inc	Chicago
Union Carbide Corp	Amex
Union Carbide Corp	Amex
Upjohn Co	Chicago
Virginia Elec & Pwr Co	Philadelphia
Warner Lambert Co	Amex
Western Un Corp	Philadelphia
Westinghouse Elec Corp	Amex
Weyerhaeuser Co	Chicago
Xerox Corp	Chicago
Xerox Corp	Pacific

February-May-August Rotation

AMF Inc	Amex
American Elec Pwr Inc	Chicago
American Hosp Supply	Chicago
AMP Inc	Chicago
Boise Cascade Corp	Chicago
CBS Inc	Chicago

Colgate Palmolive Corp	Chicago
Commonwealth Edison Co	Chicago
Consolidated Edison NY	Amex
Dr Pepper Co	Amex
El Paso Co	Amex
General Foods Corp	Chicago
Grace W R & Co	Amex
Heublein Inc	Pacific
Holiday Inns Inc	Chicago
Honeywell Inc	Chicago
Manville Corp	Chicago
Louisiana Ld Expl Co	Philadelphia
Mgic Invt Corp	Chicago
Mgic Invt Corp	Amex
McDonnell Douglas Corp	Pacific
National Distill & Chem	Amex
Occidental Pete Corp	Chicago
Penny J C Inc	Amex
Reynolds Metals Co	Pacific
Schering Plough Corp	Pacific
Searle G D & Co	Amex
Skyline Corp	Chicago
Southern Co	Chicago
Sterling Drug Inc	Amex
Tenneco Inc	Amex
Tiger Intl Inc	Amex
Tosco Corp	Amex
Transamerica Corp	Philadelphia
UAL Inc	Chicago
Walter Jim Corp	Chicago
Woolworth F W Co	Philadelphia
Zenith Radio Corp	Amex

to the nearest five expiration dates. To make the categorization by exercise price, we first designate one option (with exercise price K) on a given underlying stock to be the at-the-money option. This option is chosen such that any other option with exercise price K' satisfies $|S - K| \geq |S - K'|$, with $K > K'$ in the case of equality. All other options on the underlying stock are then assigned to cells sequentially by exercise price, relative to the at-the-money option.

At each date of analysis, valid observations consist of options that have both closing bid and closing ask prices on the Interactive Data Corporation Analytics data base. This criterion removes restricted options and options for which there is essentially no market (for example, options whose market price is less than \$0.0625, the minimum option price on the exchanges). Hence, in every cross section there are a maximum of 122 observations in each cell.

To increase the number of observations we used different dates of analysis with each date differing by (approximately) one month. In this manner we can retain approximately the same maturity schedule of the options. For example, we used analysis dates of September 4, October 2, November 6, and December 7—all in 1981. In each case, the shortest maturity options expire two weeks from the date of analysis, the next shortest maturity options expire six weeks from the date of analysis, and so on. In this manner, we claim the observations within each cell are comparable but as independent as possible.

Figure 4–1 shows the total number of data points in the two-dimensional grid.

Estimation Procedures

To determine the benefits from using the adjustments we need to estimate various parameters. We treat these in turn:

1. *The instantaneous standard deviation, σ, of the underlying security for use in the Black-Scholes formula*: We estimate σ as the sample standard deviation of previous forty-five days of logarithmic returns.[6]
2. *Cumulants of the lognormal distribution.* These are obtained as simple functions of the instantaneous standard deviation (see Jarrow and Rudd 1981).

Figure 4–1. Grid of Observations

Time to Maturity \ Exercise Price	In-the- Money				At-the- Money				Out-of-the- Money			
Two weeks	2	2	5	37	113	159	53	12	2	1	0	386
Six weeks	0	0	4	39	142	199	133	60	17	6	1	601
Ten weeks	0	0	2	24	115	190	146	79	30	5	1	592
Fourteen weeks	1	2	3	20	112	177	156	107	44	15	6	643
Eighteen weeks	0	0	3	26	127	198	162	100	27	17	6	666
	3	4	17	146	609	923	650	358	120	44	14	2888

3. *Cumulants of the actual underlying stock process*: Notice, these cumulants are relevant to the distribution of the stock at expiration. Hence, because of the unknown stock process we estimate these cumulants from the sample moments of the underlying security returns over periods that equal the remaining time to maturity. For example, when estimating the cumulants of the stock distribution to evaluate a call expiring in two weeks we use two-week stock returns.

This implies that longer-term options typically require older data to maintain an acceptable number of observations. Unfortunately, it is recognized generally that data more than a few years old has little predictive information because of changing company characteristics and market conditions.[7] Our partial solutions to these problems are (a) to restrict options to a maximum of twenty-weeks maturity, and (b) to use fewer observations for the longer maturity options, with a minimum of twenty.

4. The *risk-free rate* was the ninety-day treasury-bill rate applicable at each date of analysis.

Directional Tests

Here we attempt to determine whether the adjustments improve (remove any biases in) the Black-Scholes formula. Let X represent the difference between the market price (defined as the average of the closing bid and ask prices) and the Black-Scholes price, Δ_1 represent the variance adjustment, Δ_2 represent the combined variance and skewness adjustments, and Δ_3 the combined variance, skewness, and kurtosis adjustments; that is,

$$X = C - C(A)$$
$$\Delta_1 = e^{-rt}(\kappa_2(F) - \kappa_2(A))a(K)/2$$
$$\Delta_2 = \Delta_1 - e^{-rt}(\kappa_3(F) - \kappa_3(A))a'(K)/6$$
$$\Delta_3 = \Delta_2 + e^{-rt}[\kappa_4(F) - \kappa_4(A) + 3(\kappa_2(F) - \kappa_2(A))^2]a''(\kappa)/24$$

where C is the observed market price of the call options.

We now examine the bivariate random variables (X, Δ_1), (X, Δ_2) and (X, Δ_3), and classify each according to the signs of the first and second components. For example, if $X > 0$, and $\Delta_1 > 0$ (that is, we observe $(+, +)$), then the variance adjustment is considered beneficial since the market price is greater than the Black-Scholes price and the variance adjustment tends to correct this tendency. Of course, the variance adjustment may "overshoot" so that the absolute error is smaller without the adjustment; that is,

$|C - C(A)| < |C - C(A) - \Delta_1|$). In this test we are not concerned with the absolute error, but whether the inclusion of the adjustments correct any biases in the Black-Scholes model. Similarly, the bivariate observation $(-, -)$ is also considered beneficial, while events $(-, +)$ and $(+, -)$ are counterproductive.

We can test the significance of the adjustments using a one-tail sign test.

$$H_0: P[(+,+)] + P[(-,-)] \leq P[(+,-)] + P[(-,+)]$$

against

$$H_1: P[(+,+)] + P[(-,-)] > P[(+,-)] + P[(-,+)].$$

The test stastistic is the number of $(+,+)$ and $(-,-)$ observations, the number of times the adjustment improves Black-Scholes.

Figures 4–2, 4–3, and 4–4 show values of the test statistic for the variance, variance plus skewness, and the combined adjustments. Each of the three adjustments is typically beneficial, however it is noticeable that the

Figure 4–2. Statistic Values for Adjustment Δ_1

Time to Maturity	In-the-Money				At-the-Money				Out-of-the-Money			
Two weeks	0	2	4	11	53	106 ***	25	1	0	0	0	202
Six weeks	0	0	2	16	77	126 ***	71	24	6	3	1	326
Ten weeks	0	0	2	11	60	124 ***	96 ***	44	11	2	0	350
Fourteen weeks	0	0	2	13	57	124 ***	97 ***	73 ***	21	7	5	399
Eighteen weeks	0	0	0	11	67	124 ***	96 **	61 *	16	15	3	393
	0	2	10	62	314	604 ***	385 ***	203 **	54	27	9	1670

*Significant at the 95-percent level.
**Significant at the 99-percent level.
***Significant at the 99.5-percent level.

Figure 4–3. Statistic Values for Adjustment Δ_2

Time to Maturity	In-the-Money				At-the-Money				Out-of-the-Money			
Two weeks	2	0	2	18	51	107 ***	23	2	0	0	0	205
Six weeks	0	0	3	22	70	124 ***	67	26	7	3	1	323
Ten weeks	0	0	2	12	62	121 ***	99 ***	46	13	3	0	358
Fourteen weeks	1	2	1	13	53	122 ***	94 **	63 *	19	7	5	380
Eighteen weeks	0	0	1	14	62	124 ***	95 *	59 *	13	11	2	381
	3	2	9	79	298	598 ***	378 ***	196 *	52	24	8	1647

*Significant at the 95-percent level.
**Significant at the 99-percent level.
***Significant at the 99.5-percent level.

Figure 4–4. Statistic Values for Adjustment Δ_3

Time to Maturity	In-the-Money				At-the-Money				Out-of-the-Money			
Two weeks	2	0	3	15	57	104 ***	34	9	1	0	0	225
Six weeks	0	0	3	23	69	136 ***	69	29	11	4	1	345
Ten weeks	0	0	1	14	58	119 ***	100 ***	49 *	13	3	1	358
Fourteen weeks	1	2	1	12	54	111 ***	90 *	61	18	7	5	362
Eighteen weeks	0	0	1	13	64	120 ***	97 **	60 *	13	11	2	381
	3	2	9	77	302	590 ***	390 ***	208 ***	56	25	9	1671

*Significant at the 95-percent level.
**Significant at the 99-percent level.
***Significant at the 99.5-percent level.

adjustment arising from the skewness of the security process is, on average, less beneficial than the other two adjustments. It is discouraging to note how few of the individual cell statistics are significant. On the assumption that aggregation over the different maturities yields independent observations across exercise prices, the at-the-money and just-out-of-the-money statistics are significant at the 99.5 percent level. From this set of data, the statistical evidence for equation 4.6 over all maturities and exercise prices is marginal at best. However, for the at- and out-of-the-money options the performance is better. Although in terms of total numbers, our formula 4.6 improves upon Black-Scholes approximately 60 percent of the time, because of the dependence between formula prices this aggregate number is not convincing.

From the investor's point of view, because of the existence of the bid-ask spread and transactions costs, simply knowing that the Black-Scholes price under- or overvalues the option is insufficient information to trigger a profitable trade. Figure 4–5 shows the average bid-ask spread for our sample of 2,888 options. Since the spread frequently is larger than the difference between the market price (average of bid and ask prices) and the Black-Scholes price (figure 4–6 shows this average difference), it is more interesting to question whether equation 4.6 performs better when there are significant pricing discrepancies.

Consequently, we then restricted the analysis to those options where Black-Scholes prices are anomalous with respect to market prices. We defined an anomaly whenever the Black-Scholes price was either (a) greater than the ask price plus ten cents, or (b) less than the bid price minus ten cents. We chose the value of ten cents because it represents the typical minimum transaction cost for an individual investor.[8] Hence, an investor observing a Black-Scholes price meeting these criteria would suspect that the market value of the option is incorrectly priced to such an extent that a profitable opportunity exists. The performance of 4.6 in these circumstances is indicative of whether the Black-Scholes model is truly isolating mispriced

Figure 4–5. Average Bid-Ask Spread

Time to Maturity	In-the-Money				At-the-Money				Out-of-the-Money		
Two weeks	1.00	0.62	0.52	0.48	0.38	0.20	0.11	0.11	0.09	0.06	0.0
Six weeks	0	0	0.69	0.49	0.41	0.23	0.12	0.10	0.08	0.09	0.06
Ten weeks	0	0	0.38	0.51	0.40	0.23	0.13	0.12	0.12	0.13	0.06
Fourteen weeks	0.50	0.69	0.50	0.56	0.40	0.27	0.17	0.14	0.15	0.14	0.21
Eighteen weeks	0	0	0.66	0.56	0.45	0.28	0.19	0.16	0.18	0.16	0.12

Figure 4–6. Average Difference between Midmarket and Black-Scholes Prices.

Time Maturity \ Exercise Price	In-the-Money				At-the-Money				Out-of-the-Money		
Two weeks	0.36	−0.24	−0.08	−0.03	−0.04	−0.06	0.06	0.35	0.24	0.09	0.0
Six weeks	0.0	0.0	−0.10	0.06	0.06	0.01	0.0	0.11	0.09	0.0	−0.07
Ten weeks	0.0	0.0	0.05	0.03	0.04	−0.12	−0.07	0.01	0.12	−0.10	0.09
Fourteen weeks	0.21	0.19	0.48	0.04	0.09	−0.06	−0.03	−0.02	0.06	0.03	−0.04
Eighteen weeks	0.0	0.0	0.19	0.08	0.10	−0.01	−0.08	−0.05	−0.17	−0.21	−0.21

options or simply providing erroneous values because of model mis-specification.

The results, shown in figures 4–7, 4–8, and 4–9 are far more encouraging. We can reject the null hypothesis in most cells where there are a significant number of observations at the 95 percent level or above. Overall, the approximate formula 4.6 reverses the anomaly almost 70 percent of the time; for the at- and out-of-the-money options we can reject the hypothesis that 4.6 adds only random noise at high levels of significance (see figure 4–9). This result also suggests that significant differences between market and Black-Scholes prices can be partially attributed to departures from lognormality (serial dependence, skewness, and kurtosis) in the underlying security process, particularly for out-of-the-money options.

Conclusion

This chapter describes an exploratory test of the Jarrow-Rudd option formula. Our tentative conclusion is that knowledge of the adjustments, Δ_1, Δ_2, and Δ_3 enables the investor on average to improve the Black-Scholes option price as a predictor of the option's fair value.

We have stressed that our test is far from definitive—particularly in that we are only concerned with the sign, rather than magnitude, of any differences between formula and market price. Moreover, there are a number of caveats to the procedure. First, we have used closing prices, which are subject to nonsimultaneity between the underlying security and option, although knowledge of the bid-ask spread mitigates this problem to some extent. Second, we have used Friday as our day of analysis. In our data there is some indication that Friday closing prices are of lesser quality than closing prices from other days.[9]

Figure 4–7. Δ_1 Statistic Values When Black-Scholes Anomalous

Time to Maturity	In-the-Money				At-the-Money				Out-of-the-Money			
Two weeks	0/1	0/0	1/1	1/10	13/28	46/61***	7/12	1/5	0/1	0/0	0/0	69/119
Six weeks	0/0	0/0	0/0	5/10	28/52	73/105***	36/55*	6/17	5/9	1/1	0/0	154/249
Ten weeks	0/0	0/0	0/0	4/7	31/48*	81/117***	55/71***	15/25	4/9	2/2	0/0	192/279
Fourteen weeks	0/0	0/0	0/1	4/6	27/48	80/108***	71/96***	35/48***	12/18	2/6	1/2	232/333
Eighteen weeks	0/0	0/0	0/0	2/5	34/68	85/122***	68/97***	38/53***	12/15	11/11	2/2	252/373
	0/1	0/0	1/2	16/38	133/244*	365/513***	237/331***	95/148***	33/52*	16/20	3/4	899/1353

*Significant at the 95-percent level.
**Significant at the 99-percent level.
***Significant at the 99.5-percent level.

Figure 4–8. Δ_2 Statistic Values When Black-Scholes Anomalous

Exercise Price / Time to Maturity	In-the-Money					At-the-Money				Out-of-the-Money		
Two weeks	1/1	0/0	0/1	4/10	13/28	*** 46/61	7/12	2/5	0/1	0/0	0/0	73/119
Six weeks	0/0	0/0		7/10	24/52	*** 69/105	* 34/55	7/17	5/9	1/1	0/0	147/249
Ten weeks	0/0	0/0		5/7	29/48	*** 80/117	*** 55/71	16/25	5/9	2/2	0/0	192/279
Fourteen weeks	0/0	0/0	0/1	3/6	24/48	*** 79/108	*** 67/96	32/48	10/18	2/6	1/2	218/333
Eighteen weeks	0/0	0/0		2/5	33/68	*** 83/122	*** 69/97	* 34/53	11/15	7/11	1/2	240/373
	1/1	0/0	0/2	21/38	123/244	*** 357/513	*** 232/331	91/148	31/52	12/20	2/4	870/1353

*Significant at the 95-percent level.
**Significant at the 99-percent level.
***Significant at the 99.5-percent level.

Figure 4–9. Δ_3 Statistic Values When Black-Scholes Anomalous

Exercise Price *Time to Maturity*	*In-the-Money*				*At-the-Money*				*Out-of-the-Money*			
Two weeks	1/1	0/0	0/1	4/10	13/28	** 40/61	8/12	4/5	1/1	0/0	0/0	71/119
Six weeks	0/0	0/0	0/0	9/10	27/52	*** 76/105	* 35/55	9/17	7/9	1/1	0/0	164/249
Ten weeks	0/0	0/0	0/0	5/7	26/48	*** 80/117	*** 55/71	17/25	5/9	2/2	0/0	190/279
Fourteen weeks	0/0	0/0	1/1	2/6	25/48	*** 74/108	*** 64/96	*** 29/35	9/18	2/6	1/2	207/333
Eighteen weeks	0/0	0/0	0/0	2/5	35/68	*** 80/122	*** 69/97	** 35/53	11/15	7/11	1/2	240/373
	1/1	0/0	1/2	22/38	126/244	*** 350/513	*** 231/331	94/148	* 33/52	12/20	2/4	872/1353

*Significant at the 95-percent level.
**Significant at the 99-percent level.
***Significant at the 99.5-percent level.

Further we have used the most naive procedures for estimating the moments of the true process. More careful estimation techniques will probably improve the performance of the approximate formula, although any improvement may be partially offset by use of a more sophisticated variance estimator for the variance of the underlying security in the Black-Scholes formula. Finally, our experimental design, while preserving as much as possible independence between observations, does not use available data very efficiently. To increase the observations in many of the cells to a desirable number we require a year or more of data. Nevertheless, in spite of these difficulties, the results presented earlier are justification for proceeding to more sophisticated empirical tests.

Notes

1. For example, a partial list includes Black and Scholes (1973), Merton (1973), Cox (1975), Cox and Ross (1976), Geske (1979), and Rubinstein (1980).

2. Option-valuation models based on the empirical distribution of stock prices have been proposed (for example, Kassouf 1969 and the model by Gastineau and Madansky reported in Gastineau 1975). It may be argued that the differences between, for instance, the Black-Scholes and Gastineau-Madansky prices demonstrate the importance (or lack) of the departures from lognormality. Unfortunately, to our knowledge, no tests (or even derivation) of the Gastineau-Madansky model have appeared in the literature.

3. See Jarrow and Rudd (1983) for further details.

4. For any distribution, $\mu_4(F) = k_4(F) + 3k_2(F)^2$. Consequently, the third adjustment term reflects the differing "unadjusted" kurtosis between the two distributions.

5. See Cox and Rubinstein (1983) for the definition of a payout-protected option. For organized exchanges, this would correspond to an American call option whose underlying stock has no dividend payments over the life of the option. The above approach could easily be generalized to include constant dividend yields for European options or American options where the conditions are such that it is never optimal to exercise early.

6. We could have used more sophisticated estimation procedures (for example, Beckers 1980) and hence are open to the criticism that we have biased the results in our favor. However, we have used equally naive and arbitrary procedures for estimating the cumulants of the true distribution. Hence, it is reasonable that any improvements in estimating σ could be offset by better techniques for estimating the cumulants.

7. A better solution to these difficulties would be to build a predictive model for each of the cumulants.

8. See, for example, Phillips and Smith (1980).

9. In a limited experiment we tested the model on Monday closing prices. A casual examination of the data indicated that average spreads were smaller and the Black-Scholes model fitted better.

References

Beckers, C. "An Empirical Test of Security Price Volatility Estimators Incorporating High, Low, and Closing Price Observations." Unpublished Manuscript. University of California, Berkeley, 1980.

Black, F. "Fact and Fantasy in the Use of Options," *Financial Analysts Journal* 31 (1975): 36–72.

Black, F., and Scholes, M. "The Pricing of Options and Corporate Liabilities." *Journal of Political Economy* 81 (1973): 637–659.

Cox, J. "Notes on Option Pricing I: Constant Elasticity of Variance Diffusions." Stanford University, Mimeographed. 1975.

Cox, J. and Ross, S. "The Valuation of Options for Alternative Stochastic Processes." *Journal of Financial Economics* 3 (1976): 145–166.

Cox, J. and Rubinstein, M. *Option Markets*, Englewood Cliffs, N.J.: Prentice-Hall, 1983, forthcoming.

Gastineau, G. *The Stock Options Manual*, New York: McGraw-Hill, 1975.

Geske, R. "The Valuation of Compound Options." *Journal of Financial Economics* 7 (1979): 63–81.

Jarrow, R. and Rudd, A. "Approximate Option Valuation for Arbitrary Stochastic Processes," *Journal of Financial Economics* 11 (1983).

Kassouf, S. "An Econometric Model for Option Price with Implications for Investor's Expectations and Audacity." *Econometrica* 37 (1969): 685–694.

Kendall, M. and Stuart, A. *The Advanced Theory of Statistics I* (Distribution Theory) 4th ed., New York: Macmillan, 1977.

MacBeth, J. and Merville, L. "Tests of the Black-Scholes and Cox Call Option Valuation Models." *Journal of Finance* 35 (1980): 285–303.

Merton, R., "Theory of Rational Option Pricing," *Bell Journal of Economics and Management Science* 4 (1973): 141–183.

Phillips, S. and Smith, C. "Trading Costs for Listed Options: The Implications for Market Efficiency," *Journal of Financial Economics* 8 (1980): 179–201.

Rubinstein, M. "Displaced Diffusion Option Pricing." Mimeographed. University of California, Berkeley, 1980.

5

Tests of Market Efficiency for American Call Options

Edward C. Blomeyer and
Robert C. Klemkosky

The option-pricing model developed by Black and Scholes (1973) has been one of the major contributions to financial theory in recent years. It has also been widely adopted and utilized by investor practitioners. However, previous authors have observed that the Black-Scholes model gives biased model prices when used to price unprotected American call options, which do not adjust the exercise price for cash-dividend distributions. This bias may be due, in part, to violation of the Black-Scholes assumptions of European option contracts with no dividend distributions on the underlying stock prior to expiration of the contract.[1]

Roll (1977) developed a valuation formula for unprotected American call options with a known single-dividend distribution prior to expiration of the option contract, and this chapter provides a comparative performance evaluation of the Black-Scholes and Roll option-pricing models. The objectives of this chapter are twofold. First, the ability of each model to identify overvalued and undervalued option contracts on an ex-post basis is examined by using the hedging technique suggested by Black-Scholes (1972). Next, weak-form option-market efficiency is tested by using each model to identify overvalued/undervalued option contracts, forming hedged positions between the option and the underlying stock, and holding portfolios of hedges over a one-month holding period. The hedge returns are then calculated and adjusted for actual transaction costs to the market's most cost-efficient trader, an arbitrageur. Transaction-by-transaction option and stock-price information is used in this study, which eliminates synchronization and false transaction-quotation problems associated with using daily closing quotations.

The Roll Valuation Model

If an unprotected American call option is written on a stock that pays no dividend prior to the option expiration date, the Black-Scholes model can be

---
The authors wish to acknowledge helpful comments from H.E. Johnson.

applied directly since the option should not be exercised early.[2] If the same stock should have a cash-dividend distribution prior to the option expiration date, the Black-Scholes model prices will be biased downwards due to the possibility of early exercise of the option to capture the dividend payment. The degree of this model-price bias is sensitive to the size of the dividend relative to the exercise price, the time to the ex-dividend date, and the stock-return variance rate. The roll valuation model uses a combination of three hypothetical European call options that exactly match the contingencies faced by the unprotected American call option holder, and the values of all three hypothetical options can be solved for directly. The following notation is that proposed by Roll (1977):

$S =$ the current stock price net of the known dividend discounted at the risk-free rate from the ex-dividend date,

$X =$ the exercise price,

$T =$ the time until the expiration date,

$\sigma^2 =$ the variance rate of the return on S,

$r =$ the risk-free rate of interest,

$D =$ the known dividend, and

$t =$ the time to the ex-dividend date.

The Roll-valuation-model price, C can be given as:[3]

$$C(S,X,T,\sigma,r,D,t,S^*) = C_A + C_B - C_C \qquad (5.1)$$

where:

$$C_A = S \cdot N(d_1) - e^{rT} \cdot X \cdot N(d_2), \qquad (5.2)$$

$$C_B = S \cdot N(d_3) - e^{-rt} \cdot S^* \cdot N(d_4), \qquad (5.3)$$

$$C_C = S \cdot (d_5,d_1) - e^{-rT} \cdot X \cdot N(d_6,d_2)$$
$$-e^{rt} \cdot (S^* + \alpha D - X) \cdot N(d_6), \qquad (5.4)$$

$$d_1 = \frac{\ln\left\{\dfrac{S}{X}\right\} + \left\{r + \dfrac{\sigma^2}{2}\right\}T}{\sigma\sqrt{T}}, \qquad d_2 = d_1 - \sigma\sqrt{T},$$

$$d_3 = \frac{\ln\left\{\dfrac{S}{S^*}\right\} + \left\{r + \dfrac{\sigma^2}{2}\right\}t}{\sigma\sqrt{t}}, \qquad d_4 = d_3 - \sigma\sqrt{t},$$

$$d_5 = \frac{\ln\left\{\dfrac{S}{S^*}\right\} + \left\{r + \dfrac{\sigma^2}{2}\right\}t}{\sigma\sqrt{t}}, \text{ and } d_6 = d_5 - \sigma\sqrt{t}.$$

$N(d_i)$ is the univariate cumulative normal-probability distribution function, $N(d_i d_j)$ is the bivariate cumulative normal-probability distribution function with correlation coefficient $\sqrt{(t/T)}$, equation 5.2 is the Black-Scholes option-pricing model, equation 5.4 involves the compound-option valuation formula developed by Geske (1979), and S^* is the solution to:

$$S^* \cdot N(d_7) - e^{-r(T-t)} \cdot X \cdot N(d_8) - S^* - \alpha D + X = 0. \qquad (5.5)$$

Where:

$$d_7 = \frac{\ln\left\{\dfrac{S^*}{X}\right\} + \left\{r + \dfrac{\sigma^2}{2}\right\}\left\{T - t\right\}}{\sigma\sqrt{(T-t)}}, \text{ and } d_8 = d_7 - \sigma\sqrt{(T-t)}.$$

Equation 5.5 gives the ex-dividend date stock price, S^*, above which the option would be exercised early to caputre the dividend payment.

Ex-Post Comparative-Model Performance Evaluation

If a call-option pricing model correctly identifies the equilibrium-option pricing process, then the model could be used to identify options that are overvalued or undervalued in the marketplace. Since the market forces should cause the mispriced options to return to an appropriate equilibrium call price, a trading strategy could be employed that uses the pricing model to develop an appropriate short or long position in the mispriced call with a resultant positive-holding period return. The ex-post performance tests in this section provide a comparative evaluation of the Black-Scholes and Roll models' ability to identify overvalued and undervalued call options. If one model consistently develops higher holding-period returns, then that model demonstrates superior ex-post performance.[4]

Data

Transaction-by-transaction stock and option-price information for Chicago Board Option Exchange (CBOE) listed options written on eighteen New York Stock Exchange (NYSE) listed stocks were obtained from Francis Emory Fitch, Inc. The twelve trading days, during the period July 1977 to June 1978, were selected one per month from the week following the third Friday of the month that is the option-contract expiration week, with all options under examination having at least three weeks remaining until expiration. Additionally, all options under examination had exactly one ex-dividend date occurring prior to the expiration date. This limited most option contracts under observation to ninety days or less to expiration.[5] Initially, the data sample contained approximately 18,000 option transactions, with transaction times reported to the nearest minute. When multiple transactions occurred at a particular minute, only the first transaction was considered for inclusion in the performance tests. After filtering out restricted options and multiple-option transactions, 9,108 option transactions remained for evaluation.[6]

Options included in this study had to be actively traded in order to provide an adequate number of observations for transaction-by-transaction performance evaluation. Also, the options had to be written on stocks that paid a quarterly dividend throughout the examination period. Additionally, a stratification of dividend yields was required to effectively evaluate the ex-post performance difference between the Black-Scholes and Roll models.

The risk-free interest rate was the mean of the bid-asked quotations listed in the *Wall Street Journal*, on the day before the transaction observation date, for a treasury bill maturing at approximately the same date as the option expiration date. Dividend information was taken from *Moody's Dividend Record*, with the actual dividend declared during the life of the option contract used in the ex-post tests. The stock price input to both the Black-Scholes and Roll models was the market price of the stock net of the actual dividend declared discounted at the risk-free rate over the time period elapsing between the transaction date and the ex-dividend date. This adjustment to the stock price assumes that the market price of the stock drops by the amount of the dividend on the ex-dividend date, an assumption that is supported by evidence presented by Durand and May (1960), and contrary to evidence presented by Elton and Gruber (1970).

Variance Estimation

An implied variance technique is used in this study to provide stock-return variance estimates for the Black-Scholes and Roll models. Chiras and

Manaster (1978) suggest that the implied standard deviations should be weighted by the price elasticity of an option with respect to its implied standard deviation. The weighting function given by Chiras and Manaster is:

$$\text{WISD} = \frac{\sum\limits_{j=1}^{N} ISD_j \dfrac{\delta c_j}{\delta \sigma_j} \dfrac{\sigma_j}{c_j}}{\sum\limits_{j=1}^{N} \dfrac{\delta c_j}{\delta \sigma_j} \dfrac{\sigma_j}{c_j}}, \tag{5.6}$$

where:

$N =$ the number of options recorded on a particular stock for the observation date,

$\text{WISD} =$ the weighted implied standard deviation for a particular stock return on the observation date,

$ISD_j =$ the implied standard deviation for option j written on the stock, and

$\dfrac{\delta_j c_j \sigma_j}{\delta \sigma_j c_j} =$ the price elasticity of option j with respect to its implied standard deviation.

The advantages of using WISDs are twofold. First, Chiras and Manaster (1978) have indicated that WISDs are better estimators of future standard deviations than are historical standard deviations. Second, the calculations of a WISD does not require the gathering of historical stock return information.

The WISD is calculated by using the first transaction of the day for all options written on a particular stock that are not in a restricted trading status. If an option did not trade before noon, it was not included in the WISD calculation. A numerical-search routine is used that solves for σ_s by equating the market price of the call plus or minus $.005 to the Black-Scholes price given by equation 5.2. Occasionally, the market price of the call is too low to permit convergence by a model price. These options were eliminated from the WISD calculation. An average of 5.8 option transactions were included in each WISD calculation. With three exceptions, at least three-standard-deviation estimates were included in the WISD calculations.[7]

The WISD given by equation 5.6 is the standard-deviation input to the Black-Scholes model. For the Roll model, a WISD cannot be calculated directly since a numerical-search routine must be used to find S^*, the indifference stock price. Consequently, the WISD from equation 5.6 was used as the standard-deviation input to the Roll model. Since the Black-Scholes model is the correct pricing relationship for an unprotected European call option, this introduces a bias into the call prices given by the Roll model. For a given set of option parameters, the Black-Scholes model gives a higher implied variance than would the Roll model. This higher implied variance will bias the Roll-model call prices upwards since the partial derivative of the call price with respect to the variance, $\delta C/\delta \sigma^2$, is greater than zero. The magnitude of this bias, although it should be small, cannot be determined empirically since the Roll-model call prices are higher than Black-Scholes-model call prices due to the possibility of early exercise of the call option.

Methodology

Beginning with the first transaction of the day for a particular option, a model call price is calculated using equation 5.2 for the Black-Scholes model and equation 5.1 for the Roll model. The stock-price input to both models is the price of the simultaneous (rounded to the minute) or previous stock transaction. The model call option price is then compared to the market price. If the model price is higher (lower) than the market price, the call is undervalued (overvalued) and a long (short) position is taken in the call with a corresponding short (long) position in the stock. Using the hedging technique suggested by Black and Scholes (1972) the investment in the hedge is given by:

$$V_{H1} = C - \frac{\partial C}{\partial S}S < 0 \qquad (5.7)$$

if the option is undervalued, and:

$$V_{H2} = \frac{\partial C}{\partial S}S - C > 0 \qquad (5.8)$$

if the option is overvalued. The hedge position is then maintained until the next option transaction at which time it is closed out at the new transaction prices, a return is calculated, and a new hedge is formed. The excess return on a hedge held from time t until $t + 1$ for an initially undervalued call is given by:

$$R_H = C_{t+1} - C_t - \frac{\partial C}{\partial S}\{S_{t-1} - S_t\} - \{e^{r\Delta t} - 1\}V_{H1} \qquad (5.9)$$

and, for an initially overvalued call the return is given by:

$$R_H = \frac{\partial C}{\partial S}\{S_{t+1} - S_t\} - \{C_{t+1} - C_t\} - \{e^{r\Delta t} - 1\}V_{H2} \qquad (5.10)$$

The hedge ratio, $\partial C/\partial S$, is:

$$\frac{\partial C}{\partial S} = N(d_1) \qquad (5.11)$$

for the Black-Scholes model, and:

$$\frac{\partial C}{\partial S} = N(d_1) + N(d_3) - N(d_5, d_1) \qquad (5.12)$$

for the Roll model. The expected returns given by equations 5.9 and 5.10 are zero only if the call prices at time t and $t + 1$ are the model prices, the hedge is adjusted continuously, and all other Black-Scholes assumptions are met.

Boyle and Emanuel (1980) have demonstrated that discretely adjusted Black-Scholes hedge-excess returns will have a zero mean and positive skewness, resulting in about 68 percent of all hedge-excess returns being negative. If the discretely adjusted hedges are established at market prices, the hedge-excess returns need not have these distributional characteristics since the contribution to the hedge return of the difference between model and market prices may dominate these distributional characteristics. However the expected hedges excess return is positive if the model is successful at identifying overvalued and undervalued call options and the hedge is established properly.

The dollar return on the hedge is then scaled by the absolute size of the investment, which is:

$$\text{Percent } R_H = \frac{R_H}{|V_H|} \qquad (5.13)$$

The returns given by equation 5.13 are aggregated across all transactions on all options written on a particular stock over all twelve observation days to provide a total return figure. Mean-holding-period returns are then calculated for both of the total-return figures.

Table 5–1
Ex-Post Mean-Holding-Period-Return Summary for Option Hedges Written on One Stock across Twelve Trading Days

	Stock						
Statistic[a]	BLY	DIS	BGH	HAL	TXN	KM	UPJ
Percent dividend yield	.6	.7	1.7	2.0	2.1	2.2	3.5
Mean-percent implied variance	20.60	8.17	7.24	4.57	7.34	7.10	4.87
Black-Scholes model							
Mean-percent return	.152[b]	.117[b]	.074[b]	.040	.074[b]	.103[b]	.060[b]
	(5.23)	(3.82)	(5.24)	(1.49)	(4.93)	(2.49)	(2.01)
Percent profitable							
transactions	47.4	47.4	55.4	51.2	54.5	58.0	51.0
Roll model							
Mean-percent return	.152[b]	.117[b]	.073[b]	.040	.073[b]	.103[b]	.064[b]
	(5.23)	(3.82)	(5.17)	(1.49)	(4.87)	(2.49)	(2.19)
Percent profitable							
transactions	47.4	47.4	55.8	51.2	55.0	58.0	58.5
Test of significance (t-value)	.00	.00	.05	.00	.05	.00	−.11
Total number of transactions	819	310	733	283	644	255	337

[a]This table summarizes the transaction-by-transaction mean-holding-period returns for all option hedges written on one stock over all twelve trading days. The transaction-by-transaction holding-period returns are calculated by equation 5.13 in the text. The t-statistic is reported in parenthesis. The value tests for

Results of Ex-Post Performance Tests

A return summary for hedges involving all options written on each of the eighteen stocks across all twelve trading days is presented in table 5–1. The mean-holding-period returns realized from the Roll model exceeded those realized from the Black-Scholes model for seven of the eighteen stocks, with none of the differences between the mean-holding-period returns for the two models significant at the .05 level.[8] For both the Black-Scholes and Roll models, fifteen of the mean-holding-period returns were significantly different from zero at the .05 level and positive.[9]

Since the Roll model explicitly allows for the early exercise of an American call option, the Roll model should outperform the Black-Scholes model for options written on high-dividend-yield stocks. To investigate this hypothesis, the options were stratified into three portfolios based upon the dividend yield of the underlying stocks. The dividend yields were estimated by dividing the total dollar amount of the dividends actually paid during the one-year observation period by the median opening stock price for the twelve observation days. The low-dividend-yield portfolio contained options written

					Stock					
HON	*DOW*	*DD*	*RCA*	*UTX*	*OXY*	*GW*	*ITT*	*ATT*	*F*	*GM*
4.1	4.4	4.9	4.9	5.3	5.4	5.8	6.2	7.3	7.6	10.4
6.09	9.17	3.28	8.34	5.88	11.23	17.40	4.79	1.29	3.59	3.45
.070[b]	.138[b]	.048[b]	.070[b]	.105[b]	.093[b]	.066	.062[b]	.038	.067[b]	.035[b]
(4.62)	(3.77)	(3.25)	(2.70)	(2.66)	(4.38)	(.51)	(2.34)	(1.81)	(3.28)	(3.75)
52.9	56.6	53.8	59.5	46.9	63.1	58.6	60.7	54.7	60.5	56.4
.086[b]	.142[b]	.044[b]	.070[b]	.086[b]	.093[b]	.112	.062[b]	.030	.058	.041[b]
(5.93)	(3.90)	(2.99)	(2.72)	(2.37)	(4.38)	(.87)	(2.36)	(1.45)	(2.86)	(4.63)
59.9	57.1	54.2	61.0	68.1	63.1	60.3	61.4	57.3	59.6	65.3
−.78	−.08	.19	−.01	.35	.00	−.25	−.01	.29	.30	−.52
733	539	740	543	213	811	237	427	234	337	913

significance of the difference between the mean-holding-period returns generated by using the Black-Scholes model and the Roll model.

[b]Mean returns significantly different from zero at the .05 level.

on Bally (BLY), Burroughs (BGH), Disney (DIS), Halliburton (HAL), K-Mart (KM), and Texas Instruments (TXN). All of these stocks had dividend yields between .6 percent and 2.2 percent. The medium-dividend-yield portfolio consisted of options written on Dow Chemical (DOW), Dupont (DD), Honeywell (HON), Radio Corporation of America (RCA), and Upjohn (UPJ). The dividend yield for these stocks ranged from 3.5 to 4.9 percent. For the high-dividend-yield portfolio, the dividend yields ranged from 5.3 to 10.4 percent. Included in this portfolio were options written on American Telephone and Telegraph (ATT), Ford Motor Company (F), General Motors (GM), Gulf and Western (GW), International Telephone and Telegraph (ITT), Occidental Petroleum (OXY), and United Technologies (UTX). The actual dividend-yield estimates for each of the eighteen stocks, along with the arithmetic mean of the implied return variance rates for each stock, are summarized in table 5–1.

The Roll model collapses into the Black-Scholes model when the ex-dividend-date indifference stock price becomes infinite. This indifference stock price, $S*$, is highly sensitive to the ratio of the expected discounted dividend to the exercise price, De^{-rt*}/X, and to the stock-return variance rate, σ_s^2. If the ratio $De^{-rt}*/X$ is sufficiently small, or σ_s^2 is sufficiently large, it is highly unlikely that early exercise will occur, and the Roll model reduces to the Black-Scholes model. Consequently, small performance differences should be observed between the Black-Scholes and Roll models for options written on high-variance, low-dividend-yield stocks, such as BLY and large performance differences should occur between the two models for options written on low-variance, high-dividend-yield stocks, such as ATT or GM. Examination of table 5–1 indicates that this supposition is partially supported by the results. Also, the sensitivity of S^* to the stock-return variance rate is indicated by observing the almost nonexistent model-performance difference for options written on OXY, a stock that has a high return variance and a high dividend yield. For options written on OXY, the Roll model reduced to the Black-Scholes model, giving identical call prices, for eleven of the twenty-four option contracts examined. For the remaining thirteen option contracts, both models gave almost identical call prices.

For the 3,044 option hedges written on low-dividend-yield stocks, the mean-holding-period returns produced by the Black-Scholes model and the Roll model were .099 percent and .098 percent, respectively. For the medium-dividend-yield portfolio, the mean returns for all 2,892 hedges were .076 percent for the Black-Scholes model and .080 percent for the Roll model. And, for the 3,172 option hedges written on high-dividend-yield stocks, the mean returns were .064 percent for the Black-Scholes model and .067 percent for the Roll model. All of the mean returns were significant at the .05 level, with the t-values ranging from 5.11 to 9.35, with none of the mean returns generated by the two models for the three portfolios being significantly different from each other at the .05 level.

Examination of table 5–1 indicates that both models produced identical return streams for options written on BLY, DIS, HAL, and KM. Consequently, the performance difference between the two models for the low-dividend-yield portfolio is due solely to options written on BGH and TXN. For the high-dividend-yield portfolio, the Black-Scholes model outperformed the Roll model for options written on F, ATT, and UTX. The Roll model produced superior performance for options written on GM, GW, and ITT. The Roll model produced its best performance, relative to the Black-Scholes model, on GM, which had the highest dividend yield of all stocks under examination.

It was anticipated that the Roll model would significantly outperform the Black-Scholes model for options written on high-dividend-yield stocks. However, the results reported in this section do not support this contention. As was expected, the largest performance differential between the two models occurred for options written on medium- to high-dividend-yield stocks. However, the Black-Scholes model generated mean-holding-period returns, which exceeded those generated by the Roll model, for three of the seven high-dividend-yield stocks and one of the five medium-dividend-yield stocks. These results suggest that the Roll model is not superior to the Black-Scholes model in its ability to identify overvalued and undervalued call options.

Comparative Model-Pricing-Bias Evaluation

Several authors have reported that the Black-Scholes model gives systematically biased model prices, and Roll (1977) suggests that this bias may be partially due to the possibility of early exercise of an unprotected American call option.[10] Since the decision to exercise an American call option at the ex-dividend date should be influenced by the degree to which the option is in/out-of-the-money, the Black-Scholes and Roll models could have differing pricing bias characteristics. To examine the model-pricing bias, the degree to which an option is in/out-of-the-money was compared to the degree to which the model price differs from the market price. Using the technique suggested by MacBeth and Merville (1979), the following quantities were computed for each option transaction. The percent to which an option is in/out-of-the-money is given by:

$$M = \frac{S - Xe^{-rt^*}}{Xe^{-rt^*}} , \qquad (5.14)$$

and, the percent to which the option is overvalued/undervalued relative to the market is given by:

$$P = \frac{C_{market} - C_{model}}{C_{model}} . \qquad (5.15)$$

Examination of a graphical relationship between equations 5.14 and 5.15 for the Black-Scholes and Roll models indicated that both models had virtually identical pricing-bias characteristics. Both of the models tended to undervalue, relative to the market, out-of-the-money call options and priced fairly well at-the-money and in-the-money call options. These results are exactly opposite to the out-of-the-money bias for options with less than ninety days to maturity reported by MacBeth and Merville (1979) and are in accordance with the out-of-the-money bias reported by Black (1975) and Merton (1976).

MacBeth and Merville observed a linear relationship between the degree to which an option is in/out-of-the-money and its implied variance, with out-of-the-money options having lower implied variances than in-the-money options. By linear regression they estimated an at-the-money variance, which is higher than out-of-the-money implied variance, and used this variance estimate as the input to the Black-Scholes model. Since

$$\frac{\partial C}{\partial \sigma} > 0,$$

this variance estimate systematically biases the out-of-the-money model prices upwards, increasing the degree to which the Black-Scholes model overvalues out-of-the-money options. The implied variance weighting function used in this study does not impose this type of bias.

The Black-Scholes and Roll models appeared to have almost identical in/out-of-the-money pricing-bias characteristics, which suggests that this bias is not due to the possibility of early exercise of the call option. MacBeth and Merville (1980) have demonstrated that the magnitude and direction of the out-of-the money pricing bias is sensitive to the stochastic process governing the stock-price distribution, which suggests that the in/out-of-the-money pricing bias is a stock-return-variance-related problem.

Ex-Ante Tests of Market Efficiency

In the previous section, trading rules using both the Black-Scholes and Roll option pricing models developed, on average, statistically significant and positive-holding-period excess returns. These results suggested that the pricing models were successful in identifying overvalued/undervalued call options. It is possible that a trader could use the option-pricing models to identify overvalued/undervalued calls and earn an economic profit. If his profit is abnormally high for the amount of risk undertaken, the market is inefficient to the trader and his trading rule. Previous studies using option-pricing models to identify overvalued/undervalued call options and then testing for market efficiency have produced contradictory conclusions. Black-Scholes (1972) could not reject the hypothesis that the market was efficient. Galai (1977) detected some inefficiencies, and Chiras and Manaster (1978) concluded that the market was inefficient for the period under examination. Phillips and Smith (1980) suggested that Galai and Chiras-Manaster had underestimated transactions costs, and after adjustment for actual transactions costs, market efficiency could not be rejected.

In this section, option-market efficiency is examined using trading rules involving the Black-Scholes and Roll models to identify overvalued/undervalued call options. Holding-period excess returns are adjusted by transactions costs for the market's most efficient trader, an arbitrageur. If the arbitrageur can consistently earn a positive excess return on portfolios on hedges, market efficiency can be rejected.

Methodology

The objective of the ex-ante tests is to duplicate the activities of an actual trader and to determine if this trader could earn an abnormal economic profit. Consequently, realistic delays between identification of possibly profitable investment opportunities and the actual execution of the hedge position must be incorporated. Additionally, a filter rule should be employed to ensure that only options that are significantly mispriced are considered for investment. Finally, the holding periods should be lengthy enough to reduce the effects of transactions costs. Galai (1977) demonstrated that transactions costs estimates of one percent washed out daily holding-period returns. Thus, a one-month holding period is used in this study.

For the market-efficiency tests, the same transaction-by-transaction data used in the ex-post performance tests is incorporated, with several modifications. First, the initial three hours of the trading day are reserved for computing a variance estimate using equation 5.6. As in the ex-post tests, an implied variance is computed using option and stock-price information for the first option transaction of the day. If a particular option does not trade before noon, it is not included in the implied variance calculation. As in the ex-post tests, options in a restricted trading status are not included in the implied variance estimate. Next, options written on stocks that have an ex-dividend date occurring during the one month holding period are eliminated from consideration. Finally, a reasonable time delay between identification of an appropriately mispriced option and execution of the hedged position is needed. Stock and option-price information for the next transactions occurring at least five and fifteen minutes after identification of the mispriced option was used to form the hedge position. No adjustment is made to the stock transaction prices to ensure compliance to the "uptick" rule.[11] After these modifications to the data file, 2,211 option transactions, out of 9,108 option transactions in the original data file, remained for evaluation.

Beginning with the first transaction of the day, and continuing for three hours until noon, stock and option transaction-price information is gathered for computation of an implied-variance rate using equation 5.6. Beginning at noon, and continuing throughout the remainder of the trading day, model prices are calculated using equation 5.2 for the Black-Scholes model and equation 5.1 for the Roll model. To ensure that the option is sufficiently mispriced, a filter rule is used before identifying the call option as undervalued or overvalued. The market-efficiency tests are performed using both a five-percent and ten-percent filter. To be considered as sufficiently undervalued, the model price must exceed the market price by the amount of the filter. If the market price exceeds the model price by the amount of the filter, the option is considered to be overvalued. If the option is undervalued (overvalued), a long (short) position is taken in the option and a corresponding short (long) position is taken in the stock. For an undervalued option, the investment in the hedge is given by equation 5.7, and for an overvalued option, the investment in the hedge is given by equation 5.8.

The hedge position is maintained over the one-month holding period and is closed out at the opening stock and option transaction prices for the next transaction day, which is one month later. The dollar return on the hedge formed from an undervalued call, held over the one-month holding period, time t to time $t + 1$, is given by:

$$R_H = C_{t+1} - C_t - \frac{\partial C}{\partial S}\{S_{t+1} - S_t\}. \tag{5.16}$$

For an overvalued call, the dollar holding-period return is computed by:

$$R_H = \frac{\partial C}{\partial S}\{S_{t+1} - S_t\} - \{C_{t+1} - C_t\}. \tag{5.17}$$

The hedge ratio, $\partial C/\partial S$, is given by equation 5.11 for the Black-Scholes model and equation 5.12 for the Roll model. The dollar return on the hedge is scaled by the absolute size of the investment, and the percent holding-period return on the hedge is calculated by equation 5.13. The percent holding-period returns are aggregated across all hedges for all eighteen stocks for each of the eleven one-month holding periods, and portfolio holding-period returns are calculated.

The hedge positions given by equations 5.7 and 5.8 are riskless only if the hedge is formed at model prices, not market prices, and the hedges are adjusted continuously. Since neither of these conditions hold for the ex-ante tests, the hedge returns given by equations 5.16 and 5.17 are not entirely riskless returns.

Black-Scholes (1972) argue that all risk associated with a hedge position is diversifiable risk and that portfolios of hedges should earn a risk-free rate of return. Both Black-Scholes (1972) and Galai (1977) present empirical evidence to support this contention. The authors regress holding-period returns for portfolios of hedges on an appropriate stock-market index and report significant intercepts and insignificant slope coefficients. Consequently, portfolios of hedges should earn a risk-free rate of return. However, recent evidence presented by Boyle-Emanuel (1980) suggests that portfolios of discretely adjusted option hedges may contain some systematic risk that would prohibit rejecting market efficiency if the excess-hedge returns, net of transactions costs, are positive. If the excess returns, net of transactions costs are negative, market efficiency can be accepted.

To determine if the trader can earn an economic profit above the risk-free rate of return, the holding-period return must be adjusted for all transactions costs associated with entering and exiting the hedge position. Phillips and Smith (1980) present a summary of CBOE and NYSE transactions costs for arbitrageurs, option-market makers, and individual traders. The transactions cost adjustments suggested by Phillips and Smith for arbitrageurs are used in this study. The bid-ask spread is the difference between an offer to buy and an offer to sell and represents the cost of liquidity to the trader. Since the trading rule used in this study does not dictate that transactions occur on the wrong side of the spread, the correct transactions cost adjustment is one-half of the mean bid-ask spread.[12] Phillips and Smith report mean bid-ask spreads of .62 percent for NYSE-listed stocks, 4.51 percent for CBOE-listed options with prices of more than $.50 per option, and 29.85 percent for options with prices of less than $.50 per option. Additionally, the arbitrageur incurs floor-trading and clearing costs of $1.50 to $1.70 per option contract and $1.00 to $4.00 per round lot of stock. For this study, mean trading and clearing costs of $1.60 per option contract and $2.50 per round lot of stock are assumed. The hedge position in the stock will always be less than a round lot, however, no additional charge associated with odd-lot purchases and sales are included in the transactions cost estimates. The New York State transfer tax, which varies from zero to $6.25 per round lot, and the SEC transactions fee, which is .003 percent of the sale, have been ignored.

In establishing the hedge position, it is assumed that the arbitrageur has use of the proceeds from short sales of stock and has no net capital charges accociated with long positions. If these assumptions are not met, the transactions costs would be increased. The total transactions costs (TC) associated with entering and exiting a hedge position for one option contract is given by:

$$TC = .31 \frac{\partial C}{\partial S} \{S_t + S_{t+1}\} + 2.255 \{C_t + C_{t+1}\} + 8.20, \quad (5.18)$$

if the market price of the call is greater than fifty cents. When the market price of the call is below fifty cents, the transactions costs per hedge position is computed by:

$$TC = .31 \frac{\partial C}{\partial S} \{S_t + S_{t+1}\} + 14.925 \{C_t + C_{t+1}\} + 8.20. \quad (5.19)$$

The decision to use equations 5.18 or 5.19 is based upon the market call price at the time the hedge is established.

The dollar holding-period returns given by equations 5.16 and 5.17 are adjusted for transactions costs and transformed into excess returns. For an initially undervalued option, the dollar holding-period excess return on the hedge is given by:

$$R_H = C_{t+1} - C_t - \frac{\partial C}{\partial S}\{S_{t+1} - S_t\} - \{e^{r\Delta t} - 1\}V_{H1} - TC, \qquad (5.20)$$

and, for an initially overvalued call by:

$$R_H = \frac{\partial C}{\partial S}\{S_{t+1} - S_t\} - \{C_{t+1} - C_t\} - \{e^{r\Delta t} - 1\}V_{H2} - TC. \quad (5.21)$$

The term Δt represents the actual holding period, expressed in years. The dollar returns given by equations 5.20 and 5.21 are scaled by the absolute size of the investment in the hedge using equation 5.13, and these percent excess returns are aggregated across all hedges for each of the eleven one-month holding periods. Mean-holding-period excess returns are then calculated.

A total of eight trading rules, resulting from using two option-pricing models, two filters, and two time delays between identification and execution of the hedge position, are available for ex-ante performance evaluation.

Results of the Ex-Ante Tests

The ex-post performance tests reported in the previous chapter presented evidence that both the Black-Scholes and Roll models were successful in identifying overvalued and undervalued call options. The results would suggest that the percent mean-holding-period returns, unadjusted for risk or transactions costs, should be positive. Table 5–2 presents the grand mean of the one-month holding-period returns calculated for all hedges for each of the eight trading rules. All of the grand-mean holding-period returns are positive and significant at the .05 level. Although not reported in tabular form, mean-holding-period returns were also calculated for each of the eleven one-month holding periods and eight trading rules. For trading rules involving the Black-Scholes model, twenty-eight of the forty-eight holding-period returns were positive and significantly different from zero at the .05 level. For the Roll model, twenty-nine of the mean-holding-period returns were positive and statistically significant, with one of the holding-period returns negative and significantly different from zero. Overall, fifty-seven of the eighty-eight mean-holding-period returns were positive and statistically significant, while one of the mean-holding-period returns was negative and statistically significant. The large percentage of positive and significant unadjusted holding-period returns suggests that the Black-Scholes and Roll models are successful at identifying overvalued/undervalued call options.

When the holding-period returns are adjusted for the risk-free rate of return and transactions costs by equations 5.20 or 5.21, the predominance of positive holding-period returns disappears. For fifty-eight of the eighty-eight holding periods the mean excess returns were negative and significantly different from zero at the .05 level. Twelve of the mean-excess holding-period returns were positive and statistically significant. The percent grand-

Table 5–2
Ex-Ante Grand-Mean-Return Summary for Portfolios of Option Hedges Held over Eleven One-Month Holding Periods Beginning July 1977

Statistic[a]	Grand-Mean Holding-Period Return	Grand-Mean Excess-Holding-Period Return
(a) Percent mean returns for the Black-Scholes model and:		
5 percent filter, 5-minute delay	1.24[b]	−1.06[b]
	(10.47)	(−9.50)
5 percent filter, 15-minute delay	1.23[b]	−1.06[b]
	(10.37)	(−9.52)
Number of hedged positions	1324	1324
10 percent filter, 5-minute delay	1.67[b]	−1.06[b]
	(8.95)	(−5.96)
10 percent filter, 15-minute delay	1.66[b]	−1.07[b]
	(8.85)	(−6.03)
Number of hedged positions	777	777
(b) Percent mean returns for the Roll model and:		
5 percent filter, 5-minute delay	1.15[b]	−1.05[b]
	(9.57)	(−9.39)
5 percent filter, 15-minute delay	1.13[b]	−1.06[b]
	(9.42)	(−9.47)
Number of hedged positions	1317	1317
10 percent filter, 5-minute delay	1.64[b]	−.96[b]
	(8.67)	(−5.42)
10 percent filter, 15-minute delay	1.63[b]	−.97[b]
	(8.58)	(−5.51)
Number of hedged positions	768	768

[a]This table summarizes grand-mean one-month holding-period returns, and holding-period excess returns for portfolios of option hedges where the option is initially identified as overvalued or undervalued by equation 5.2 for the Black-Scholes model and equation 5.1 for the Roll model. The mean-excess-holding-period returns are net of transactions costs. The five- and fifteen-minute delays are minimum time lapses between hedged-position identification and execution at prevailing market prices. The t statistic is reported in parenthesis.

[b]Mean-holding-period returns significantly different from zero at the .05 level.

mean-excess holding-period returns computed across all eleven holding periods for each trading rule are presented in table 5–2. For all eight trading rules the grand-mean excess returns are negative, indicating that an arbitrageur could not have earned an abnormal return during the period under examination. For trading rules involving the Black-Scholes model, the arbitrageur would have earned, on average, an excess return of a negative 1.06 percent of his total investment over a one-month holding period. By using trading rules involving the Roll model, his mean one-month holding-period excess return would have been a negative 1.01 percent of his total investment. Since the mean-holding-period excess returns are negative, the hypothesis that the option market is efficient for trading rules involving the Black-Scholes or Roll pricing models cannot be rejected.

The degree to which an average option contained within a portfolio of hedges is mispriced is determined by the filter used in the investment-opportunity identification process, and it would be expected that increasing the size of the filter would increase the holding-period returns. Also, if options are efficiently priced, market forces should cause a mispriced option to return quickly to the equilibrium price, and the holding-period returns should decrease as the delay between identification of a mispriced option and execution of the hedged position increases. Examination of the grand-mean holding-period excess returns in table 5–2 indicates that mean excess returns do become slightly less negative as the filter is increased from five to ten percent for a given delay as was predicted. As the delay between identification and execution of a hedge is increased from five to fifteen minutes, the mean excess returns become slightly more negative, or remain constant. This same phenomenon can also be observed for the grand-mean holding-period returns in table 5–2. However, these changes in mean excess returns are statistically insignificant.

Summary and Conclusions

This chapter has examined the comparative performance of the Black-Scholes and Roll option-pricing models on both an ex-post and ex-ante basis. The purpose of the ex-post tests was to determine if the Roll option-pricing model could better identify overvalued and undervalued call options than could the Black-Scholes model. The results indicated that both models were successful at identifying mispriced call options, with a statistically insignificant ex-post performance difference between the two models. Also, both models displayed almost identical pricing biases by undervaluing, relative to the market price, out-of-the-money call options and pricing fairly well at- and in-the-money options. These results suggested that the systematic pricing bias observed in the Black-Scholes model is not a dividend bias.

The results of the ex-ante performance tests supported option-market efficiency. Although holding-period returns were positive, on average, an arbitrageur could not earn an abnormal return when adjusted for risk and transactions costs. For each of the eight trading rules examined, the mean excess returns were negative.

The implications of these results are twofold. First, the Black-Scholes model is an acceptable pricing alternative to the mathematically complex Roll model. Researchers and practitioners can use the simpler Black-Scholes model for pricing unprotected American call options without concern about the introduction of a severe dividend bias. Additionally, option markets appear to be efficient to the arbitrageur using the trading rules involving the Black-Scholes and Roll pricing models. Studies by Galai (1977) and Chiras and Manaster (1978) that rejected option-market efficiency may have underestimated transactions costs, as is suggested by Phillips and Smith (1980). Also, these studies used daily stock and option closing quotations, which may have affected these conclusions.

The Black-Scholes model performs very well in identifying overvalued or undervalued call options. However, the option market is not inefficient to traders using the Black-Scholes model in identifying investment opportunities.

Notes

1. Biased Black-Scholes model prices have been noted by Black-Scholes (1972), Merton (1976), Galai (1977), and MacBeth and Merville (1979, 1980).

2. A proof of this proposition is in Merton (1973).

3. In Roll (1977) the exercise price on the second option was given as $S^* + \alpha D$. The correct exercise price of S^* was noted by Whaley (1981).

4. Implicit in this methodology is that the hedge is correctly established. If we assume that the Roll model is correct, then the hedge established by the Black-Scholes model will be incorrect. An incorrectly established hedge could generate positive or negative average returns, however, if the average returns are positive, the variance rate of the returns should be large.

5. The one exception to this rule was that options written on Honeywell (HON) during the months November 1977 through January 1978 expired in May 1978. These longer expiration options were included because HON did not declare dividends on a strictly quarterly basis during the observation period.

6. During the time period of this study, the CBOE restricted opening transactions on options that were more than five dollars out-of-the-money and with a price of less than fifty cents per option on a per-share basis.

7. For Halliburton (HAL), only one implied-variance calculation was available for November 1977 and two calculations for February 1978. For DuPont (DD), no implied variances could be calculated for June 1978. The WISD computed for May was used for June model-price computations.

8. By the *central-limit-theorem* the difference between the two return-series means is approximately normally distributed in repeated sampling with variance of $\sigma_1^2/n_1 + \sigma_2^2/n_2$, where σ_j^2 is the sample variance.

9. The actual distribution of the hedge returns examined in this chapter is slightly positively skewed and highly leptokurtic. For the Roll model, the distribution of all 9,108 hedge returns had skewness of .61 and kurtosis of 58.8. The Black-Scholes hedges had skewness and kurtosis of .60 and 57.5, respectively. We have chosen to report significant t-statistics as if the hedge returns were normally distributed. Also, the hedge returns are not independent, which would bias the reported t-statistics upwards.

10. Black (1975), Merton (1976), and MacBeth and Merville (1979, 1980), report that the Black-Scholes model produces biased model prices that are systematically related to the degree to which the option is in/out-of-the money. Black-Scholes (1972) report that model prices are systematically related to the stock-return variance rate, and Galai (1977) reports a pricing bias that is systematically related to the dividend yield of the stock.

11. The Securities and Exchange Commission (SEC) permits short selling of a stock only on a positive price change from the previous transaction price or an *uptick*.

12. If the hedge position was established at the same moment that the overvalued/undervalued call was identified, the option transaction prices would usually be at the wrong side of the bid-ask spread, and the correct transaction-cost adjustment would be the full value of the bid-ask spread. Since this study provides a waiting period between hedge identification and execution, transactions occur on the wrong side of the hedge 50 percent of the time, on average, and the transaction-cost adjustment is one-half of the bid-ask spread.

References

Black, F. "Fact and Fantasy in the Use of Options," *Financial Analysts Journal* 31 (1975): 36–72.

Black, F., and Scholes, M. "The Pricing of Options and Corporate Liabilities." *Journal of Political Economy* 81 (1973): 637–659.

_____. "The Valuation of Options Contracts and a Test of Market Efficiency." *Journal of Finance* 27 (1972): 399–417.

Boyle, P., and Emanuel, D. "Discretely Adjusted Option Hedges." *Journal of Financial Economics* 8 (1980): 259–282.

Chiras, D., and Manaster, S. "The Information Content of Option Prices and a Test of Market Efficiency." *Journal of Financial Economics* 6 (1978): 213–234.

Cox, J., and Ross, S. "The Valuation of Options for Alternative Stochastic Processes." *Journal of Financial Economics* 3 (1976): 145–166.

Durand, D., and May, A. "The Ex-Dividend Behavior of American Telephone and Telegraph Stock." *Journal of Finance* 15 (1960): 19–31.

Elton, E., and Gruber, M. "Marginal Stockholders' Tax Rates and the Clientele Effect." *Review of Economics and Statistics* 52 (1970): 68–74.

Galai, D. "Tests of Market Efficiency of the Chicago Board Options Exchange." *Journal of Business* (1977): 167–197.

Geske, R. "The Valuation of Compound Options." *Journal of Financial Economics* 7 (1979): 63–81.

MacBeth, J., and Merville, L. "Tests of the Black-Scholes and Cox Option Valuation Models." *Journal of Finance* 35 (1980): 285–303.

————. "An Empirical Examination of the Black-Scholes Call Option Pricing Model." *Journal of Finance* 34 (1979): 1173–1186.

Merton, R. "Option Pricing When Underlying Stock Prices are Discontinuous." *Journal of Financial Economics* 3 (1976): 125–144.

————. "Theory of Rational Option Pricing." *Bell Journal of Economics and Management Science* 4 (1973): 141–183.

Phillips, S., and Smith, C. "Trading Costs for Listed Options: The Implications for Market Efficiency." *Journal of Financial Economics* 8 (1980): 179–201.

Roll, R. "An Analytic Valuation Formula for Unprotected American Call Options on Stocks with Known Dividends." *Journal of Financial Economics* 5 (1977): 251–258.

Whaley, R. "On the Valuation of American Call Options on Stocks with Known Dividends." *Journal of Financial Economics* 9 (1981): 207–211.

Part II
The Valuation
of Debt and
Commodity Options

6

An Equilibrium Model of Bond Pricing and a Test of Market Efficiency

Michael J. Brennan and
Eduardo S. Schwartz

In two previous and related papers (Brennan and Schwartz, 1979, 1980) the authors have reported the results of estimating a particular equilibrium model of bond pricing using quarterly data on Canadian government bonds for the period 1964 to 1979. This chapter reports the results of applying a similar model to the pricing of U.S. government bonds for the period 1958 to 1979 using data from the Center for Research Security Prices (CRSP) Government Bond File. The chapter also extends the previous empirical analysis by evaluating the ability of the pricing model to detect underpriced and overpriced bonds: the data reveal a strong relation between price prediction errors and subsequent bond returns.

The bond-pricing model is described briefly in the following section: it relies on the assumption that there are only two independent stochastic factors that determine bond prices and, therefore, the shape and position of the yield curve at any point in time. Then, in the spirit of the option-pricing model (Black-Scholes 1973, Merton 1973) and arbitrage-pricing theory (Ross 1976), this assumption is shown to imply restrictions on the relative rates of return of bonds of different coupon and maturity. These restrictions take the form of a partial differential equation that must be satisfied by the equilibrium values of all default-free bonds. Solution of this equation yields bond prices and, therefore, the term structure of interest rates or yield curve, in terms of the underlying factors or state variables. In the present chapter these unknown state variables are replaced by two interest rates, the *short rate* and the *consol rate*.

Since the coefficients of the differential equation depend upon the parameters of the stochastic process for the underlying state variables, these parameters must be estimated before the model can be implemented. This task is undertaken in the subsequent section, which also reports the results of estimating the single, utility function dependent, market price of risk

This chapter first appeared in the *Journal of Financial and Quantitative Analysis*, 15 October, 1982, pp. 301–329 and is reprinted with permission. The authors gratefully acknowledge financial support from the Institute for Quantitative Research in Finance and thank Bruce Dietrich-Campbell for computer-programming assistance.

parameter that enters the model. In the next section the ability of the model to make predictions of bond prices and yields is evaluated, and evidence is found of an omitted *third factor* that affects bond prices: this finding is congruent with those of the aforementioned Canadian study. The following section compares the predictive performance of several different rules for forecasting bond returns conditional on forecasts of the exogenously determined state variables. The final section of the chapter relates the bond-pricing errors to subsequent bond returns. A strong relationship between pricing errors and bond returns is found even outside the sample period over which the pricing model was estimated. Whether or not this is interpreted as evidence of market inefficiency and a profit opportunity will depend upon one's belief in the adequacy of the underlying equilibrium model and the accuracy of the price data.

The Bond-Pricing Model

It is assumed that the prices of all default-free bonds at any moment in time may be expressed in terms of the values of two, possibly unknown, stochastic factors, u_1, and u_2, which follow continuous sample paths.[1] Thus, the price of a bond with a continuous coupon rate c, face value of unity, and maturity τ can be written as $G(u_1, u_2, \tau, c)$.

The instantaneously riskless interest rate, the *short rate*, is the yield on the currently maturing discount bond and is defined by:

$$r(u_1, u_2) = \lim_{\tau \to 0} \frac{-\ln G(u_1, u_2, \tau, 0)}{\tau}. \qquad (6.1)$$

Similarly, the *consol rate* is defined as the yield on a bond whose maturity is infinite:

$$l(u_1, u_2) = \frac{c}{G(u_1, u_2, \infty, c)}. \qquad (6.2)$$

If equations 6.1 and 6.2 can be inverted and the state variables u_1 and u_2 expressed as twice differentiable functions of the potentially observable interest rates, r and l, then, as pointed out by Cox, Ingersoll, and Ross (1978), bond prices may be expressed as functions of the proxy-state variables r and l, and the value of any default-free bond written as $B(r, l, \tau; c)$. In what follows it will be convenient to suppress the coupon-rate argument and to write the bond value simply as $B(r, l, \tau)$.

The price change on a bond over any short interval of time, and therefore its rate of return, will depend upon the corresponding change in the state variable proxies, r and l. These are assumed to follow a stochastic process of the general type:

$$dr = \beta_1(r,l,t) \, dt + \eta_1(r,l,t) \, dz_1$$
$$d_l = \beta_2(r,l,t) \, dt + \eta_2(r,l,t) \, dz_2 \qquad (6.3)$$

where t denotes calendar time and dz_1 and dz_2 are increments to a standard Wiener process, so that $E[dz_1] = E[dz_2] = 0$, $E[dz_1 \cdot dz_2] = \rho dt$ and $E[dz_1^2] = E[dz_2^2] = dt$; ρ is the instantaneous correlation between the processes.

It then follows from Ito's Lemma[2] that the instantaneous return on a bond is given by:

$$\frac{dB + c \, dt}{B} = \mu \, dt + \frac{B_r}{B} \eta_1 \, dz_1 + \frac{B_l}{B} \eta_2 \, dz_2 \qquad (6.4)$$

where:

$$\mu = (B_r\beta_1 + B_l\beta_2 + 1/2B_{rr}\eta_1^2 + 1/2B_{ll}\eta_2^2 + B_{rl}\rho\eta_1\eta_2 - B_\tau + c)/B \qquad (6.5)$$

and subscripts denote partial derivatives.

Since the instantaneous returns on all default-free bonds are by assumption from equation 6.4 perfect linear functions of the two stochastic increments dz_1 and dz_2, the absence of arbitrage possibilities can be shown to imply:

$$\mu - r = \lambda_1 \frac{B_r}{B} \eta_1 + \lambda_2 \frac{B_l}{B} \eta_2 \qquad (6.6)$$

where λ_1 and λ_2, the market prices of short-term and consol-rate risk, respectively, are at most functions of r, l, and t. The important aspect of condition 6.6 is that λ_1 and λ_2 are the same for all bonds at any particular instant in time. Recognizing that μ is the expected instantaneous rate of return on the bond, it is seen that 6.6 expresses the risk premium as the sum of two components that depend on the sensitivity of the bond return to changes in the short and consol rates, respectively: the correspondence with arbitrage-pricing theory is apparent.

The value of a consol bond paying a continuous coupon at a rate of one dollar per period is $B(r,l,\infty,1) \equiv l^{-1}$, and its derivatives with respect to r and l are readily computed. Substitution of these derivatives for the consol bond into equations 6.5 and 6.6 yields the following expression for the market price of consol-rate risk:

$$\lambda_2(r,l,t) = \frac{-\eta_2}{l} + (\beta_2 - l^2 + r_l)/\eta_2 \qquad (6.7)$$

Finally, substitution for $\mu(\cdot)$ from 6.5 and for $\lambda_2(\cdot)$ from 6.7 into the equilibrium condition 6.6 yields the following partial differential equation that must be satisfied by the value of all default-free bonds:

$$1/2B_{rr}\eta_1^2 + B_{rl}\rho\eta_1\eta_2 + 1/2B_{ll}\eta_2^2 + B_r(\beta_1 - \lambda_1\eta_1)$$
$$+ B_l(\eta_2^2/l + l^2 - r_l) - B_\tau + c - Br = 0 \qquad (6.8)$$

The bond value must also satisfy an appropriate boundary condition determining its maturity value, $B(r,l,0)$. Note that it is not actually necessary to solve this equation more than once in order to value all straight default-free bonds, for if the equation is solved with $B(r,l,0) = 1$ and $c = 0$, the resulting values of $B(r,l,\tau)$ will be the values of discount bonds with par value of unity, or discount factors that give the present value of one dollar due in τ periods when the current short and long rates are r and l, respectively. By applying these discount factors to the promised payments on any straight default-free bond, its model value may be calculated directly. If the bond contains option-like features, such as call, retraction, or exchange provisions, then it also may be valued using equation 6.8 by appending the appropriate boundary conditions that define its payoffs. In this chapter we are concerned only with straight bonds.

Model Estimation

The coefficients of the partial-differential equation 6.8 depend upon four functions that derive from the stochastic process for r and l: β_1, η_1, η_2, and ρ. They also depend upon $\lambda_1(\cdot)$, the market price of short-term interest-rate risk. We shall take up first the estimation of the stochastic process and then the estimation of $\lambda_1(\cdot)$.

The Stochastic Process

The specific form of the stochastic process 6.3 that was assumed for purposes of estimation was:

$$dr = (a_1 + b_1(l - r)) \, dt + r\sigma_1 \, dz,$$

$$d_l = l(a_2 + b_2 r + c_2 l) \, dt + l \, \sigma_2 \, dz_2. \tag{6.9}$$

This formulation presupposes that the scale of the unanticipated increment in each of the interest rates is proportional to the current value of that rate, an hypothesis that is tested below. The coefficient of dt in the short-rate equation reflects the essence of expectations-based theories of the term structure, which is that long rates are based upon expectations about future short-interest rates. If such expectations are rational, the short rate will have a tendency to regress towards the current value of the long rate so that $b_1 > 0$. The coefficient of dt in the consol-rate equation was obtained by treating $\lambda_2(\cdot)$, the market price of consol-rate risk, as a linear function of r and l, and solving equation 6.7 for $\beta_2(\cdot)$. It should be observed that $\beta_2(\cdot)$ does not enter the partial-differential equation and hence does not affect bond prices.[3] It may be noted also that if $a_1 < 0$, this formulation allows the possibility that r may become negative, a circumstance that is theoretically unacceptable if money exists. Despite this, the above formulation was retained in view of its empirical tractability, and it should be regarded as a linearized approximation to the true stochastic process. Our interest here is not in the stochastic process as such but in the predictive ability of the bond-pricing model that results from it.

For empirical purposes the system 6.9 was replaced by the discrete approximation:

$$\frac{r_t - r_{t-1}}{r_{t-1}} = \frac{a_1}{r_{t-1}} + b_1 \left(\frac{l_{t-1}}{r_{t-1}} - 1 \right) + \xi_{1t}$$

$$\frac{l_t - l_{t-1}}{l_{t-1}} = a_2 + b_2 r_{t-1} + c_2 l_{t-1} + \xi_{2t} \tag{6.10}$$

This system of equations was estimated using monthly data on interest rates from the CRSP Government Bond File for the period December 1958–December 1979. r was taken as the annualized yield to maturity (percent) on the U.S. government treasury bill whose maturity was closest to thirty days on the last trading day of each month. The consol rate l was approximated by the annualized yield to maturity on the highest yielding U.S. government bond with a maturity exceeding twenty years. If no such bond was available in a particular month then the highest yielding bond with a maturity of more than fifteen years was used instead.[4]

The system was estimated using an iterative Aitken (1935) procedure that yields the maximum likelihood estimator.[5] The parameter estimates for different subperiods are reported in table 6–1 along with some diagnostic statistics. We observe first that the estimated value of a_1, although predominantly negative, is small, less than 0.2 percent in absolute value. Combining this with the estimate of b_1 of about 0.1, it is seen that the change in r at $r = 0$ will be positive so long as the consol rate exceeds about 2 percent. It is to be hoped therefore that the misspecification that allows negative values of r will have only slight consequences for bond values.

The estimated values of σ_1 and σ_2 for the two half-periods are quite similar; on the other hand, the correlation coefficient estimate exhibits much less stability. In the consol-rate equation the estimates of b_2 and c_2 are of opposite sign and approximately equal magnitude. This confirms the finding of Shiller (1979) that when long rates are high relative to short rates they tend to move down in the subsequent period. The estimates of a_1 and b_1 in the short-rate equation are of potentially greater importance for the bond-pricing model since they enter directly into the partial-differential equation. The instability of the estimates between the two halves of the sample period therefore has potentially serious consequences for the model. These will be explored later.

If the joint stochastic process for the two interest rates (equation 6.9) were correctly specified the disturbances in the two equations 6.10 would be serially independent. Table 6–1 reports the serial correlations of the errors from the two equations as well as Durbin's (1970) h-statistic: the latter takes account of the effect of the presence of a lagged dependent variable and is normally distributed for large samples. The errors from both equations are negatively serially correlated; the correlation is statistically significant for the short-rate equation but appears to be confined to the first half of the sample period. The negative serial correlation found in these data contrasts with a finding of positive serial correlation of similar Canadian data,[6] though the Canadian data were quarterly rather than monthly. Ignoring measurement error, serial correlation of the errors from the estimated stochastic process suggests either that the functional form of the stochastic process is misspecified, or that the current values of r and l are not sufficient statistics for the joint distribution of future values of r and l, and, therefore, if the true process is to be estimated in Markov form as is necessary for the derivation of the partial-differential equation, then at least one additional state variable must be introduced.[7] On the other hand, negative serial correlation is symptomatic of measurement errors. In the following section we shall say more about the existence of state variables in addition to r and l.

The assumption that η_1 and η_2 were proportional to r and l was tested using a procedure suggested by Park (1966): the logarithm of the squared error was regressed on the logarithm of the corresponding interest rate.

$$\ln \hat{\xi}_{1t}^2 = \delta_1 + \gamma_1 \ln r_{t-1}$$
$$\ln \hat{\xi}_{2t}^2 = \delta_2 + \gamma_2 \ln l_{t-1} \tag{6.11}$$

Table 6–1
Estimation of the Stochastic Process
(standard errors in parenthesis)

Period	a_1	b_1	a_2	b_2	c_2	σ_1	σ_2	ρ	$\rho(\xi_{1t}\xi_{1t-1})$	$\rho(\xi_{2t}\xi_{2t-1})$	DH_1^*	DH_2^*	γ_1	γ_2
Dec 1958–Dec 1979	-.0887 (.0526)	.1102 (.0301)	.00891 (.0069)	.00358 (.0017)	-.0037 (.0020)	.1133	.0298	.2063	-.195	-.064	-3.52	-1.022	-.6269 (.3710)	.7503 (.5711)
Dec 1958–June 1969	-.1809 (.0754)	.1882 (.0480)	.0151 (.0200)	.00468 (.0037)	-.0062 (.0067)	.1286	.0233:	.0519	-.239	-.032	-3.183	-.364	-1.9363 (.6704)	3.9373 (1.701)
July 1969–Dec 1979	-.0135 (.0826)	.0377 (.0369)	.0319 (.0221)	.00444 (.00229)	-.0074 (.0039)	.0914	.0349	.3923	-.043	-.067	-.526	-.748	-.2489 (.7837)	-1.1807 (1.6619)
Dec 1958–March 1964	-.4667 (.1594)	.3357 (.0907)	.2142 (.0725)	.00869 (.00567)	.0588 (.0202)	.1619	.0205	.2126	-.160	.018	-1.830	.146	-1.3433 (1.2774)	-8.270 (6.889)
April 1964–June 1969	-.1079 (.0593)	.2729 (.0796)	.00078 (.0252)	.0038 (.0069)	-.0022 (.0087)	.0688	.0248	-.1637	-.104	-.022	-1.066	-.175	-1.3955 (1.9133)	8.656 (2.200)
July 1969–Sept 1974	-.0350 (.1103)	.0551 (.0578)	.1233 (.0614)	.0120 (.0055)	-.0283 (.0129)	.1031	.0415	.3778	-.034	-.040	-.308	-.320	+.2869 (1.110)	-.3579 (3.002)
Oct 1974–Dec 1979	.0361 (.1375)	.0118 (.0525)	.1675 (.0713)	.0089 (.0033)	-.271 (.0109)	.0777	.0243	.4423	.026	-.032	.231	-.259	-.6625 (1.137)	4.348 (4.286)

*Durbin's *h*-statistic.

Under the null hypothesis that the process is correctly specified γ_1 and γ_2 will be equal to zero: the estimated values are shown in table 6–1 and, at least for the total sample period, the null hypothesis is not rejected.

Estimation of $\lambda_1(\cdot)$

$\lambda_1(\cdot)$, the market price of short-term interest-rate risk, was assumed to be an intertemporal constant for purposes of estimation. The details of the estimation procedure are reported elsewhere.[8] The principle employed was to solve the partial-differential equation 6.8 with $c = 0$ and boundary condition $B(r,l,0) = 1$ using a numerical procedure. The resulting present-value factors were used to value the bonds represented each month on the CRSP Government Bond File, and the estimated value of λ_1 was that that minimized the price-prediction errors. A generalized least-squares procedure was employed to take account of serial and contemporaneous correlation of the errors. To implement this procedure all of the bonds to be valued each month were assigned to one of ten basic portfolios according to maturity, portfolio j $(j = 1, \ldots, 10)$ consisting of all bonds whose maturity fall between $(j - 1)$ and j years. Within each of the basic portfolios each bond received equal weight. Bonds whose maturity exceeded ten years were ignored in the estimation because the paucity of observations for the longer maturities posed problems for the estimation of the variance-covariance matrix.

The ordinary (nonlinear) least-squares estimator that minimized the squared monthly price-prediction errors for the ten basic portfolios was formed and the resulting errors were then used to estimate the variance-covariance matrix for the generalized least-squares estimator.

Estimates of λ_1 were obtained using two different sets of parameters from the stochastic process in the partial-differential equation: those in panel A of table 6–2 were derived using the parameters of the stochastic process estimated over the whole sample period, the different estimates in this panel depending on the sample subperiod over which bond price predictions were made. The estimate of λ_1 in panel B was obtained by pricing bonds over the first half of the sample period relying on parameter estimates of the stochastic process that were also obtained from the first half of the sample period. We shall refer to this model, which was derived using only data from the first half of the sample period, as the *first-half estimator*, and its performance over the second half of the sample period will be evaluated later in this chapter.

It should be clearly recognized that the estimates of λ_1 presented in table 6–2 were derived treating the parameters of the stochastic process as known rather than as estimated. This means of course that the standard errors are misstated, and it is the difference in the stochastic-process parameters that accounts in substantial part for the difference between the estimates of λ_1 for

Table 6–2
Estimation of the Market Price of Short-Term Interest-Rate Risk (λ_1)

Period	$\lambda*$	$SE(\lambda*)$	Number of Observations
A. Stochastic Process Parameter Estimates: December 1958–December 1979			
December 1958–December 1979	−0.450	0.028	2016
December 1958–June 1969	−0.674	0.023	960
July 1969–December 1979	−0.283	0.031	1049
December 1958–March 1964	−0.671	0.043	480
April 1964–June 1969	−0.593	0.021	471
July 1969–September 1974	−0.322	0.068	479
October 1969–December 1979	−0.216	0.013	561
B. Stochastic Process Parameter Estimates: December 1958–June 1969			
December 1958–June 1969	−1.185	0.019	960

Table 6–3
Two Estimates of ($\beta_1 - \lambda_1\eta_1$) for December 1958 through June 1969

$\beta_1 - \lambda_1\eta_1 =$	a_1	$+ b_1l$	$- (b_1 + \lambda_1\sigma_1)r$	
	−0.0887	+ .1102l	− 0.0338r	December 1958–December 1979
	−0.1809	+ .1882l	− 0.0358r	December 1958–June 1969

the period December 1958 through June 1969 reported in panels A and B. λ_1 enters the partial-differential equation 6.8 only as part of the term ($\beta_1 - \lambda_1\eta_1$) and it is to be expected therefore that different estimates of the drift function β_1 will tend to be offset by differences in the resulting estimates of λ_1. This effect is illustrated in table 6–3, which shows that despite the large difference in the estimates of λ_1 for December 1958 through June 1969 obtained using the different stochastic-process estimates, the coefficients of r in the term ($\beta_1 - \lambda_1\eta_1$) are quite similar.

Bond-Price and Yield Predictions

The differential equation 6.8 was solved with $c = 0$ and boundary condition $B(r,l,0) = 1$ using the estimates of the stochastic process parameters and λ_1, which were obtained from the whole sample period: these are the parameters given in the first lines of tables 6–1 and 6–2. The resulting present-value factors were used to price all outstanding bonds[9] with maturities up to twenty

**Table 6–4
Bond-Price and Yield Predictions for December 1958 through
December 1979**

		Prices[a]		Yields	
Year	Number of Observations	Mean Error[b] ($)	Root Mean Square Error ($)	Mean Error (%)	Root Mean Square Error (%)
Full Period	11669	.18	1.58	.08	.59
1958[c]	27	−.03	1.29	.32	.38
1959	33	−.50	1.74	.67	.71
1960	35	−.19	.65	.04	.18
1961	38	−.42	.63	.11	.23
1962	40	.02	.75	−.15	.33
1963	40	−.11	.60	.01	.21
1964	38	−.23	.71	.12	.28
1965	35	−.81	1.22	.43	.52
1966	33	−.44	.77	.25	.35
1967	34	−.91	1.24	.55	.71
1968	33	.18	1.26	.08	.63
1969	36	−2.21	2.50	1.39	1.55
1970	40	.27	.43	−.27	.83
1971	42	−.01	.52	−.14	.72
1972	43	−1.12	1.48	.38	.54
1973	45	1.70	2.40	−.38	.73
1974	51	2.01	3.23	−.27	1.10
1975	60	.94	1.54	−.23	.32
1976	71	1.89	2.37	−.66	.72
1977	81	.68	1.51	.01	.39
1978	87	.20	1.59	.48	.94
1979	94	.17	1.91	.67	1.31

Note: Parameter estimates are from whole-sample period.
[a]Per $100 par value.
[b]Actual-predicted.
[c]December.

years for the last trading day of each month of the sample period. The root
mean-square price-prediction error is reported in the first line of table 6–4,
which is constructed on the assumption that each bond has a par value of one
hundred dollars. A predicted yield to maturity was also calculated based on
the predicted bond price, and the root-mean-square error of this predicted
yield is also reported. The balance of the table reports the prediction errors
for December of each year of the sample period. It is apparent that there is
considerable intertemporal variation in the predictive ability of the model,
although it is encouraging to note that there is no tendency for the model
error to grow systematically with time.

Table 6–5
Bond Price and Yield Predictions for July 1969 through December 1979 Using First-Half Estimator

Year	Number of Observations	Prices[a] Mean Error[b] ($)	Prices[a] Root Mean Square Error ($)	Yields Mean Error[b] (%)	Yields Root Mean Square Error (%)
Full Period	7045	2.53	3.90	−.71	1.07
1969[c]	36	−1.09	1.31	.92	1.21
1970	40	1.65	2.07	−.87	1.10
1971	42	1.48	1.89	−.70	.93
1972	43	.19	.52	−.07	.36
1973	45	3.28	4.43	−.89	1.16
1974	51	4.02	5.65	−1.01	1.58
1975	60	3.18	4.24	−1.10	1.16
1976	71	4.01	4.96	−1.44	1.49
1977	81	2.87	4.06	−.82	.99
1978	87	2.13	3.83	−.20	1.00
1979	94	2.55	4.52	−.18	1.33

[a]Per $100 par value.
[b]Actual-predicted.
[c]December.

While the errors reported in table 6–4 are from within sample predictions, table 6–5 reports the errors from using the first-half estimator to predict bond prices in the second half of the sample period. As one would expect, these out-of-sample prediction errors are somewhat greater—roughly twice as great as those of the within-sample predictions.

Model Error Analysis

If the assumptions of the valuation model discussed in the opening section of this chapter were correct and if λ_1 were truly an intertemporal constant, then the price-prediction errors would be serially and cross-sectionally independent. Table 6–6 reports both the serial correlations and the contemporaneous correlations of the pricing errors for the ten basic portfolios over the whole sample period. Their systematic nature points either to an incorrect functional form for the model or to the omission of relevant-state variables in addition to those represented by r and l. The choice of an incorrect functional form for joint stochastic process 6.3 or for λ_1, which was assumed to be a constant, would lead to pricing errors that were systematically related to r and l. We have already adverted to the possible existence of omitted state

Table 6–6
Contemporaneous Correlation of Valuation Errors for Ten Basic Portfolios for Total Sample Period: $\lambda_1 = -.45$

Portfolio Maturity (years)	1	2	3	4	5	6	7	8	9	10
1	1.00									
2	.87	1.00								
3	.74	.90	1.00							
4	.52	.74	.89	1.00						
5	.24	.49	.69	.86	1.00					
6	.38	.57	.67	.71	.62	1.00				
7	.31	.52	.67	.77	.69	.81	1.00			
8	−.31	−.19	−.05	.14	.45	.07	.02	1.00		
9	−.41	−.11	.10	.33	.65	.25	.37	.90	1.00	
10	−.46	−.25	−.08	.20	.47	.05	.23	.94	.94	1.00
Serial correlation	.75	.78	.85	.88	.91	.88	.90	.97	.91	.96

variables in relation to the serial correlation of the errors in the estimated stochastic process of r and l.

To gain further insight into the causes of the price-prediction errors, they were factor analyzed. The factor-analysis model assumes that the errors $u_{pt}(p = 1, \ldots, 10; t = 1, \ldots, 253)$ may be expressed as:

$$u_{pt} = \Sigma_k h_{pk} f_{kt} + e_{pt} \tag{6.12}$$

where h_{pk} is the loading of the error from portfolio p on factor k, f_{kt} is the factor score in period t, and e_{pt} is a residual error that is serially and cross-sectionally independent.

The factor analysis revealed only one important common factor that accounted for 86.7 percent of the total variance and had a serial correlation of 0.92; the second factor accounted for a further 7.8 percent of the variance. Factor loadings on the first factor for the ten basic portfolios are given in table 6–7.

To assess whether the errors are due merely to an incorrect functional form of the model, the factor score was regressed on the contemporaneous values of the proxy state variables r and l. While the ordinary least-squares regression suggested a strong relation (table 6–8), after adjustment for serial correlation the factor was found to be related only to l. This is consistent with some misspecification of the functional form; however the large unexplained component in the factor score suggests also the omission of relevant-state variables.

Table 6–7
Factor Loadings of Portfolio Errors for Total Period

	Portfolio									
	1	2	3	4	5	6	7	8	9	10
Loading	−0.03	−0.21	0.59	0.98	1.36	1.74	1.98	2.71	2.68	3.11

Table 6–8
Regression of Factor Score on r and l
(*t-ratios in parentheses*)

	a	b	c	$\hat{\rho}^a$	R^b
Ordinary Least-Squares Regression	−2.85 (16.76)	−0.14 (3.5)	0.58 (11.6)		.52
Cochrane-Orcutt	−2.41 (4.63)	0.04 (0.80)	0.36 (3.60)	0.86	$.10^2$
		$f_t = a + br_t + cl_t$			

[a]Serial correlation.
[b]In terms of changes.

If a state variable that has been omitted is to be relevant to bond pricing it must be that it affects one of the elements of the model that has been assumed to be independent of any state variables except r and l. The candidates are the elements of the joint stochastic process 6.3, βi, ηi ($i = 1,2$), and ρ, as well as λ_1, the market price of short-term rate risk.

It is not possible to test whether λ_1 is related to the factor score and hence an omitted state variable, since we have no period-by-period estimate of λ_1. However we can test whether the drift terms of the process, $\beta i(i = 1,2)$, are related to the factor by regressing the errors from the regressions 6.10 on the lagged-factor score:

$$\hat{\xi}_{it} = h_{1i} + h_{2i}f_{t-1} \quad (i = 1,2). \tag{6.13}$$

The results reported in table 6–9 fail to reveal any significant relation, and it does not appear that we have lost anything by representing expectations about future values of r and l solely in terms of their current values. However further analysis suggests that the factor does appear to be associated with uncertainty about expected future interest rates.

Table 6–9
Regression of Error on Lagged Factor Score

	h_1	h_2	R^2
$r{:}\hat{\xi}_{1t}$	−0.003	−0.008	0.1
	(0.41)	(1.19)	
$l{:}\hat{\xi}_{2t}$	0.000	0.0007	0.00
	(0.08)	(0.39)	
	$\hat{\xi}_{it} = h_{1i} + h_{2i} f_{t-1}$		

Table 6–10
Regression of Logarithm Squared Error on Logarithm of Squared Lagged Factor Score
(*t-ratios in parentheses*)

	k_1	k_2	R^2
$r{:}\ln \hat{\xi}_{1t}^2$	−6.13	0.17	0.01
	(36.06)	(1.89)	
$l{:}\ln \hat{\xi}_{2t}^2$	−8.18	0.22	0.02
	(48.94)	(2.20)	
	$\ln \hat{\xi}_{it}^2 = k_{1i} + k_{2i} \ln f_{t-1}^2$		

To test whether the state variable is affecting interest-rate uncertainty as represented by σ_1 and σ_2, which were taken as constants in the model,[10] the logarithm of the squared errors from the regressions 6.10 were regressed on the logarithm of the squared lagged-factor score:

$$\ln \hat{\xi}_{it}^2 = k_{1i} + k_{2i} \ln f_{t-1}^2 \ (i = 1,2) \qquad (6.14)$$

The results reported in table 6–10 allow us to reject the null hypothesis that the variance rates are independent of the factor score. Thus the valuation model is misspecified insofar as it assumes constant rather than stochastic variance rates. On the other hand it should be recalled that the model was fitted over twenty years, a very long period to assume parameter stationarity, and the very high serial correlation of the factor score suggests that our two factor model may yet be quite adequate over short periods of time.

Conditional Predictions of Returns

To gain insight into the ability of the valuation model to predict changes in bond prices conditional on changes in r and l with and without a factor-score adjustment, rates of return were calculated for each month from December 1958 to December 1979 for each of the ten basic portfolios: each portfolio $(p = 1, \ldots, 10)$ consists of all taxable bonds with a time to maturity of between p and $(p - 1)$ years at both the beginning and end of the month under consideration. These rates of return were compared with the predictions of four different rules that are based on the valuation model.

Under the first three prediction rules the valuation model is used to yield a prediction of the future value of the portfolio and the predicted rate of return is defined by:

$$\hat{R}_{pt} = (\hat{y}_{pt} + c_{pt} - y_{pt-1})/y_{pt-1} \tag{6.15}$$

where c_{pt} is the aggregate coupon payment for the month, and y_{pt-1} is the actual value of the portfolio at the end of the previous month. The first three rules differ in the way $\hat{y}_{pt}$, the predicted value of the portfolio at the end of the current month, is calculated.

Define $B_{pt}(r_t, l_t)$ as the model value of portfolio p at the end of month t conditional on the values of r and l. Then:

$$\text{Rule 1: } \hat{y}_{pt} = B_{pt}(r_t, l_t).$$

Rule 1 assumes that the current price-prediction error will be eliminated by the end of the month.

$$\text{Rule 2: } \hat{y}_{pt} = B_{pt}(r_t, l_t) + \rho_p u_{pt-1}$$

Rule 2 recognizes that the price-prediction errors are serially correlated and adjusts the model prediction by the serial correlations reported in table 6-6.

$$\text{Rule 3: } \hat{y}_{pt} = B_{pt}(r_t, l_t) + h_p f_t$$

Rule 3 adjusts the model value using the actual factor score, which is treated as a state variable like r and l.

Rule 4 is identical to rule 1, except that y_{pt-1}, the actual value of the portfolio, is replaced by its model value, $B_{pt-1}(r_{t-1}, l_{t-1})$. The predicted rate of

Table 6–11
Monthly Rate of Return Prediction Errors for Ten Basic Portfolios, December 1958–December 1979

Maturity (years)	Standard Deviation of Monthly Returns (percent)	Prediction Rule			
		1	2	3	4
		Root-Mean-Square Error			
1	0.27	0.30	0.16	0.30	0.17
2	0.53	0.58	0.33	0.48	0.38
3	0.76	0.96	0.48	0.53	0.50
4	0.95	1.25	0.59	0.51	0.62
5	1.09	1.71	0.71	0.74	0.74
6	1.31	1.96	0.81	0.55	0.83
7	1.43	2.15	0.90	0.58	0.94
8	1.24	3.06	0.63	0.58	0.65
9	1.28	3.25	1.13	0.83	1.14
10	1.45	3.76	0.98	0.82	0.99

return is thus the same as the model rate of return conditional on the change in the state variables.

The root-mean-square prediction errors for the four rules are reported in table 6–11. Rule 1, which assumes that the pricing error will disappear in one month, performs worst—worse even than the naive rule that the expected rate of return is constant.[11] This is not surprising in view of the previously noted persistence of the errors. The performance of rules 2 and 4 is approximately the same although the former relies on assumed knowledge of the serial correlation structure of errors and the latter ignores the pricing errors altogether. Only rule 3, which presumes knowledge of the factor score, performs significantly better—and then only for portfolios with maturities longer than five years.

In summary, it appears that the factor score is of very great importance in predicting absolute bond prices—compare rules 1 and 3. On the other hand it is of very little importance in predicting rates of return because its serial correlation is so high—compare rules 3 and 4.

Price-Prediction Errors and Bond Returns

To this point we have examined the price-prediction errors of the valuation model under the implicit assumption that they were attributable entirely to deficiencies in the valuation model itself, rather than to market inefficiencies, which would imply the existence of profit opportunities, or even to errors in the price quotations, which would imply the existence of apparent profit opportunities. In this section we take the opposite viewpoint and, treating the pricing errors as possible manifestations of market inefficiency, we test whether they are related in any systematic fashion to subsequent bond returns. Since the issue of market efficiency is a vexed one we do not wish to be dogmatic about the implications of our finding of such a systematic relation. Within the context of our equilibrium model this finding does not imply market inefficiency. This is not to say however that there do not exist other valuation models that would account for this anomaly, or even that the phenomenon is not due merely to the quality of the price quotations.

The discrete time approximation to the exact expression 6.4 for the instantaneous rate of return on a bond is:

$$R_j = E[R_j] + S_{1j}\Delta Z_1 + S_{2j}\Delta Z_2 \qquad (6.16)$$

where the subscript j denotes the particular bond, R_j is the one period rate of return, ΔZ_1 and ΔZ_2 are the (standardized) unanticipated changes in r and l, respectively, and $S_{1j} = B_r\eta_1/B$, $S_{2j} = B_l h_2/B$.

The corresponding discrete time approximation to the equilibrium condition 6.6 is:

$$E[R_j] - r = \lambda_1 S_{1j} + \lambda_2 S_{2j} \qquad (6.17)$$

where $E[R_j]$ is the one-period equilibrium expected return on the bond[12] and r is the one-period riskless interest rate.

Combining equations 6.16 and 6.17 we obtain:

$$R_j - r = (\lambda_1 + \Delta Z_1)S_{1j} + (\lambda_2 + \Delta Z_2) S_{2j}. \qquad (6.18)$$

Motivated by equation 6.18 the regression model estimated each month t was:

$$R_{jt} - r_t = a_{0t} + a_{1t}S_{1jt} + a_{2t}S_{2jt} + a_{3t}E_{jt} + e_{jt} \qquad (6.19)$$

where E_{jt} is the price-prediction error for bond j at the beginning of month t. Under the null hypothesis of market efficiency $a_{3t} = 0$. This hypothesis was tested by constructing the means of the time series of the coefficients of equation 6.19 and calculating the t-statistic in the manner first suggested by Fama and MacBeth (1973) in a related context. The results are reported in tables 6–12 through 6–15.

In table 6–12 the valuation error E_{jt} was constructed from parameter estimates obtained from the whole sample period and the regressions 6.19 were estimated using all taxable bonds with maturities up to twenty years. To control for possible misspecification of the valuation model and the coupon

Table 6-12
Bond-Returns and Price-Prediction-Errors; Valuation Model Estimated over December 1958 to December 1979: All Taxable Bonds with Maturities Less Than Twenty Years

(t-ratios in parentheses)

	Holding Period = One Month						Holding Period = Three Months					
	Intercept ($\times 10^{-3}$)	S_{1jt}	S_{2jt}	$COUP_{jt}$ ($\times 10^{-3}$)	MAT_{jt} ($\times 10^{-3}$)	E_{jt}	Intercept ($\times 10^{-3}$)	S_{1jt}	S_{2jt}	$COUP_{jt}$ ($\times 10^{-3}$)	MAT_{jt} ($\times 10^{-3}$)	E_{jt}
December 1958 to December 1979	.485 (2.53)	-.0233 (-.56)	.0201 (1.11)				.814 (1.09)	-.0585 (-.44)	.0638 (1.18)			
	-1.22 (-3.72)	-.114 (-2.41)	.0352 (1.60)			.136 (7.88)	-1.44 (-1.79)	-.139 (-1.08)	.0675 (1.16)			.274 (7.74)
	-.817 (-2.14)	-.145 (-2.08)	-.0448 (-.35)	-.104 (-2.02)	-.0304 (-.61)	.146 (9.98)	-.933 (-1.02)	-.129 (-.81)	-.0519 (-.18)	-.0915 (-.79)	-.0595 (-.53)	.311 (8.93)
December 1958 to June 1969	.385 (1.99)	-.0328 (-.51)	.0197 (.84)				.147 (.20)	-.125 (-.67)	.106 (1.43)			
	-.0370 (-.14)	-.0489 (-.74)	.0536 (2.22)			.0646 (3.69)	-.440 (-.62)	-.150 (-.86)	.184 (2.54)			.146 (3.75)
	.175 (.68)	-.140 (-1.14)	-.124 (-.54)	-.184 (-3.11)	-.0812 (-.95)	.105 (6.05)	.453 (.64)	-.179 (-.70)	-.0579 (-.11)	-.322 (-2.39)	-.125 (-.65)	.243 (5.64)
July 1969 to December 1979	.586 (1.76)	-.0136 (-.27)	.0206 (.73)				1.47 (1.12)	-.0193 (-.13)	.0626 (.78)			
	-2.43 (-4.11)	-.180 (-2.65)	.0166 (.45)			.209 (7.30)	-2.11 (-1.47)	-.125 (-.79)	.0117 (.12)			.386 (5.80)
	-1.83 (-2.56)	-.150 (-2.25)	.0359 (.33)	-.0229 (-.27)	.0211 (.42)	.188 (8.13)	-.799 (-.41)	-.108 (-.69)	.00243 (.01)	-.0931 (-.42)	.0105 (.10)	.310 (6.21)

Table 6-13

Bond-Returns and Price-Prediction-Errors; Valuation Model Estimated over December 1958 to June 1969: All Taxable Bonds with Maturities Less Than Twenty Years

(t-ratios in parentheses)

Holding Period = One Month

Period	Intercept $(\times 10^{-3})$	S_{1jt}	S_{2jt}	$COUP_{jt}$ $(\times 10^{-3})$	MAT_{jt} $(\times 10^{-3})$	E_{jt}
December 1958 to December 1979	.441 (1.97)	−.0346 (−.67)	.0220 (1.04)			
	−2.04 (−5.73)	−.312 (−4.82)	−.0863 (−2.77)	−.113 (−2.17)	−.0767 (−1.70)	.152 (8.25)
	−1.95 (−4.31)	−.387 (−5.11)	−.320 (−2.40)			.173 (10.87)
December 1958 to June 1969	.385 (1.69)	−.0457 (−.56)	.0218 (.81)			
	−.336 (−.98)	−.157 (−1.69)	.0206 (.72)	−.200 (−3.28)	−.128 (−1.64)	.0657 (3.46)
	−.350 (−1.11)	−.364 (−2.91)	−.363 (−1.53)			.122 (6.39)
July 1969 to December 1969	.499 (1.28)	−.0234 (−.37)	.0221 (.68)			
	−4.50 (−6.21)	−.469 (−5.30)	−.195 (−3.62)	−.0234 (−.28)	.0250 (−.56)	.239 (8.04)
	−3.58 (−4.30)	−.412 (−4.80)	−.277 (−2.32)			.225 (9.07)

Holding Period = Three Months

Period	Intercept $(\times 10^{-3})$	S_{1jt}	S_{2jt}	$COUP_{jt}$ $(\times 10^{-3})$	MAT_{jt} $(\times 10^{-3})$	E_{jt}
December 1958 to December 1979	.757 (.78)	−.0958 (−.53)	.0704 (1.07)			
	−3.51 (−3.26)	−.521 (−2.75)	−.145 (−1.74)	−.0619 (−.53)	−.159 (−1.49)	.283 (7.81)
	−2.83 (−2.52)	−.565 (−2.89)	−.600 (−1.80)			.341 (9.29)
December 1958 to June 1969	−.0453 (−.05)	−.203 (−.76)	.117 (1.32)			
	−1.35 (−1.31)	−.440 (−1.62)	.119 (1.31)	−.286 (−2.11)	−.226 (−1.24)	.146 (3.37)
	−.804 (−.90)	−.657 (−2.16)	−.549 (−.95)			.258 (5.61)
July 1969 to December 1969	−1.37 (.82)	−.0387 (−.19)	.0693 (.73)			
	−.545 (−2.85)	−.562 (−2.47)	−.368 (−2.84)	−.0977 (−.43)	−.0453 (−.48)	.436 (6.39)
	−3.19 (−1.32)	.462 (−2.02)	.450 (−1.65)			.361 (6.81)

Table 6–14

Bond-Returns and Price-Prediction Errors; Valuation Model Estimated over December 1958 to December 1979: All Taxable Bonds with Maturities Less Than Ten Years

(*t-ratios in parentheses*)

	Intercept	S_{1jt}	S_{2jt}	$COUP_{jt}$	MAT_{jt}	h^*_{jt}	E_{jt}
	\(\times 10^{-3}\)			\(\times 10^{-3}\)	\(\times 10^{-3}\)		
December	.516	−.0135	.0171				
1958 to	(2.97)	(−.37)	(.87)				
December	.548	−.00646	−.00538			−.0267	
1979	(3.24)	(−.18)	(−.12)			(−.46)	
	−1.23	−.126	−.0429				.423
	(−3.98)	(−2.87)	(1.72)				(7.66)
	−1.28	−.134	.0638			.0352	.143
	(−4.28)	(−3.11)	(1.92)			(.93)	(7.93)
	−.872	−.176	−.107	−.0770	−.0532		.140
	(−2.36)	(−2.35)	(−.69)	(−1.64)	(−.87)		(9.46)
	−.974	−.195	−.0989	−.0709	−.0654	.0551	.142
	(−2.72)	(−2.65)	(−.63)	(−1.55)	(−1.07)	(2.07)	(9.80)
December	.449	−.00985	.0129				
1958 to	(2.64)	(−.18)	(.50)				
June 1969	.413	−.00174	−.0513			−.0777	
	(2.48)	(−.03)	(−1.11)			(−1.68)	
	−.164	−.0718	.0702				.071
	(−.70)	(−1.25)	(2.61)				(4.00)
	−.209	−.0742	.0690			−.00532	.075
	(−.89)	(−1.27)	(1.92)			(−.14)	(4.20)
	.122	−.210	−.273	−.165	−.135		.104
	(.50)	(−1.58)	(−.97)	(−3.06)	(−1.31)		(5.99)
	.112	−.220	−.284	−.168	−.144	.00854	.107
	(.46)	(−1.68)	(−1.02)	(−3.15)	(−1.40)	(.32)	(6.06)
July	.584	−.0173	.0213				
1969 to	(1.91)	(−.36)	(.72)				
December	.685	−.0112	.0412			.0250	
1979	(2.31)	(−.24)	(.51)			(.23)	
	−2.32	−.182	.0152				.213
	(−4.12)	(−2.73)	(.36)				(6.78)
	−2.37	−.194	.0585			.0763	.21
	(−4.40)	(−3.09)	(1.04)			(1.16)	(6.99)
	−1.88	−.141	.0612	.0125	.0298		.17
	(−2.73)	(−2.10)	(.47)	(.16)	(.46)		(7.45)
	−2.08	−.170	.0889	.0275	.0139	.102	.17
	(−3.13)	(−2.58)	(.66)	(.37)	(.21)	(2.23)	(7.83)

Holding Period = One Month

Intercept	S_{1jt}	S_{2jt}	$COUP_{jt}$	MAT_{jt}	h^*_{jt}	E_{jt}
			Holding Perod = Three Months			
$(\times 10^{-3})$			$(\times 10^{-3})$	$(\times 10^{-3})$		
.753	−.0597	.0628				
(1.07)	(−.48)	(1.14)				
.813	−.0702	−.186			.141	
(1.19)	(−.57)	(2.36)			(1.73)	
−1.59	−.139	.0579				.300
(−2.15)	(−1.13)	(.94)				(7.58)
−1.67	−.162	.180			.166	.303
(−2.29)	(−1.32)	(2.61)			(2.57)	(7.69)
−1.23	−.190	−.213	−.0347	−.113		.302
(−1.42)	(−1.12)	(−.62)	(−.34)	(−.87)		(9.25)
−1.34	−.211	−.148	−.0246	−.126	.125	.309
(−1.58)	(−1.26)	(−.43)	(−.25)	(−.97)	(2.77)	(9.44)
.302	−.0912	.0952				
(.44)	(−.52)	(1.28)				
.356	−.114	.282			.197	
(.54)	(−.67)	(2.91)			(2.27)	
−.597	−.174	.208				.158
(−.88)	(−1.06)	(2.90)				(4.11)
−.552	−.184	.328			.125	.159
(−.83)	(−1.14)	(3.50)			(1.80)	(4.09)
.439	−.281	−.377	−.261	−.235		.277
(.65)	(−1.01)	(−.62)	(−2.29)	(−1.07)		(5.69)
.462	−.296	−.326	−.259	−.251	.0753	.230
(.69)	(−1.08)	(−.52)	(−2.28)	(−1.14)	(1.46)	(5.69)
1.26	−.0330	.0682				
(1.07)	(−.23)	(.82)				
1.43	−.00278	−.0318			−.167	
(1.13)	(−.02)	(−.12)			(−.49)	
−2.45	−.156	.0202				402
(−1.76)	(−1.04)	(.20)				(5.47)
−2.61	−.197	.157			.244	.394
(−1.94)	(−1.33)	(1.05)			(1.38)	(5.72)
−1.58	−.130	.135	−.0150	.0599		.280
(−.82)	(−.83)	(.45)	(−.08)	(.40)		(5.51)
−2.11	−.175	.231	.0327	.0434	.217	.287
(−1.15)	(−1.13)	(.80)	(.19)	(.29)	(2.26)	(5.82)

Table 6–15

Bond-Returns and Price-Prediction-Errors; Valuation Model Estimated over December 1958 to June 1969: All Taxable Bonds with Maturities Less Than Ten Years

(*t-ratios in parentheses*)

	Intercept	S_{1jt}	S_{2jt}	$COUP_{jt}$	MAT_{jt}	h_{jt}^*	E_{jt}
	$(\times 10^{-3})$			$(\times 10^{-3})$	$(\times 10^{-3})$		
December	.474	−.0211	.0185				
1958 to	(2.39)	(−.49)	(.82)				
December	.334	−.0440	−.0114			−.0336	
1979	(2.12)	(−1.23)	(.44)			(−.77)	
	−2.34	−.308	−.0907				.158
	(−5.67)	(−5.10)	(−2.54)				(7.96)
	−2.20	−.288	−.0872			−.0145	.154
	(−5.41)	(−5.12)	(−2.41)			(−.43)	(7.73)
	−1.92	−.385	−.336	−.0839	−.0842		.164
	(−4.31)	(−5.00)	(−2.11)	(−1.76)	(−1.54)		(10.16)
	−1.98	−.470	−.642	−.0454	−.188	−.0760	.164
	(−4.40)	(−.538)	(−3.40)	(−1.01)	(−2.91)	(−2.27)	(10.24)
December	.451	−.0148	.0143				
1958 to	(2.29)	(−.23)	(.47)				
June 1969	.291	−.0550	−.00438			−.0447	
	(1.84)	(−1.16)	(.14)			(−1.01)	
	−.421	−.165	.0294				.0704
	(−1.35)	(−2.10)	(.96)				(3.66)
	−.413	−.153	.0298			−.00726	.0703
	(−1.32)	(−2.17)	(.98)			(−.18)	(3.64)
	−.341	−.378	−.434	−.189	−.149		.118
	(−1.11)	(−2.94)	(−1.53)	(−3.35)	(−1.61)		(6.14)
	−.445	−.542	−.957	−.135	−.314	−.108	.121
	(−1.49)	(−3.38)	(−2.84)	(−2.47)	(−2.96)	(−2.84)	(6.31)
July	.497	−.0275	.0229				
1969 to	(1.44)	(−.47)	(.67)				
December	.379	−.0328	.0186			.0222	
1979	(1.37)	(−.61)	(.44)			(−.29)	
	−4.28	−.454	−.213				.246
	(−5.88)	(−5.00)	(−3.36)				(7.45)
	−4.01	−.426	−.206			−.0219	.240
	(−5.56)	(−4.92)	(−3.19)			(−.40)	(7.15)
	−3.51	−.393	−.236	.0233	−.0188		.211
	(−4.30)	(−4.61)	(−1.68)	(.31)	(−.32)		(8.29)
	−3.55	−.397	−.322	.0459	−.0608	−.0429	.209
	(−4.25)	(−4.84)	(−1.96)	(.64)	(−.84)	(−.78)	(8.23)

Holding Period = One Month

				Holding Period = Three Months			
Intercept	S_{1jt}	S_{2jt}	$COUP_{jt}$	MAT_{jt}	h^*_{jt}	E_{jt}
$(\times 10^{-3})$			$(\times 10^{-3})$	$(\times 10^{-3})$		
.709	−.0860	.0675				
(.82)	(−.53)	(1.00)				
.427	−.125	−.0511			−.0740	
(.59)	(−.85)	(.76)			(−.74)	
−3.38	−.465	−.205				.314
(−3.02)	(−2.66)	(−2.24)				(7.64)
−3.02	−.417	−.198			.0103	.309
(−3.38)	(−2.60)	(−2.25)			(.15)	(7.64)
−2.81	−.535	−.663	−.0217	−.180		.331
(−2.62)	(−2.81)	(−1.78)	(−.21)	(−1.49)		(9.47)
−2.71	−.633	−.0126	−.0418	−.385	−.151	.326
(−2.50)	(−3.10)	(−2.89)	(.41)	(−2.65)	(−2.31)	(9.35)
.241	−.133	.102				
(.28)	(−.57)	(1.14)				
−.103	−.211	.0989			.0480	
(−.15)	(−.97)	(1.15)			(−.45)	
−.134	−.421	.124				.154
(−1.46)	(−1.74)	(1.37)				(3.63)
−1.22	−.411	.131			.00170	.149
(−.149)	(−1.82)	(1.58)			(.02)	(3.87)
−.574	−.606	−.652	−.264	−.254		.242
(−.67)	(−2.02)	(−1.00)	(−2.21)	(−1.25)		(5.63)
−.706	−.862	−.0168	−.156	−.588	−.225	.246
(−.83)	(−2.43)	(−2.30)	(−1.27)	(−2.69)	(−3.07)	(5.67)
1.09	−.0569	.0751				
(.76)	(−.31)	(.77)				
−3.15	−.145	−.0632			−.0822	
(−.22)	(−.77)	(.57)			(−.37)	
−5.50	−.568	−.383				.449
(−2.88)	(−2.59)	(−2.76)				(5.89)
−5.15	−.554	−.339			.0512	.406
(−2.95)	(−2.73)	(−2.53)			(−.38)	(5.55)
−3.67	−.461	−.263	−.00402	.00603		.316
(−1.50)	(−2.07)	(−.82)	(−.02)	(−.05)		(5.65)
−3.70	−.491	−.577	.0461	−.139	−.132	.315
(−1.47)	(−2.32)	(−1.42)	(.26)	(−.77)	(−1.07)	(5.85)

rate ($COUP_{jt}$) and maturity (MAT_{jt}) of the individual bonds were included as independent variables in some of the regressions. The left half of the table reports the results obtained when bond returns were calculated on a monthly basis; the right half of the table reports results obtained using quarterly rates of return. In either case the independent variables including the price-prediction error were calculated as of the beginning of the observation interval.

The results reported in table 6–12 indicate a highly significant relationship between the valuation error and the rate of return over the next time interval—approximately 15 percent of the error is corrected during the next month and 30 percent over the next quarter. The results are quite insensitive to the inclusion of the coupon and maturity variables, which suggests that they are not explicable in terms of model misspecification.

Since the price-prediction error used in the regressions reported in table 6–12 was derived from a valuation model that was estimated over the whole sample period, the prediction errors are not true ex-ante forecasts and it is possible that the results are attributable to testing the model on the data for which it was estimated. To investigate this issue the preceding analysis was repeated with the difference that the price-prediction error was computed using the first-half estimator, which it will be recalled used only data from the period December 1958 to June 1961. The results obtained using the first-half estimator are reported in table 6–13, which follows the same format as table 6–12. It may be seen from this table that the price-prediction error continues to have a highly significant effect on the subsequent return even outside the period over which the model was estimated; moreover the coefficients of the price-prediction errors are very similar to those reported in the previous table.

Although inclusion of bond coupon and maturity in the cross-sectional regressions was found to have no significant effect on the coefficient of the price-prediction error, model misspecification remains the most plausible explanation of our findings. Since we have found evidence of model misspecification in the systematic behavior of the price-prediction errors and, related this, to a possible omitted-state variable that could be proxied for by the factor, it is worth exploring whether this could have accounted for our results.

Assuming that the omitted-state variable can be represented by the factor extracted from the price-prediction errors and that this factor affects bond prices in a linear fashion, the expression corresponding to 6.16 for the rate of return on a bond is:

$$R_j = E[R_j] + S_{1j}\Delta Z_1 + S_{2j}\Delta Z_2 + h_j^*\Delta f \qquad (6.16')$$

where h_j^* is the transformed factor loading for bond j[13] and Δf is the unanticipated change in the factor score. The corresponding equilibrium condition 6.17 becomes:

$$E[R_j] - r = \lambda_1 S_{1j} + \lambda_2 S_{2j} + \lambda_3 h_j^* \qquad (6.17')$$

Combining 6.16' and 6.17' we obtain:

$$R_j - r = (\lambda_1 + \Delta Z_1)S_{1j} + (\lambda_2 \Delta Z_2)S_{2j} + (\lambda_3 + \Delta_f)h_j^* \quad (6.18')$$

and the corresponding regression equation is:

$$R_{jt} - r_t = a_{0t} + a_{1t}S_{1jt} + a_{2t}S_{2jt} + a_{3t}h_j^* + a_{4t}E_{jt} + e_{jt}. \quad (6.19')$$

The transformed factor loading for each bond, h_j^*, was based on its maturity and the price-prediction-error factor loadings reported in table 6–7. Since these factor loadings were available only for maturities up to ten years the regressions were restricted to bonds of maturity less than ten years.

Tables 6–14 and 6–15 report the regression results and correspond to tables 6–12 and 6–13 respectively, except for the inclusion of the transformed factor loading as an independent variable and the restriction of the sample to maturities of less than ten years. Addition of the factor loading has no significant effect on the results.

It does not seem that the results can be easily explained in terms of model misspecification. If they are not due to model misspecification then the data suggest market inefficiency and whether true profit opportunities existed depends upon whether the bond prices used were true end-of-month transaction prices at which further transactions could have been made.

Notes

1. A more complete description of the bond-pricing model may be found in Brennan and Schwartz (1979).

2. See McKean (1968).

3. This is analogous to the standard result in the option-pricing literature that the value of an option does not depend on the expected rate of return on the underlying stock. See Brennan and Schwartz (1979), appendix.

4. The highest yielding bond was chosen to mitigate the problem posed by "flower" bonds whose yields are distorted (bid down) on account of the privilege they offer of redemption at par for payment of estate duty.

5. See Drhymes (1971).

6. Brennan and Schwartz (1980).

7. Strictly speaking, it would still be possible to derive the partial-

differential equation if there were additional state variables so long as they affected only $\lambda_2(\cdot)$.

8. Brennan and Schwartz (1981) appendix A.

9. Excluding flower bonds.

10. See equation 6.9.

11. The root-mean-square error for this rule is given by the standard deviation of returns, assuming that the mean is known.

12. The values of λ_1 estimated earlier in the chapter presuppose that the unit of time is one year. Therefore if the rate of return in equation 6.17 is measured on a monthly or quarterly basis the value of λ_1 in equation 6.17 would be one-twelfth or one-quarter of the value reported here.

13. $h_i^* = h_j/B_j$ where h_j is the factor loading for the price prediction errors reported in table 6–7 and B_j is the price of the bond at the beginning of the period: the transformation is required because equation 6.18' is in terms of rates of return, not prices.

References

Aitken, A.C. "On Least Squares and Linear Combinations of Observations." *Proceedings of the Royal Society of Edinburgh* 55 (1935): 42–48.

Black, F., and Scholes, M. "The Pricing of Options and Corporate Liabilities." *Journal of Political Economy* 81 (1973): 637–659.

Brennan, M.J., and Schwartz, E.S. "Duration, Bond Pricing and Portfolio Management." Mimeographed. University of British Columbia 1981.

———. "Conditional Predictions of Bond Prices and Returns." *Journal of Finance* 35 (1980): 405–417.

———. "A Continuous Time Approach to the Pricing of Bonds." *Journal of Banking and Finance* 3 (1979): 133–155.

Cox, J.; J. Ingersoll; and S. Ross. "A Theory of the Term Structure of Interest Rates" Mimeographed, Stanford University 1978.

Dhrymes, P.J. "Equivalence of Iterative Aitken and Maximum Likelihood Estimators for a System of Regressors Equations." *Australian Economic Papers* 10 (1971): 20–24.

Durbin, J. "Testing for Serial Correlation in Least Squares Regression When Some of the Regressors are Lagged Dependent Variables." *Econometrica* 38 (1970): 410–421.

Fama, E., and MacBeth, J. "Risk, Return, and Equilibrium: Empirical Tests." *Journal of Political Economy* 71 (1973): 607–636.

McKean, H.D., Jr. *Stochastic Integrals.* New York: Academic Press, 1968.

Merton, R.C. "Theory of Rational Option Pricing." *Bell Journal of Economics and Management Science* 4 (1973): 141–183.

Park, R.G. "Estimation with Heteroscedastic Error Terms *Econometrica* 34 (1966): 88.

Ross, S.A. "The Arbitrage Theory of Capital Asset Pricing." *Journal of Economic Theory* 13 (1976): 341–360.

Shiller, R.J. "The Volatility of Long-Term Interest Rates and Expectations Models of the Term Structure." *Journal of Political Economy* 87 (1979): 1190–1219.

7

The Risk of Bank-Loan Portfolios

Richard A. Brealey,
Stewart D. Hodges, and
Michael J.P. Selby

Many financial institutions face a variety of interesting and important problems that concern the management of a risky loan portfolio. This chapter examines the nature of these risks. In particular, it looks at the distribution of returns on a diversified loan portfolio and considers how returns are affected by a variety of factors, such as the maturity of the debt and the capital structure and business risk of the borrowers.

It is well known that any corporate liability can be viewed as a combination of options. Both Black and Scholes (1973) and Merton (1973) showed that, as long as there are no interest or dividend payments, the common stock of a levered corporation is equivalent to a European call option. Thus, the shareholders have the option at maturity to repurchase the bondholders' claim on the firm by paying off the face value of the debt. Subsequently, Merton (1974) derived the value of a risky pure-discount bond and showed how this value is affected by changes in the nature of the firm and its capital structure.

Our analysis in this chapter is in the spirit of Merton's 1974 paper on discount bonds. However, unlike Merton, we focus on the behavior of diversified loan portfolios and we are interested in the time-series properties of the returns on these portfolios. In addition, we are concerned with coupon debt rather than pure-discount debt. The effect of intermediate coupon payments is to transform the common stock into a compound call option. At every coupon date the stockholders have the option of either buying the next option by paying the coupon or forfeiting the firm to the bondholders. The final option is to repurchase the bondholders' claim on the firm by paying both the principal and the final coupon.

Since the distribution of returns on a single coupon loan is in itself a complex sum of truncated distributions, the distribution of returns on a portfolio of such loans is analytically intractable. We therefore employ simulation to estimate the behavior of such a portfolio.[1]

Empirical Studies of Returns on Risky Loans

There have been a number of empirical studies of the risk premia on bonds, but since they largely predate the development of a consistent theory of contingent liabilities, they are inevitably somewhat ad hoc in character. Moreover, almost the only matter on which they are agreed is that there exists a risk premium.

The classic analysis of Fisher (1959) suggested that a large fraction of the variation in the yield spread between corporate and government bonds could be explained in terms of various proxies for default risk (earnings variability, length of solvency, and leverage) and a proxy for marketability (volume of bonds outstanding).

Fisher did not examine the effect of bond maturity. However, subsequent work by Johnson (1967) suggested that in the period 1900–1944 most bond defaults occurred at maturity and there was a significant relationship between the yield spread and maturity. Johnson concluded that the spread normally rose with maturity but that in periods of unusual economic uncertainty the spread was greater for bonds that were just about to become due.

Rather than working in terms of annual yields, Silvers (1973) and, more recently, Boardman and McEnally (1981) have estimated the certainty-equivalent values of the payments on corporate bonds.[2] Although the estimated certainty-equivalent coefficients generally decline with the time to payment, it is difficult to compare these results with those of Johnson. One reason for this is that there is no simple relationship between the yield spread, the (future) certainty-equivalent coefficients, and the difference between the price of a government and corporate bond. In addition the certainty-equivalent coefficients were estimated as a function of time to payment rather than as a function of the period to the bond's maturity. Both Silvers and Boardman and McEnally included a proxy for marketability in their regressions, but in contrast to Fisher's study its coefficient was seldom significant.

The Value of a Coupon Bond

We have noted that the value of a coupon bond is equal to the value of the firm less the value of a compound option. To value this option we need to make some assumptions about the assets used to form the hedge and about the precise character of the contingent claim.

The former consist of the standard assumptions of the Black-Scholes option-valuation model:

1. The value of company assets follows a random walk in continuous time with a constant known variance rate proportional to the square of the value.
2. The risk-free interest rate is known and constant through time.
3. Markets are frictionless and trading takes place in continuous time.

Our second set of assumptions is less standard. We assume that companies are financed by a combination of common stock and a single noncallable coupon loan. To economize on computing requirements, we also assume that coupon payments on this loan are made at two yearly intervals.

The bondholders' claim also depends on the restrictive convenants imposed on the issuer. Black and Cox (1976) pointed out that the regular interest payment serves as a hurdle that, if not jumped safely, gives the lender the opportunity to demand immediate repayment. However this hurdle would serve little purpose if the borrower was permitted to sell assets to pay interest. For this reason most bond indentures place restrictions on the sale of assets. We shall make the extreme assumption that this restriction is absolute, so that the borrower must issue stock to pay interest. This requirement reduces the riskiness of the bonds but it also provides an incentive for the ailing company to default early to avoid pumping in additional equity.

Bondholders are also concerned that the company should not distribute a substantial proportion of the assets to stockholders in the form of dividends. In the case of most publicly issued bonds the company is permitted to distribute cumulative income. In private placements or term loans, however, there may be a total ban on dividend payments. In our simulations we assume such a ban on dividends.

Finally, since we are in part interested in the effect of approaching maturity on bond values, we assume that no further loans are issued until the current loan is repaid. In practice most companies have debt outstanding with a variety of maturities and, subject to restrictions on the total degree of leverage or interest cover, may refund maturing debt and issue new debt periodically.

Our assumptions of a ban on the sale of assets, on the payment of dividends, and the issue of further debt serve to reduce the riskiness of each loan but, on the other hand, make companies less like one another in their capital structures (since a limited ban on these actions is likely to bear less heavily on the successful company). While these assumed restrictions are more extreme than those that are usually imposed, they are more realistic than the absence of any such restrictions.

Immediately after payment of the penultimate coupon the bond resembles a pure-discount bond and the boundary condition is that at maturity the bondholders receive the minimum of the value of the firm's assets or the face value of the debt and final coupon.

At all times before the penultimate coupon, the stockholders own a compound option. The boundary condition at each payment date is that the bondholders receive the minimum of (a) the value of the firm's assets or (b) the coupon plus the value of the bond after stockholders have put up the additional funds and paid the coupon. Thus, the value of the coupon bond can be obtained by solving recursively for the values at each boundary.

To calculate these bond values we use the approach suggested by Geske (1977) and described in appendix 7A. Geske derives a formula for the value of a coupon bond that contains multivariate normal-distribution functions, and one where the size of the highest dimensional distribution function is the number of nested options. Geske also points out that for certain correlation structures the multivariate normal integral can be factorized conveniently into a product of lower-order normal integrals.

The Simulation Model

To simulate the returns on a portfolio of loans, we proceed as follows. We specify a portfolio with an equal initial investment in each of thirty-two loans. Each of these loans has the following known characteristics:

$\sigma^2 =$ the variance rate of the returns on the company's assets.

$\rho^2 =$ the proportion of the variance of asset returns that is explained by the market factor.

$T =$ the maturity of the loan (in years).

$r_f =$ the risk-free interest rate.

$r =$ the rate of drift in the logarithm of the company's assets; that is, $E (\log (V_{t+1}/V_t))$.

$d =$ the face value of the loan discounted at the risk-free rate and expressed as a proportion of the market value of the firm's assets. (This measure of leverage was referred to by Merton in his 1974 paper as the *quasi-debt ratio*).

At each biennial coupon date we simulate the value of each company's assets and then, using Geske's formula for valuing compound options, we calculate the value of each bond. Thus we have a picture of the behavior of one *buy-and-hold* bond portfolio up to the time of maturity. We then repeat the exercise on 400 independent samples to give a distribution of returns on a portfolio of thirty-two loans.

The next step is to divide the portfolio into two smaller portfolios of sixteen loans each and to calculate the distribution of returns on the sixteen-loan portfolios. Similarly we can go on to estimate the distribution of eight-, four-, two-, and one-loan portfolios.

A Note on Sampling Procedures

Our simulations provide information on returns for loans with maturities that vary from two to ten years. They include thirty-two loans of each maturity for each of 400 simulations of different ten-year periods. Loans of different maturity are treated as if they were alternative loans issued on the same dates and by identical firms.

When forming loans into portfolios, we consider at one extreme a single portfolio of thirty-two loans for each of 400 simulations and at the other extreme thirty-two portfolios of one loan each for each of 400 simulations. The one-loan portfolios are subsets of the thirty-two loan portfolios.

When estimating the moments of portfolio returns, we pool the returns on all similar portfolios. Thus the standard deviation of returns on one-loan portfolios is calculated from $32 \times 400 = 12,800$ observations. However, because the 32 observations for each period are all influenced by the same market factor these 12,800 observations are not independent of each other.

It is important to bear in mind that the sampling error on such simulations can be quite large. However, as a check that our broad conclusions are not a consequence of sampling error, we repeated the base-case simulations with a different set of random numbers.

The Choice of Parameters—The Base Case

While our choice of parameters was somewhat arbitrary, we selected values that are broadly typical of quoted companies. Our base-case parameters are as follows:

Description	Symbol	Value
The annual standard deviation of the continuously compounded returns on the firm's assets	σ	.25
The proportion of the variance of asset returns explained by the market factor	ρ^2	.30
The risk-free interest rate (annually compounded)	r_f	.12
The coupon rate (equivalent to a payment of $25.44 every two years)	C	.12
The expected-risk premium for each firm's assets	$r\text{-}\log(1 + r_f)$	.05
The debt ratio, where debt payments are discounted at the risk-free rate	d	.40
Loan maturity	T	two years–ten years

The Bounds on Loan Prices

At each coupon date the price of the loan has an upper bound, which is equal to the value of a default-free loan. The nondefaulting loan has a lower bound, which is equal to the asset value at which it would just pay the firm to default on the loan service rather than raise the required funds from the shareholders. Table 7–1 shows these lower bounds on the price of a nondefaulting ten-year loan under our base-case assumptions. Notice that at the final date the firm will pay off the loan as long as the assets are worth more than the $100 principal plus the $25.44 coupon. Two years before maturity the company must decide whether to make the penultimate coupon payment of $25.44. If it does so, it acquires the option to purchase the assets two years later for $125.44. Table 7–1 shows that it will be justified in making this coupon payment as long as the value of the assets exceeds $117.35. You can also see from table 7–1 that the lower bound on the price of nondefaulting loans declines further as the period to maturity increases.

The Distribution of Returns

Figure 7–1 shows histograms from our simulations for the internal rates of return on two-year loans (the top pair) and on ten-year loans (the bottom pair). To show a reasonable number of cases of default, we have chosen the histograms corresponding to an initial leverage of $d = 0.60$, rather than $d = 0.40$. However, the general form of the distribution is similar for other levels of leverage. The histograms on the left-hand side are from holding single loans and those on the right are from holding a portfolio of thirty-two loans. The horizontal scale gives the annual percentage return relative to the initial promised return (that is, the yield to maturity at issue). The vertical scale measures the percentage of occurrence in each class internal, and a

Table 7–1
Lower Bounds on Cum-Dividend Price of a Nondefaulting Loan (Base Case)

Year	Lower Bound on Cum-Dividend Price	Equivalent Upper Bound On Promised Yield
2	$114.89	14.2%
4	115.17	14.5
6	115.76	15.2
8	117.35	16.8
10	125.44	–

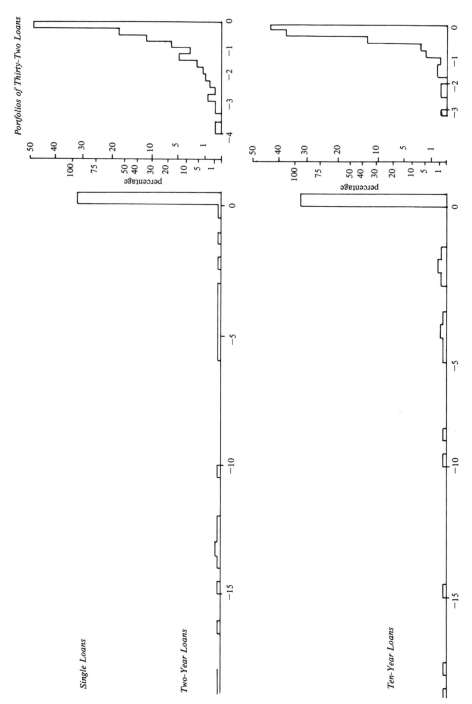

Figure 7–1. Histograms of Realized Internal Rates of Return

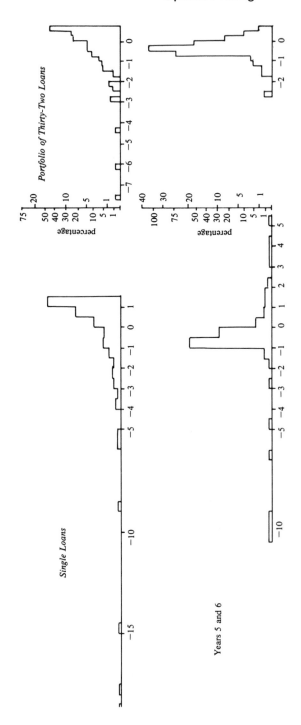

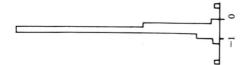

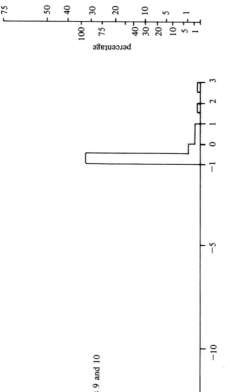

Figure 7–2. Histograms of Subperiod Returns

nonlinear scale has been chosen to make the all-important tails of the distribution more visible.

Two features of figure 7–1 are worth noting. First, all the distributions, even for portfolios of loans, are extremely negatively skewed. Second, all the histograms have been drawn to the same horizontal scale, and it is clear that the benefits of forming a diversified portfolio of loans are considerable.[3]

Figure 7–2 shows how the probability distribution of returns changes over the life of a ten-year loan. As before, the left-hand histograms are for a single loan and the right-hand ones are for a portfolio of thirty-two loans. All the histograms are for loans to companies with an initial leverage of $d = 0.60$.

The top pair of figures shows the simulated returns (relative to the initial yield to maturity) over the first two years. The best that can happen is that the loan becomes almost safe and this provides the upper bound on possible positive returns. A much wider range of possibilities exists on the downside, where the risk premium may widen or a loan may actually default. Not surprisingly, therefore, the distributions are quite negatively skewed.

The middle pair of histograms shows the returns for years five and six.[4] The modal point consists of those loans that had already become relatively safe and therefore provide approximately the default-free interest rate. There are other companies whose loans had become very risky in the preceding years that subsequently recover. These loans provide much higher returns than the initial yield to maturity. Finally some firms experience deteriorating fortunes in years five and six and their loans give much lower returns than the initial yield to maturity. Thus in the middle years of the loan's life there is room for both good and bad performance and as a result the distribution of returns is fairly symmetric.

Finally, the bottom pair of histograms shows the realized returns over the final two-year period. Over this period loans must either yield exactly their promised return or else default. Many loans have by now become very safe and simply offer the risk-free rate. Others may be offering risk permia of various amounts. Premature default will have already taken place if the assets of the company failed to reach the critical values shown in table 7–1 and these provide a limit to how risky a loan may be and still remain extant. In the example illustrated no loan may offer a yield that is more than 4.7 percent above its promised yield. As a result the histogram shows a positively skewed distribution of required returns, bounded below by the risk-free rate, but with a long negative tail corresponding to actual defaults.

**The Effect of Diversification
on the Distribution of Loan Returns**

The instantaneous returns on loans are by assumption multivariate normal with the market movement explaining thirty percent of their variances.

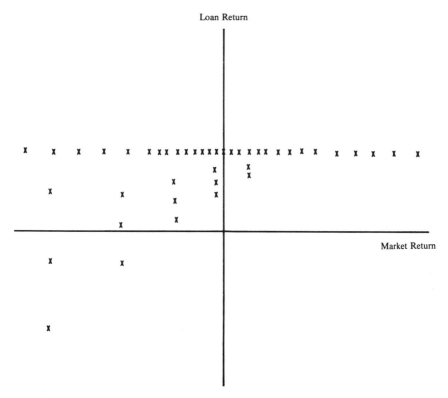

Figure 7–3. Relationship between Loan and Market Return

However, over any finite period the distribution of returns on the loan portfolio is a complex sum of lognormal distributions that are both truncated and correlated. For example, figure 7–3 shows that the return on a loan can never exceed the promised yield regardless of the market return. On the other hand, the return can fall short of the promised yield and is more likely to do so when the market return is negative. This results in a nonlinear relationship between different loan returns, which lowers the correlation with the market and causes the variance to decline more rapidly with the number of securities.

The histograms in figure 7–1 provided some indication of the effect of loan portfolio diversification but table 7–2 shows more clearly how large this effect can be. The first column shows that for a two-year holding period the risk of a portfolio containing both the debt and the equity can be reduced by approximately 45 percent, which is what we would expect given the 0.30 R^2 with the market. The remaining columns show that in the case of loan portfolios, diversification provides a much larger proportionate reduction in

Table 7-2
The Effect of Diversification on Risk

Number of Securities	*Index of Standard Deviation*		
	Debt and Equity	*Two-Year Loan*	*Ten-Year Loan*
1	100	100	100
2	81	69	38
4	70	49	26
8	63	36	17
16	59	25	13
32	57	19	10

Note: The summary data in this table are extracted from table 7B-1.

risk and this effect is particularly marked when return is measured over the life of a ten-year loan. We observe that in practice banks and lending institutions seek to diversify their loan portfolios very widely indeed: table 7-2 suggests that they are right to do so.

As we saw with the sample histograms, single-loan portfolios are characterized by strong negative skewness and leptokurtosis. Portfolio diversification always reduces both the skewness and kurtosis but the extent to which it does so depends on the holding period. Since over the period of the loan it must either give the promised return or default, a portfolio of loans held to maturity will still be characterized by a marked degree of skewness and kurtosis. On the other hand, just before maturity many long-term loans may stand at a significant discount, and in the final period a number of these will offer above-average returns. Thus, in this final period, the returns on a diversified portfolio of loans may actually be positively skewed.

More detailed information on the effect of diversification on the distribution of returns is provided in table 7B-1.

Promised and Realized Yield Spreads

Table 7-3 summarizes the spread between the yield to maturity on risky loans and the yield on risk-free loans. Under base-case assumptions the equilibrium spread varies between 4.6 and 10.6 basis points depending on maturity. This spread is substantially less than the actual spreads on corporate loans. While this difference may be partially due to the very restrictive covenants that we assume, it is also consistent with Fisher's suggestion that a significant proportion of the observed variations in spread is due to differences in marketability.

Table 7–3
Promised and Realized Yield Spreads (Base Case)
(*in percentage*)

	Maturity (Years)				
	2	4	6	8	10
Promised Spread	.046	.091	.104	.106	.104
Realized Spread	.034	.067	.086	.082	.085

Note: The summary data in this table are extracted from table 7B–2.

If there is a chance of default, then the average realized yield to maturity will fall short of the promised yield. This differential depends not only on the terms and risk of the loan but also on the expected risk premium on the stock. Table 7–3 shows that under our base-case assumptions roughly a quarter of the yield spread over government bonds represents the difference between promised and realized returns. The remainder represents the premium that the lender receives for bearing risk.

If the present value of the exercise price is held constant, the value of a call option must increase with maturity. Hence the issue price of the risky loan falls monotonically with maturity. In this sense long-term loans offer a larger risk premium.

Merton (1974) has pointed out that in the case of discount bonds there is no such simple relationship betwen maturity and measures of the annual risk premium. The results in table 7–3 are consistent with this, since neither the promised nor expected yield increases monotonically with maturity.

We shall see later that if the leverage is high, then the issue price of the debt declines relatively slowly with maturity. In these circumstances, the yield spread can decline throughout the range of maturities with which we are concerned. This result is consistent with Johnson's observation that yield spreads are more likely to decline with maturity in periods of economic crisis. It is also, however, a reminder of the problems involved in any empirical analysis of yield spreads.

We now look at how the average realized return varies through the life of the loan. For example, consider first the relationship between ten-year loans with two years to run and newly issued two-year loans. There are two differences between these loans. First, in the case of the ten-year loans the passage of time brings about some cross-sectional dispersion in the degree of leverage even though at the time of issue the leverage of each company was identical. Second, the regular injection of cash reduces the average leverage of ten-year loans.

Table 7–4
Realized Yield Spread by Years (Base Case)
(*in percentage*)

Years	Two-Year Loan	Ten-Year Loan
0–2	.034	.176
2–4		.099
4–6		.070
6–8		.028
8–10		.012

Note: The summary data in this table are extracted from table 7B–2.

   These changes have opposite effects on the expected return of the ten-year loan. The increasing dispersion in leverage is equivalent to a dispersion in the exercise price of the shareholders' option. Since the average value of a number of options with different exercise prices exceeds the value of a single option with the average exercise price, this increasing dispersion tends to reduce the expected value of the loan and to increase the expected subsequent return.

   In contrast, the regular cash injection reduces the average degree of leverage. This tends to make the ten-year loan less risky in its last two years and, therefore, reduces its expected return. Table 7–4 shows that the effect of this shifting mean greatly outweighs the effect of the shifting dispersion. The average return in the final two years of a ten-year loan is not only substantially lower than the average return on a two-year loan but is also very close to the risk-free rate.

   Given the above observation, we should not be surprised that the average return declines throughout the life of a loan. However, one of the interesting features of table 7–4 is just how large this decline can be. For example, the average return in the first two years of a ten-year loan is not only about sixteen basis points higher than the average return in the final two years, it is also higher than the promised yield over the life of the loan. Thus these variations in the average return during the life of the loan can be much larger than the yield spread between corporates and governments.

   We shall see in a later section that this decline in the return is matched by a similar decline in the loan's systematic risk.

Default Experience

If a company issues a discount loan and there are no dividend payments on the equity, the number of defaults will increase with loan maturity and all

Table 7–5
Default Experience
(*in percentage*)

	Maturity of Loan (Years)				
	2	4	6	8	10
Total Defaults	.21	.48	.46	.52	.46

Note: The summary data in this table are extracted from table 7B–2.

defaults will occur at maturity. Conversely, if a company issues a coupon loan and there are no restrictions on dividends, companies will have an incentive to default at the first coupon date. Thus the proportion and timing of defaults depend critically on the covenants imposed by the borrower.

With our intermediate case of coupon loans, with prohibitions on the payment of dividends and the sale of assets, there is no such simple relationship between default and maturity. Thus, table 7–5 shows that with the base-case simulations, the proportion of loans defaulting increases from 0.21 percent for two-year loans to 0.48 percent for four-year loans, but the annual injection of cash is sufficiently large that the default rate on longer loans remains approximately the same. Moreover, table 7–6 shows that the prospective cost of these cash injections is such that the majority of defaults on these longer loans occur during the first half of the loan's life and only a relatively small proportion takes place at maturity.

Systematic Risk

Suppose that the assets have a beta of one. Then at any point in time the hedge ratio of the compound call option is equal to the beta of the common

Table 7–6
Defaults of Ten-Year Loans by Year (Base Case)

Year	Percentage of Defaults
2	.08
4	.15
6	.09
8	.05
10	.09

Note: The summary data in this table are extracted from table 7B–2.

Table 7–7
Expected Systematic Risk

	Maturity (Years)	
Beginning Year	Two	Ten
0	.007	.025
2		.015
4		.009
6		.004
8		.002

Note: The summary data in this table are extracted from table 7B–3.

stock multiplied by the ratio of the value of the equity to the value of the assets. From this we can derive the beta of the loan.

These betas are shown in table 7–7. Notice that the systematic risk of a typical corporate loan is uniformly very low. On the other hand, most banks finance their loan portfolios largely with deposits, so that the beta of the underlying equity may be ten to twenty times that of the debt it supports. If our base-case assumptions are correct, this would still imply a much lower beta for bank stocks than is usually estimated. On the other hand, not only have we assumed unusually restrictive covenants, but, as we shall see, minor changes in the parameter assumptions can have substantial effects on the beta of a corporate-loan portfolio and, therefore, on the implied beta of bank stocks.

As we should expect, there are quite large proportional changes in systematic risk throughout the life of the loan. Thus, although the systematic risk on a ten-year loan at the time of issue is very low, it is nevertheless thirteen times the expected risk of the same loan two years before maturity. Thus changes in the growth rate of bank-loan portfolios or in their maturity structure may induce quite large variations in the systematic risk of the underlying equity.

Since the option-pricing model can be derived from the capital-asset-pricing model, the instantaneous expected risk premium on a loan is proportionate to the loan's systematic risk. While this is clearly not true of expected premia over any finite period, figure 7–4 shows that the expected two-year risk premia are roughly a linear function of the betas at the beginning of each period.

Sensitivity Analysis

Table 7–8 summarizes briefly the sensitivity of loan returns to the choice of parameters. We draw attention briefly to the following features:

Table 7-8
Sensitivity Analysis of Promised Yield Spreads and Default Rates

		Maturity (Years)		
		Two	Six	Ten
Base case	Yield spread	.046%	.104%	.104%
	percentage defaults	.21	.46	.46
Leverage = 60%	Yield spread	.849%	.733%	.517%
	percentage defaults	4.12	4.75	4.80
Standard deviation	Yield spread	.541%	.737%	.696%
= .35	percentage defaults	1.77	3.57	4.32
Coupon = 8%	Yield spread	.046%	.150%	.149%
(Annually)	percentage defaults	.21	.67	.61
Risk premium = 7%	Yield spread	.046%	.104%	.104%
	percentage defaults	.18	.25	.22

Note: The summary data in this table are extracted from tables 7B–4 through 7B–7.

Debt Ratio

The change in leverage from 40 percent to 60 percent has a very large effect on loan returns. For example, on a two-year loan the yield spread increases from .046 percent to 4.12 percent. The systematic risk of such loans increases by a factor of thirteen.

The change also affects the time pattern of returns. Since the options are no longer so deep in the money, more of the defaults occur in the early years and there is now quite a substantial variation in both expected return and risk over the life of the loan.

Standard Deviations of Asset Returns

Not surprisingly, changing the standard deviation from 0.25 to 0.35 also increases significantly the expected returns and risk. In this case, however, the additional dispersion provides an incentive for the company to keep making coupon payments to acquire a further option. Defaults, therefore, tend to occur late in the loan's life. Likewise, maturity now has a larger impact on the value of the loan.

Coupon

In table 7–8 we hold the risk-free rate constant and reduce the coupon to 8 percent. While this increases the average life of the loan, the more important

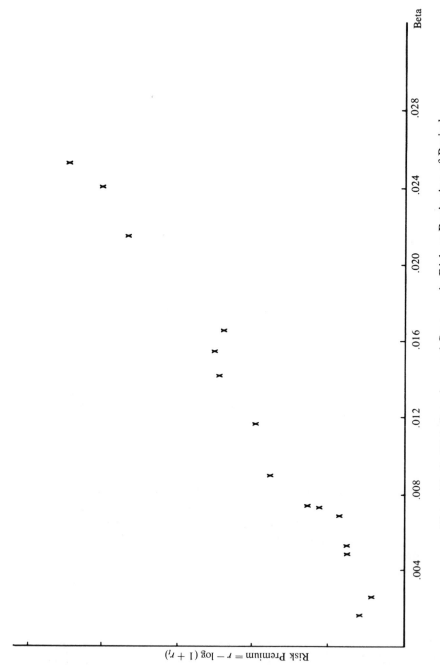

Figure 7–4. Risk Premium and Systematic Risk at Beginning of Period

effect is that it makes the loan closer to a simple option. With the lower annual cash injection, there is less incentive to default early but the default rate is substantially higher in later years. Given our assumed restrictive covenants, the regular coupon provides an important default trigger. Thus the reduction in coupon increases the promised yield on the ten-year loan from 12.046 percent to 12.149 percent. Moreover, since the annual cash injection is reduced, the required return is almost as high in the later years of the bond's life as in the early years. Clearly, the relevant characteristic is the cash-flow pattern. Given the restrictive covenants, a large sinking-fund requirement will have a similar effect on the value of the loan as a large coupon.

Expected Risk Premium on Assets

The expected risk premium on the underlying asset does not affect the value of an option. Thus the equilibrium-loan price and yield are unchanged in table 7–8. The expected returns on the option are, however, significantly changed. For example, just about all the yield spread now consists of a risk premium and only a negligible proportion represents the difference between the promised and expected return. Similarly the large cash accumulation reduces substantially the proportion of defaults in later years.

Summary and Conclusion

The purpose of this chapter was to present some basic information on equilibrium returns on corporate loans. While we use option theory to value these risky loans, the analysis is complicated by the fact that coupon loans involve compound options and we are concerned with loan portfolios rather than with single loans.

One aspect of the simulations is that we cannot rely on the central-limit theorem to produce even approximate normality in portfolio returns. The distribution of returns looks very different over different stages in the loan's life, but they are generally characterized by negative skewness and always by substantial leptokurtosis.

Because the distribution of loan returns is so different from that of the assets, diversification has a much more powerful effect on the risk of loan portfolios than on that of common stocks. These benefits justify the attention that banks in practice pay to maintaining highly diversified loan portfolios.

While the risk of the loan portfolios that we examined was very small indeed compared with that of common-stock portfolios, banks and other lending institutions are generally financing these investments with an extremely small equity base. It is, therefore, important to be aware that the risk of the loan portfolio is highly sensitive to changes in lending policy. For example, the systematic risk of making two-year loans to companies with a 60 percent debt ratio is thirteen times that of making similar loans to companies with a 40 percent ratio.

We have also shown that the change in the expected return and risk over the life of a loan can be at least as important as the variation among different loans. It is, therefore, incorrect for lenders to amortize any discount evenly over the life of the loan or to make equal bad-debt provisions in each year. Moreover, any shifts in the maturity structure of new lending may have a marked (but partly temporary) effect on portfolio risk.

A comparison of the behavior of coupon bonds with that of pure-discount bonds suggests that the pricing and subsequent returns are strongly influenced by the form of the loan covenants. Our very stringent covenants make high coupons or sinking funds very valuable features and they provide an incentive for borrowers to default long before asset values have disappeared. An attempt to model and compare the effect of actual covenants would be a very useful exercise.

Some of the effects with which we are concerned are fairly complex. For example, while the value of a risky bond declines with maturity, there is no such simple relationship between yield spread and maturity. This complicates the task of the banker who must settle on an appropriate yield for a particular loan. Similarly the absence of any simple relationship between loan maturity and the default rate at each stage of the loan's life makes it difficult to monitor the portfolio in terms of default rate. These problems are further complicated by the extreme kurtosis of the relevant distributions.

Finally, our simulations have some cautionary messages for empirical research on risky debt. Not only are the relationships quite complex but the return distribution over each bond's life is nonstationary. Also, while the differences in risk are important to a bank with a small equity base, they are generally far too small to be measured with any confidence empirically.

Notes

1. Merton, Scholes, and Gladstein (1978) have also employed simulation to estimate the distribution of option portfolio returns. The principal differences are that our interest is in deep-in-the-money options rather than near-the-money options, in compound rather than simple options, and in long-dated rather than short-dated options.

2. Silvers did, however, re-express his estimated certainty-equivalent coefficients as annual rates and these predominantly fell with maturity.

3. We should be cautious when interpreting the relative dispersion of returns on the two-year and ten-year portfolios, since these differences may depend significantly on the particular covenants that are assumed.

4. Note that these are unconditional distributions. The distribution of returns in years five and six, given the price at the beginning of the period, would not resemble figure 7–2.

Appendix 7A:
Valuation of
Risky Coupon Debt

This appendix describes how the approach suggested by Geske (1977) is used to calculate the values of the risky bonds simulated in our experiments. Consider a firm with assets currently worth V, which is financed partly by equity (worth $S(V)$) and party by debt (worth $B(V)$), so $S(V) + B(V) = V$. The debt promises to make payments X_1, X_2, ... X_M on M future dates t_1, t_2, ... t_M. The shareholders have the option to buy the firm by making the series of payments promised on the debt. They will default on the debt at any stage if it is in their interests to do so. In Geske's model the underlying assets of the firm are allowed to follow their assumed stochastic process undisturbed, and the payments to the debtholders are found by means of rights issues from the shareholders. Under these assumptions Geske shows that the value of the equity is given by:

$$S(V) = VN_M(d_{11}, d_{12}, \ldots, d_{1M}) - \sum_{i=1}^{M} X_i e^{-rt_1} N_i(d_{21}, d_{22}, \ldots, d_{2i})$$

where:

$$d_{1i} = \frac{\text{Log}\,(V/\bar{V}_i) + (r + \tfrac{1}{2}\sigma^2)t_i}{\sigma\sqrt{t_i}}, \qquad d_{zi} = d_{1i} - \sigma\sqrt{t_i}$$

where $r =$ the risk-free interest rate; $\sigma^2 =$ the variance rate on the assets; $\bar{V}_M = X_M$, and, in general, $\bar{V}_i$ is the solution to the equation:

$$S(V) = X_i \text{ at } t = t_i, \ (i = 1, 2, \ldots, M).$$

Note that $S(V)$ is the value of the equity immediately after a coupon has been raised by means of a rights issue. if at t_i the assets of the firm are worth more than $\bar{V}_i$, then it is worthwhile for the shareholders to subscribe to the immediate coupon payment X_i, to maintain their interest in the firm, which will be worth $S(V) > X_i$. The firm defaults on its debt if at any date t_i the assets are worth less than $\bar{V}_i$.

Finally, $N_n(h_1, h_2, \ldots, h_n)$ is the nth-order multivariate normal integral:

$$N_n(h_1, h_2, \ldots, h_i) = \int_{-\infty}^{h_i} \int_{-\infty}^{h_2} \cdots \int_{-\infty}^{h_n} f(x_1, \ldots, x_n)\, dx_1 dx_2 \ldots dx_n$$

where:

$$f(x_1, x_2, \ldots, x_n)$$

is the joint-probability density function of n standardized normal variates with matrix of correlation coefficients:

$$[\rho ij] = \sqrt{\frac{t_i}{t_j}}$$

Geske points out[1] that the evaluation of N_n can be reduced to an integral whose dimension is the integer part of $n/2$. This enables us to evaluate N_2 and N_3 as single integrals, and N_4 and N_5 as double integrals. We used Simpson's Rule for numerical integration to do this. For each set of assumptions the risky bond values depend only on the number of periods to run and on the value of the firm's assets at that point. For computational efficiency, we compiled tables of bond values as a function of asset value and the bond evaluation for the main simulation program was done by interpolating from these tables.

Note

1. The procedure is described by Curnow, R.N., and C.W. Dunnett. "The Numerical Evaluation of Certain Multivariate Normal Integrals." *Annals of Mathematical Statistics* (1962): 571–579.

Appendix 7B:
Detailed
Simulation Results

Table 7B–1
The Effect of Diversification on the Distribution of Loan Returns (Base Case)

| Number of Loans | Debt and Equity Years 0–2 | | Two-Year Loan | | Internal Rate of Return | | Ten-Year Loan | | | |
| | | | | | | | Years 0–2 | | Years 8–10 | |
	Percentage Per Annum	Index	Percentage Per Annum	Index	Percentage Per Annum	Index	Percentage Per Annum	Index	Percentage Per Annum	Index
1. Standard Deviation										
1	21.51	100	.309	100	.369	100	.446	100	.221	100
2	17.52	81.5	.214	69.0	.140	37.8	.332	72.8	.153	68.9
4	15.06	70.5	.152	49.0	.095	25.7	.263	57.3	.108	49.0
8	13.58	63.1	.110	35.5	.064	17.2	.218	47.8	.079	35.7
16	12.76	59.3	.077	24.9	.048	12.9	.196	43.0	.059	26.7
32	12.35	57.4	.059	19.0	.037	10.1	.183	40.2	.048	21.6
2. Skewness										
1	.56		−31.6		−27.5		−14.3		−26.2	
2	.55		−22.0		−15.3		−9.2		−14.7	
4	.51		−15.4		−13.2		−6.7		−8.4	
8	.54		−11.2		−9.5		−5.2		−5.0	
16	.59		−7.8		−7.9		−4.5		−1.6	
32	.60		−6.0		−6.8		−4.0		−1.4	
3. Kurtosis										
1	3.6		1148		940		398		2256	
2	3.6		559		271		163		930	
4	3.4		270		220		84		405	
8	3.4		142		121		52		175	
16	3.6		70		84		37		81	
32	3.5		43		63		28		44	

Note: Skewness is defined as $m_3/(m_2)^{3/2}$ and kurtosis as $m_4/(m_2)^2$

Table 7B–2
Promised and Realized Yield Spreads (Base Case)

	Maturity (Years)				
	Two	Four	Six	Eight	Ten
Issue price	99.92	99.71	99.55	99.44	99.38
Promised yield spread	.046	.091	.104	.106	.104
Average realized yield spread:					
Internal rate of return	.034	.067	.086	.082	.085
Years 0–2	.034	.095	.145	.160	.176
2–4	–	.050	.076	.096	.099
4–6	–	–	.029	.044	.070
6–8	–	–	–	.016	.028
8–10	–	–	–	–	.012
Geometric mean	.034	.071	.082	.078	.076
Percentage of issues defaulting:					
Years 0–2	.21	.19	.07	.13	.08
2–4	–	.30	.17	.13	.15
4–6	–	–	.22	.16	.09
6–8	–	–	–	.09	.05
8–10	–	–	–	–	.09
Total	.21	.48	.46	.52	.46

Table 7B–3
Expected Systematic Risk of Loans (Base Case)

	Maturity in Years				
Beginning Year	Two	Four	Six	Eight	Ten
0	.007	.017	.021	.024	.025
2	–	.007	.012	.014	.015
4	–	–	.005	.007	.009
6	–	–	–	.003	.004
8	–	–	–	–	.002

Table 7B–4
Loan Returns for Debt Ratio
($d = .60$)

	Two-Year Loan			Six-Year Loan			Ten-Year Loan		
Issue Price	98.50			97.29			96.98		
Promised yield spread	.849			.733			.517		
Realized yield spread:	μ	σ	β	μ	σ	β	μ	σ	β
Internal rate of return	.57	.52	–	.56	.33	–	.39	.27	–
Years 0–2	.57	.52	.089	.90	.82	.113	.84	.87	.116
2–4	–	–	–	.43	.51	.050	.37	.59	.055
4–6	–	–	–	.22	.26	.018	.21	.36	.027
6–8	–	–	–	–	–	–	.08	.19	.012
8–10	–	–	–	–	–	–	.03	.12	.004
Geometric mean	.57	.52	–	.52	.23	–	.30	.15	–
Percentage of issues defaulting:									
Years 0–2	4.12			2.37			2.32		
2–4	–			1.52			1.34		
4–6	–			.87			.62		
6–8	–			–			.30		
8–10	–			–			.22		
Total	4.12			4.75			4.80		

Notes: Betas are measured at beginning of period.

Means refer to thirty-two-loan portfolios. They may be slightly different from those for one-loan portfolios.

Table 7B–5
Loan Returns for Standard Deviation = 0.35

	Two-Year Loan			Six-Year Loan			Ten-Year Loan		
Issue price	99.04			96.87			95.96		
Promised yield spread	.541			.737			.696		
Realized yield spread:	μ	σ	β	μ	σ	β	μ	σ	β
Internal rate of return	.38	.37	–	.58	.30	–	.55	.29	–
Years 0–2	.38	.37	.045	.85	.89	.084	.96	.99	.091
2–4	–	–	–	.52	.78	.054	.58	.94	.063
4–6	–	–	–	.27	.52	.027	.46	.72	.043
6–8	–	–	–	–	–	–	.24	.49	.025
8–10	–	–	–	–	–	–	.11	.34	.012
Geometric mean	.38	.37	–	.54	.25	–	.47	.19	–
Percentage of issues defaulting:									
Years 0–2	1.77			.63			1.17		
2–4	–			1.41			1.14		
4–6	–			1.53			.79		
6–8	–			–			.61		
8–10	–			–			.61		
Total	1.77			3.57			4.32		

Notes: Betas are measured at beginning of period.

Means refer to thirty-two loan portfolios. They may be slightly different from those for one-loan portfolios.

Table 7B–6
Loan Returns for Coupon = 8 Percent

	Two-Year Loan			Six-Year Loan			Ten-Year Loan		
Issue price	93.16			82.99			76.67		
Promised yield spread	.046			.150			.149		
Realized yield spread:	μ	σ	β	μ	σ	β	μ	σ	β
Internal rate of return	.03	.06	–	.13	.06	–	.14	.05	–
Years 0–2	.03	.06	.007	.20	.21	.029	.25	.25	.034
2–4	–	–	–	.11	.19	.017	.15	.26	.023
4–6	–	–	–	.05	.15	.008	.12	.21	.015
6–8	–	–	–	–	–	–	.05	.12	.008
8–10	–	–	–	–	–	–	.02	.09	.004
Geometric mean	.03	.06	–	.12	.06	–	.12	.04	–
Percentage of issues defaulting:									
Years 0–2	.21			.05			.05		
2–4	–			.22			.16		
4–6	–			.40			.13		
6–8	–			–			.11		
8–10	–			–			.17		
Total	.21			.67			.61		

Notes: Betas are measured at beginning of period.
Means refer to thirty-two loan portfolios. They may be slightly different from those for one-loan portfolios.

Table 7B–7
Loan Returns For Risk Premium =0.07

	Two-Year Loan			Six-Year Loan			Ten-Year Loan		
Issue price	99.92			99.55			99.38		
Promised yield spread	.046			.104			.104		
Realized yield spread:	μ	σ	β	μ	σ	β	μ	σ	β
Internal rate of return	.04	.04	–	.09	.03	–	.10	.03	–
Years 0–2	.04	.04	.007	.16	.12	.021	.20	.16	.025
2–4	–	–	–	.07	.11	.010	.10	.16	.013
4–6	–	–	–	.02	.08	.003	.05	.12	.007
6–8	–	–	–	–	–	–	.02	.05	.003
8–10	–	–	–	–	–	–	.00	.02	.001
Geometric mean	.04	.04	–	.08	.03	–	.07	.02	–
Percentage of issues defaulting:									
Years 0–2	.18			.05			.05		
2–4	–			.09			.10		
4–6	–			.11			.03		
6–8	–			–			.03		
8–10	–			–			.01		
Total	.10			.25			.22		

Notes: Betas are measured at beginning of period.
Means refer to thirty-two loan portfolios. They may be slightly different from those for one-loan portfolios.

References

Black, F., and Cox, J. "Valuing Corporate Securities: Some Effects of Bond Indenture Provisions." *Journal of Finance* 31 (1976): 351–367.

Black, F., and Scholes, M. "The Pricing of Options and Corporate Liabilities." *Journal of Political Economy* 81 (1973): 637–654.

Boardman, C.M., and McEnally, R.W. "Factors Affecting Seasoned Corporate Bond Prices." *Journal of Financial and Quantitative Analysis* 16 (1981): 207–226.

Fisher, F. "Determinants of Risk Premiums on Corporate Bonds." *Journal of Political Economy* 68 (1959): 217–237.

Geske, R. "The Valuation of Corporate Liabilities as Compound Options." *Journal of Financial and Quantitative Analysis* 12 (1977): 541–552.

Johnson, R.E. "Term Structure of Corporate Bond Yields as a Function of Risk of Default." *Journal of Finance* 22 (1967): 313–345.

Merton, R.C. "On the Pricing of Corporate Debt: The Risk Structure of Interest Rates." *Journal of Finance* 29 (1974): 449–470.

_____. "Theory of Rational Option Pricing." *Bell Journal of Economics and Management Science* 4 (1973): 141–183.

Merton, R.C.; Scholes, M.J.; and Gladstein, M.L. "A Simulation of the Returns and Risk of Alternative Option Portfolio Investment Strategies." *Journal of Business* 51 (1978): 183–242.

Silvers, J.B. "An Alternative to the Yield Spread as a Measure of Risk." *Journal of Finance* 28 (1973): 933–955.

8 The Valuation of Commodity Options

James W. Hoag

This chapter presents the preliminary results of research conducted on the nature of options on commodities. Although much has been written recently on option pricing,[1] the basic setting has always been in terms of financial assets: stocks and options on those stocks (warrants, over-the-counter (OTC), and exchange-traded options). Fortunately, these techniques are generally applicable to the study of commodity options.

There exists an extensive literature on the motivation and interaction of participants (hedgers and speculators) in commodity-futures markets—some notable examples being Brennan (1958), Cootner (1967), and Working (1948, 1949). Partially due to lack of availability and intermittent illegality, the use of commodity options in hedging policy has not been examined in the academic (or popular) literature. One aspect of the difficulty of examining commodity options is the lack of theory for pricing of commodity options and for the entire area of commodity pricing and inventory-storage policy. In recent research, Cootner (1977) related spot-commodity prices to the optimal inventory-storage pattern and produced a model with future and spot prices endogenously computed. The value of a commodity stored by inventory holders included a premium for the inventory holder's option to sell to current consumers at the spot price or to sell to future consumers at the future spot price. Thus, commodity options are really compound options (that is, options on other options). Throughout this chapter, arbitrage relationships among prices of spot, futures, and options are considered to be implicit functions of aggregate supply (represented by inventory holdings). The underlying inventory dependence will be useful for understanding and interpreting the approximations to option value that are presented later in the chapter.

Recently, hedging practice has come to include the purchase or sale of call or put options. These efforts attempt to hedge price risks connected with

This chapter summarizes my work on commodity options from 1973 through 1978 and is based on my dissertation and subsequent papers presented at various meetings and seminars at Stanford, the University of British Columbia, and the London Graduate School of Business. Comments made during those presentations have improved this work, but results beyond 1978 are not contained herein. This chapter has also benefited from discussions with colleagues at Stanford, and especially with the late Paul Cootner. A comprehensive transaction data base for commodity-option prices has been assembled since then and results of tests using those data will soon be available.

uncertain supply and demand for raw materials used in production.[2] Hence, the pricing of these options is an important aspect in hedging policy. Although hedging motives and practice provide incentives to create option markets in these commodities, these markets are also investment or speculative vehicles for individuals and corporations. As with future markets, the delicate interplay between hedgers and speculators serves to equilibrate commodity-option prices.

In this chapter, a summary of the theory concerning the pricing of commodity options is examined in a consistent framework. Empirical results on the pricing of options on futures (London commodity options on cocoa, coffee, and sugar) and options on metals (dealer silver options) are presented. Evidence of efficient market pricing of commodity options is necessary to discuss rationally the implications of regulatory policy on social and individual welfare. Although tentative in many aspects, this chapter links the appropriate areas of commodity theory with the basic option-pricing model to provide a consistent background for research in this area.

Brief Economic History of Commodity Options

Commodity options (known then as privileges, indemnities, bids, offers, or guaranties) developed simultaneously with commodity futures markets for agricultural commodities (wheat, corn, oats, and rye) in the mid 1800s. Both options and futures along with the commodity exchanges were viewed with suspicion by farmers during the early period of trading. Legends of massive price manipulation by so-called speculators fill the popular literature of that period. Many efforts were initiated by farmers to have stage legislatures and the federal Congress ban futures and options during the period.

In 1885, the Illinois Supreme Court in the case of *Pearce* v. *Foote* declared option transactions illegal based on an 1874 Illinois statute. During this period the Chicago Board of Trade was quite ambivalent in their position, banning option transactions and subsequently ignoring and not enforcing their own ban.

By the 1892–1893 session of Congress, both the House and the Senate came within a technicality of passing bills levying a large tax on futures trading. Thereafter, the sentiment against futures trading subsided until the early 1920s.

In 1900, the court, in the case of *Booth* v. *People* (57 NE 798), held with respect to options that (see Mehl 1924, p. 7):

> The prohibition of the right to enter into contracts which do not contemplate the creation of an obligation on the part of one of the contracting parties to accept and pay for the commodity which is the purported subject matter of the contract, but only to invest him with the option or privilege to demand

the other contracting party shall deliver him the grain, if he desires to purchase it, tends materially to the suppression of the very evil of gambling in grain options which it was the legislative intent to extirpate, for the reason such evil injuriously affected the welfare and safety of the public.

Although futures received a reprieve, options received continuing attention from both government and the commodity exchanges throughout the early 1900s. In 1920, the Futures Trading Act imposed a prohibitive tax on options, which essentially halted trading in options.

The next year, the Grain Futures Act provided the government with fact-finding capability and elemental tools to deal with the commodity exchanges. In early 1926, the United States Supreme Court held that the tax on options was unconstitutional, and option trading recommenced immediately. The 1922 act permitted the collection of data on option trading during August and September 1926. It is this data that Mehl analyzes in his 1934 study of grain options. In that study, commodity options on grain futures represented on the order of 10 to 15 percent of the volume (in bushels) of grain traded in futures contracts. Mehl presents little evidence on price manipulation with options. His summary is relatively inconsistent and unsupported by his own empirical evidence:

> Priviledge trading is considered useful by many members of the grain trade in that it affords protection against price changes, makes possible the financing of speculative transactions on a small capital, . . . Its unfavorable aspects are the following: The small amount of capital required to trade in privileges encourages speculation by traders of limited financial resources. The practice of trading against privileges bought and protecting those sold causes artificial price movements.

In July 1933, options trading on the Chicago Board of Trade was suspended following a three-year decline in grain prices. After extensive hearings before Congress, the Commodity Exchange Act of 1936 banned trading in commodity options on regulated commodities. During the hearings (see, To Amend the Grain Futures Act, Hearings before the Committee on Agriculture and Forestry, U.S. Senate), Mehl filed very ambiguous "evidence" with these sentences:

> I think I shall have very little to say on the subject of privilege trading. The record of the exchanges themselves on that question over a period of years shows conclusively that the trade itself has never had any unanimity of opinion regarding the desirability of trading in privileges.

Mehl did not mention the sizable volume of options in grains shown by his study. Although the Congress did ban commodity options, there seems to be very little evidence presented either for or against option trading in the hearings.

The relevant portions of the 1936 Commodity Exchange Act are given in section 2(a), which lists the commodities regulated by the act, and section 4(c):

> It shall be unlawful for any person to offer to enter into or confirm the execution of, any transaction involving any commodity.
>
> (B) if such transaction is, is the character of, or is commonly known to the trade as, a "privilege," "indemnity," "bid," "offer," "put," "call," "advance guaranty," or "decline guaranty," or.

The only minor modifications of this act, as related to commodity options, changed and added to the list of regulated commodities during the period from 1936 to 1974.

During the period before 1974, there was *no* restriction on commodity-option transactions in unregulated commodities (those not explicitly stipulated in the Commodity Exchange Act). Commodity options have been bought and sold by reputable metals dealers. These dealer options were written on unregulated metals, such as silver, platinum, palladium, and, later, copper. Commodity options, traded on the London Commodity Exchanges (now the International Commodities Clearing House (ICCH)) and the London Metal Exchange, were also available in the United States.

Few statistics exist on the volume of usage of these options, but the existence of the instruments does indicate at least sufficient interest to cover the transaction costs of establishing the market (which, of course, could be quite low). The volume of options compared to futures transactions for soft commodities (coffee, sugar, and cocoa) traded on the ICCH is presented for the most recent years in table 8–1.

In the early 1970s, dealers came into existence to market options to the general public for investment (as opposed to hedging) purposes. These dealers attempted to satisfy a market need in terms of selling options.[3] Some dealers not only acted as brokers or clearing houses for options, they took a net (or naked) position in options without hedging that risk (see, for instance, the *SEC* v. *Goldstein, Samuelson, Inc.*). These dealers subsequently discovered the hard lessons of other merchandising firms by carrying the full-price risk of their product—commodity options. The demise of commodity-option dealers inspired renewed regulatory and public interest in commodity options.

In 1974, Congress modified the Commidity Exchange Act to create the Commodity Futures Trading Commission (CFTC). In addition, the act was changed in two important respects. Section 2(a) was modified to include:

Table 8–1
London Soft Commodities: Volume of Trading—Options and Futures Contracts

Year	Coffee		Sugar		Cocoa	
	Futures[a]	Options[b]	Futures[a]	Options[b]	Futures[a]	Options[b]
1964	63111	~0	261858	2146	142442	74
1965	89693	~0	202654	2059	248736	119
1966	64336	~0	172646	6094	389231	1099
1967	38369	~0	457491	11614	416932	515
1968	37567	~0	395557	9644	707893	1093
1969	48537	65	579479	10284	990045	1772
1970	106344	139	530870	6323	1129252	2779
1971	78240	16	676146	4311	1028948	492
1972	60341	1109	879020	6471	1027935	6666
1973	152427	7571	854045	6163	1342946	6539
1974	423528	1710	956598	8131	954370	2305
1975	228293	3313	824263	6436	742557	1538

Notes: Volume for both options and futures is measured in number of contracts traded. Futures are bought and sold easily, but the options are essentially nontradeable. Contract size and description for futures and option contracts are presented later.

Table statistics adapted from "Market Turnover Statistics," International Commodities Clearing House, Ltd., London 1976.

[a]All maturities
[b]Calls, puts, and doubles in all maturities.

All other goods and articles, except onions as provided in Public Law 85–839, and all services, rights, and interests in which contracts for future delivery are presently or in the future dealt in.

Section 4c(B) continued the ban on options on the commodities that had previously has been banned in the 1936 Commodity Exchange Act and its subsequent amendments. A new section 4c(b) regulates option transactions in the newly regulated commodities, which are:

contrary to any rule, regulation, or order of the Commission prohibiting any such transaction or allowing such transaction under such terms and conditions as the Commission shall prescribe.

The report of the Advisory Committee on Definition and Regulation of Market Instruments to the Commodity Futures Trading Commission entitled "Recommended Policies on Commodity Option Transactions" suggests rules under which option transactions would be allowed. The CFTC allowed transactions in these commodity options through April 1978, when they again prohibited all commodity-option transactions in the United States and forbade marketing of London commodity options.[4] At the time of the ban, several exchanges had submitted proposals for exchange-traded, CFTC-regulated commodity options.

In view of the concern about the viability of commodity options, a thorough examination of the evidence on the pricing of commodity options follows.

Commodity Options as Contingent Claims

A commodity option is a contract conveying the right to buy or sell a specific amount of the spot commodity or futures contract at a given price on (or before) a given date. The value of the commodity is directly contingent upon the price of the underlying commodity contract. Through the commodity price, the option is *also* contingent upon supply, demand, current inventory, and expected future harvests of the underlying commodity.

Commodity options can be written on either the spot commodity (for example, dealer precious-metals options) or on a futures contract (for example, London Soft Commodity Options). Thus it is necessary when discussing commodity options to distinguish the *underlying asset or index* upon which the option is written. If exercised, an option on spot requires delivery of the physical commodity and an option on a futures contract requires delivery of a futures contract.

The given price of purchase is typically called the *exercise price, E,* or basis for London Options. The last exercise date is the *maturity* of the option, T. The price of the underlying commodity is designated S, if a spot price, or F, if a futures price. The exercise price is always in the same units as the spot or futures price. An option to buy (sell) a unit of a commodity is a call (put) and its price or premium will be designated as $C(S,T;E)$ $(P(S,T;E))$ or for options on futures $C(F,T;E)$ $(P(F,T;E))$. If the call (put) can be exercised at any time during the period to maturity it is an *American* call (C, or American put, P). A call (put) that can only be exercised at maturity is a *European* call (c, or European put, p). Many relationships between puts and calls of both the American and European varieties are developed in Kruizenga (in Cootner 1964), Samuelson and Merton (1969), Stoll (1969), and Merton (1973).

Commodity options (puts or calls on either spot commodities or futures contracts) are limited-liability contracts. Option contracts are generally assumed to satisfy the so-called bucket-shop assumption concerning zero aggregate supply (see Merton 1973, footnote 6, for a brief history of this nomenclature). In essence the buyer and seller create a side bet on the price of the commodity. If the introduction of option trading does not change the state space spanned by the extant securities, the distribution of commodity prices in the future will be unaffected (Ross 1976). Unfortunately, without a full set of state contingent claims (currently, only unconditional futures contracts exist), this assumption may not be realistic for commodity options.

The commodity option provides one form of contingent claim on a commodity. For instance, a European call on a commodity offers to the owner one unit of the commodity on a specific, single day at a fixed price, regardless of the then current price of that commodity. Of course, the call *need not be exercised* if the commodity price is below the exercise price—the commodity can be purchased in the market. At maturity, when the price of the option is below the exercise price, the premium (original price of the option) paid to insure purchase at or below the exercise price was, ex post, paid unnecessarily.

A futures contract provides a different contingent claim on a unit of spot commodity. Specifically, a future contract requires the purchase of one unit of commodity on a specific date at a fixed price, regardless of the then prevailing price. There is, however, *no* option. The agreed-upon price[5] is due on the delivery date in payment for the goods, which are also deliverable at that time.

Both a commodity option written on a futures contract and a commodity option written on the spot commodity are contingent claims on the spot commodity. Potentially, *both* option and futures markets provide instruments for suppliers or purchasers of inventories of the commodity to hedge against some of the relevant price risks.[6] The hedge created with futures contracts and the spot commodity exchanges price risk for *basis risk*. The basis risk of a commodity (fluctuations in the difference between futures and spot prices on the same commodity) has smaller magnitude than the risk of price fluctuations. Hedges created with commodity options (at least, American options) can partially hedge the basis risk. Holders of physical inventories of a commodity can conveniently hedge inventory-price risk by writing options against inventories. Since options and futures can hedge changes in the spot price, both contingent claims depend upon the spot price (in a currently undetermined fashion).

Additionally, the current inventory of the commodity involved will also affect all prices of claims for that asset (spot, future, and option). In this chapter, inventory-carrying theory is used to estimate the carrying charges for moving the spot commodity through time. These charges are necessary to distinguish the differential benefits (costs) of holding the spot commodity, a futures contract, or a commodity option.

Payouts against the Commodity:
Carrying Charges and the Basis

The calculation of profitability for holding inventories of the spot commodity (either hedged or unhedged) rests on the determination of the influence of inventories, production, and consumption on the expected spot price. In the commodity literature, supply-of-storage theory describes this relationship.[7]

The direct costs of holding inventory include warehouse rental and insurance. These costs are thought to be relatively constant over a wide range of inventory levels. Holding inventory ties up capital. An implicit interest charge is usually included in the direct costs of carrying inventory. The difference between the futures price (a surrogate for expected spot price) and the spot price is termed the *basis*. When the direct costs of carrying inventory are netted out of the basis, there is an empirically substantiated residual component termed the *marginal convenience yield*. This relationship (the *supply-of-storage curve*) is depicted in figure 8–1. The carrying charges per unit of spot commodity ($\mathtt{c}(t)$) for the period from now until time t consists of interest plus other costs and benefits q:

$$\mathtt{c} = rS + w + i + y = rS + q$$

where $r =$ current t-period interest rate, $w =$ warehouse rent for t periods, $i =$ insurance for t periods, and $y =$ convenience yield.

Each of the components of carrying cost are familiar except for the convenience yield. The classic explanation of the convenience-yield phenomenon is that convenient inventories provide benefits to holders of inventory by reducing stockout costs. The theory contends that there is a reduction of plant downtime and start-up costs that reduces the costs of idle capital. Also, convenient inventories reduce the chance of turning away good customers (or increase the chance of adding new customers) when inventories are scarce. Thus this theory holds that consumers will pay inventory holders for reducing their costs to locate supplies in times of scarcity. While there has been no completely satisfactory explanation of the supply-of-storage phenomenon, the empirical effect exists for many commodities (for example, Brennan 1958; Working 1948, 1949).

Supply-of-storage phenomena are relevant to all markets[8] where there exists some possible *option value* to holding inventory. Mining and smelting capacity and harvest size and timing provide supply uncertainty. Uncertain demand for commodities adds to the uncertainty about expected spot price. If the price rationally can be expected to decline in the future, Cootner (1977) has shown that inventories should be held in positive quantities even if the price rises at less than the rate of interest (plus direct storage costs). The

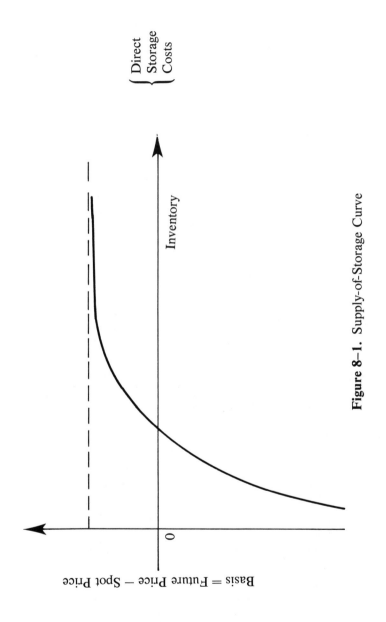

Figure 8-1. Supply-of-Storage Curve

difference between the going rate of interest (plus direct storage costs) and the rate of interest reflected in the difference between futures and spot prices can be interpreted as an option granted by consumers to inventory holders. Future consumers grant inventory holders the current use of stocks, if it is profitable to use the stocks now. If, however, the stocks are stored into the future, consumers will buy the stocks then. Inventory holders pay for this put (option to sell in the future) by selling forward (for future delivery) to consumers at a price lower than that necessary to store inventories into the future. This option value is the difference known heretofore as the *marginal-convenience yield*.

The relevant question herein is *not* the explanation of the convenience yield. The empirical existence of payouts (in the form of direct and indirect carrying charges) against the commodity requires different theoretical analysis for options written on the commodity. The values of a nonpayout-protected option may differ from the value of a payout-protected option (Merton 1973). The ability of the (American) option owner to capture this value is at issue.

Payout Effects on Commodity Option Valuation

Carrying the physical commodity and carrying the hedged commodity provide different expected rates of return. To see this, consider the strategies available for acquiring the commodity at some future time.

1. The spot commodity can be bought and held at a direct known cost by purchasing now and storing until needed. Empirically, there are some implicit benefits to this strategy (the convenience yield). The expected return is a function of the known costs (warehouse rental, insurance, and interest) and unknown benefits.
2. A future contract with sufficiently long maturity can be entered into at a known price. When the need for the commodity arises, the futures contract is sold and the spot commodity is bought in the market at that time. The expected return of this strategy is dependent upon the movement of the spot price with respect to the future price.
3. A commodity option with sufficiently long maturity can be purchased at a known premium. This option can be written on either a futures contract or the spot commodity.
   a. When the need arises for the commodity, a European option (which cannot be exercised until maturity) is sold and the commodity is purchased in the spot market at that time. European options on spot and futures contracts may have different expected returns, but the mechanics of acquiring the spot commodity are identical. The

expected return depends upon the comovement of the option and spot prices for the commodity.

    b. With an American option two strategies are possible for obtaining the commodity. The American option can be sold and the spot commodity purchased. In addition, an American option can be exercised, thus making available at the known, previously established exercise price either the spot commodity or a futures contract. If a futures contract is obtained by exercise, it is then sold, and the spot commodity is purchased. The expected return on these strategies depends on the comovement of the spot (and futures) and the option price.

4. Finally, the spot commodity can be bought in the market only when needed. Carrying costs are avoided, but the risk of spot price change is borne over that period of time.

Each of these strategies has a different rate of return contingent upon the realized state of the world (as characterized, for instance, by the size of the next harvest). Each strategy would have different risks, and dominance or arbitrage can be utilized to determine an equilibrium relationship between expected return and risk for the previous strategies.

What is not obvious from these scenarios is whether an option holder can earn the convenience yield that accrues to the holder of the spot commodity. If this is possible, it should be reflected in the premium paid for the option. This is extremely important in terms of the option-pricing models, since early developments in security option models assume that there are *no* payouts against the security and *no* unfavorable exercise-price changes.[9] Under that assumption, the value of a European and an American call are equal $(C = c)$

The following digression on stock options with payouts will assist in the analysis of commodity options with payouts. As the dividend on a stock increases (ceteris paribus), the current value of a nonpayout-protected call decreases. If the exercise price per share is increased without corresponding change in the number of shares to be purchased, the current value of a call decreases. Lack of contractual arrangements (in the option) for payout protection requires that all anticipated payouts against the stock be discounted in the value of the stock option.[10]

A commodity option is analogous to an option on a stock that pays dividends. The expected return available to the holder of a (nonpayout-protected) commodity option is different from the expected return on the spot commodity. The difference in expected rates of return to commodity option and spot holders arise from two sources: (1) different risks assumed by each asset holder, and (2) potential payouts (in the form of carrying charges) to the holder of the spot commodity. Thus, it is necessary to consider option-pricing models that incorporate the value of protection against payouts.[11]

The owner of the European commodity option cannot benefit from the convenience of having the commodity currently available at a known cost (the direct costs of storage). A holder of an American option *may* partially benefit from the convenience yield by exercising the option prematurely to earn any payouts on the spot commodity. Of course, the holder of an American commodity option may pay for the right to exercise the option at any time during the life of the option. An American call will always be worth as much as a European call, and perhaps more (Merton 1973). The differential premium on American and European commodity call options must be related to the carrying charges for holding the physical asset (the basis).

Analysis of the relationship between the payouts on commodity options (in the form of carrying charges as a function of total inventory) and the overall profitability of carrying inventory will lead to a more fundamental formula for the commodity-option price. However, it is necessary to go beyond a simple arbitrage relationship between the commodity option and spot commodity to include some overall inventory-carrying theory. In later sections, payouts on the spot commodity are incorporated into the analysis of options on the spot commodity in a simple and useful fashion.

Dynamics of Spot Prices

Before continuing on to the evaluation of commodity option prices, the dynamics of the spot price (the price for current delivery of the commodity) will be specified.

For stock-option pricing, Samuelson (1965b), Samuelson and Merton (1969), Black and Scholes (1972), and Merton (1973) assume that prices follow a relative (geometric) diffusion:

$$dS = \mu S dt + \sigma S dt.$$

In this formulation, μ and σ are assumed to be nonstochastic time-invariant constants. Cox (1975) uses models of stock dynamics with constant elasticity of variance diffusions ($0 \leq \beta \leq 2$)

$$dS = \mu(S,t)dt + \sigma S^{(\beta/2)}dz.$$

Cox and Ross (1976a) and Merton (1976) use Poisson processes and/or mixes of the above diffusions for the underlying stock processes. The form of their respective option-pricing models follows from the assumptions made about stock-price dynamics.[12]

An adequate theory of commodity-option pricing requires a description of the underlying process (either spot or futures) price dynamics. In the following paragraphs, aspects of the underlying problem of specifying the spot and futures price dynamics are examined and various important features are noted for use in approximations of commodity-option values.

Cootner (1977) specified the relationship between spot price ($S(x,t)$) and inventory (x) in a stochastic form that differs significantly from the original work on speculative prices by Samuelson (1957, 1971). Inventory (x) is assumed to follow a locally Brownian[13] process:

$$dx = \mu^x(x,t)dt + \sigma^x(x,t)dz$$

where dz is a normal Wiener process with zero drift and unit-instantaneous variance; $\mu^x(x,t)$ is the drift of inventory; and $\sigma^x(x,t)$ is the instantaneous standard deviation of inventory.[14] Using Ito's Lemma, [15] the spot-price dynamics are:

$$dS = \{S_t + \mu^x S_x + 1/2[\sigma^x]^2 S_{xx}\}dt + \{S_x\sigma^x\}dz$$

Without pursuing the solution of the optimal inventory/spot-price policy, it is apparent that the spot-price dynamics will be dependent on inventory levels and can be specified generically as:

$$dS = \mu^S(x,S,t)dt + \sigma^S(x,S,t)dz.$$

This model is sufficiently flexible to admit a basis (future/spot price) versus inventory relationship that is consistent with the general form of the (empirical) supply-of-storage curve (figure 8–1). A complete solution of that problem would be useful, but it is *not* required. The spot-process form, dynamics, and parameters are specified in sufficient generality to accomodate an approximate solution to the option-pricing problem. Several simplifying assumptions are made. The spot-price dynamics are assumed to follow the locally Brownian motion:

$$dS = \mu(S,t)dt + \sigma(S,t)dz \qquad (8.1)$$

$$\mu(S,t) \approx S_t + \mu^x S_x + 1/2[\sigma^x]^2 S_{xx} = \mu^S(x,S,t)$$

$$\sigma(S,t) \approx S_x\sigma^x = \sigma^S(x,S,t)$$

The dependence on inventory is suppressed, but not forgotten (*especially* in the empirical estimation). Starting with a simple diffusion:

$$dS = \mu Sdt + \sigma Sdz \qquad (8.2)$$

mismodels the process by oversimplification. In some respects, the degree of nonlinearity and nonstationarity of $\mu(x,S,t)$ and $\sigma(x,S,t)$ are at question. Some evidence on this empirical question exists, which indicates substantial nonlinearity and nonstationarity.[16] For the dynamics of spot price, a nonspecific locally Brownian process[17] is assumed. By adaptation of the parameters, equation 8.1 models many possible spot-commodity stochastic processes.

Valuation of Options on the Spot Commodity

The spot-price dynamics discussed in the previous section of this chapter are used here to evaluate an option on the spot commodity. The commodity option is a security C, the value of which depends on the spot price and time $C(S,t)$. The spot-commodity price $S(t)$ has dynamics given by equation 8.1 previously

$$dS = \mu(S,t)dt + \sigma(S,t)dz.$$

However, the maintenance of the spot value requires the payment of the direct carrying charges (insurance and warehouse costs) and the potential receipt of the covenience yield. The instantaneous-payout function $q(S,t)$ summarizes these costs and benefits.[18]

Consider the portfolio[19] consisting of a mixture of the spot commodity and the commodity option:

$$P = n_s S + n_c C(S,t)$$

where n_s is the number of contracts of spot; n_c is the number of commodity options, and P is the value of the portfolio. The change in the value of the portfolio (including payouts) is:

$$dP = n_s dS + n_c dC - n_s q(S,t)dt.$$

The return on the portfolio is given by:

$$\frac{dP}{P} = \alpha_s \left[\frac{dS - q(S,t)dt}{S} \right] + \alpha_c \frac{dC}{C}$$

where $\alpha_s = n_s S/P$ is the percentage of the value of the portfolio invested in spot and $\alpha_c = n_c C/P$ is the percentage of the value of the portfolio invested in commodity options:

$$\alpha_s + \alpha_c = 1$$

Assume that the option can be represented in differential form as:

$$dC = \mu_c dt + \sigma_c dz.$$

Substituting the dynamics of spot (dS) and option (dC) into the portfolio-return equation and rearranging:

$$\frac{dP}{P} = \left\{ \frac{\alpha_s(\mu(S,t) - q(S,t))}{S} + \frac{\alpha_c \mu_c}{C} \right\} dt + \left\{ \frac{\alpha_s \sigma(S,t)}{S} + \frac{\alpha_c \sigma_c}{C} \right\} dz.$$

By choosing the portfolio weights properly, the portfolio can be made riskless:

$$\frac{\alpha_s \sigma(S,t)}{S} + \frac{\alpha_c \sigma_c}{C} = 0.$$

This implies that the portfolio must earn the riskless rate of return:

$$\frac{dP}{P} = \left\{ \frac{\alpha_s(\mu(S,t) - q(S,t))}{S} + \frac{\alpha_c \mu_c}{C} \right\} dt = r dt.$$

Rearranging gives the fundamental option-valuation relationship:

$$\frac{\mu(S,t) - q(S,t) - rS}{\sigma(S,t)} = \frac{\mu_c - rC}{\sigma_c}. \tag{8.3}$$

Ito's Lemma is applied to $C(S,t)$ to specify the dynamic motion of the commodity option:

$$dC = \{C_t + \mu(S,t)C_S + \tfrac{1}{2}\sigma^2(S,t)C_{SS}\} dt +$$
$$\{\sigma(S,t)C_S\} dz \equiv \mu_c dt + \sigma_c dz. \tag{8.4}$$

Substituting the parameters μ_c and σ_c from equation 8.4 into 8.3 and rearranging gives the partial-differential equation for the value of the commodity option[20] $C(S,t)$:

$$\tfrac{1}{2}\sigma^2(S,t)C_{SS} + (rS + q(S,t))C_S - rC + C_t = 0.$$

The option-differential equation is not analytically tractable, except for very special cases of the noninterest-payout function $q(S,t)$.[21] Fortunately the market provides empirical estimates of $q(S,t)$ as the difference between futures and spot prices net of interest costs. These yield naturally to solutions using numerical methods such as finite differences.

Some minor changes facilitate solution of the equation. If time is measured from the expiration date, then $dt = -dT$. The terminal condition for the option and a boundary condition[22] at $S = 0$ completes the specification of the partial-differential equation for the spot-commodity option value:

$$\tfrac{1}{2}\sigma^2(S,T)C_{SS} + (rS + q(S,t))C_S - rC - C_T = 0$$

$$C(S,0) = \max(0, S - E)$$

$$C(0,T) = 0. \tag{8.5}$$

Evidence on the Pricing of Spot-Commodity Options

The model for pricing options on spot commodities will be tested on a sample of 388 call options written on silver.[23] The options were offered with fixed maturity dates (four series a year) and with various exercise prices near the then current price of silver.

The spot price of silver was extrapolated from the Commodity Exchange, Inc., futures market prices.[24] The daily spot and future price series extend from January 1967 to June 1974. During the period of the study (May–September 1973) the price of silver ranged from \$2.3430 per ounce to \$3.0100 per ounce without any discernible trend. The carrying charges for silver were also estimated from the current day's futures-price term structure.

The riskless rate for the maturity of the contract was estimated from the prevailing government-bond structure in much the same way that the carrying charges were estimated from the silver term structure.

Estimation of the instantaneous variance is a serious problem that affects evaluation of any option-pricing model. Black and Scholes (1972) found that estimating variance from past data caused their option-pricing formula for stocks to overprice options on high-variance stocks and underprice options on low-variance stocks. They suggested that this was evidence of measurement error or possibly nonstationarity in the variance.[25]

Obtaining a useful estimate of the instantaneous variance is difficult, but the problem is not insoluble. Accurate utilization of prior information in modeling the stochastic process of commodity-future returns is necessary to obtain unbiased estimates of the process parameters. A technique that samples the generating stochastic differential equation for price is used. An adaptive Kalman filter then computes the updated variance-parameter estimate.[26] The actual change in the variance parameter of the spot-price process over time was substantial. The estimated daily variance parameter ranged from 2.5 cents per ounce to 3.5 cents per ounce over the period of the study. Any single estimate would have provided a poor approximation to the variance parameter even during this short period.

A model option price is calculated with the same exercise price, maturity, and spot price as each of the actual option prices. The interest rate and variance were estimated from historic informaton as indicated above. For each set of parameters corresponding to a sample price, the option-valuation partial-differential equation (equation 8.5) was solved.

An example of the output of the numerical solution to the partial-differential equation is shown in Figure 8–2. It is necessary to compute a range of current spot prices and times to maturity to obtain the single necessary data point. On 11 May 1973, with silver selling at $2.43 per ounce, a 294-day option with exercise price $2.40 was priced by the model at $1,896. The option was actually selling at $2,950.

The model prices were compared to the prevailing market prices with Ordinary Least Squares (OLS) regression for descriptive purposes. Although the model explained 82 percent of the variation in market prices, the model prices were downward-biased estimates of market price.[27]

One test for market efficiency is to purchase *undervalued* options and sell *overvalued* options at market prices. Black and Scholes (1972) use this technique for testing their stock-option valuation formula. These strategies follow individual commodity options from issuance to expiration. The options are hedged with the spot commodity at the going market price to balance the portfolio position using the appropriate weights given in the theoretical-valuation formula. If the model of commodity-option pricing is valid, the riskless rate of interest would be earned on these positions. If this strategy gives significant returns over the risk-free rate, then a hypothesis of market inefficiency (before-transactions costs) might be entertained. In practical terms, the positions called for must be feasible. Execution of orders at market prices, such as the open and close, may not be feasible due to price limits in most commodity markets. Care is taken to eliminate situations that require trading when none occurred. The transactions costs of continuously adjusting these positions are large. Anyone attempting to emulate this strategy would look beyond individual positions to the entire commodity portfolio (options plus spot) and balance the costs of transacting against the potential losses of holding unbalanced positions.

A market-consensus ex-ante estimate of the variance should be necessary for the option-pricing formula to give correct values. If both the market and

Days to Exercise	0	17	35	259	277	294
20250	0	4	16	478	517	571
21000	0	10	34	641	687	749
21750	0	26	72	846	896	967
22500	0	62	151	1096	1151	1229
23250	0	152	304	1396	1453	1538
24000	0	371	588	1747	1806	1896
24750	750	902	1055	2152	2210	2304
25500	1500	1563	1651	2608	2665	2760
26250	2250	2276	2323	3114	3167	3263
27000	3000	3011	3035	3664	3713	3808
27750	3750	3755	3767	4255	4299	4392
28500	4500	4502	4508	4881	4919	5011
29250	5250	5251	5254	5537	5569	5658
30000	6000	6001	6002	6216	6243	6329

Exercise Price

Current Spot Price

Figure 8–2. $C(S, T)$ Silver Option, 11 May 1973

Table 8–2
Excess Dollar Returns from Riskless Arbitrage Portfolios per Contract per Day

Average Excess Dollar Return	Standard Error of Excess Dollar Return
−$16	$17.78

the model fully use the same information sources then the strategy would earn the riskless return. If the market uses information that the model does not, the strategy would earn no more than the riskless rate, and possibly less. If the model uses information more fully than the market, then the strategy would earn in excess of the riskless rate. This test sheds some light on the relative efficiency of the models' (vis-a-vis the market's) use of market information to estimate the instantaneous variance for the commodity.

The result of pursuing the arbitrage portfolio during the time period of the sample is given in table 8–2. Interpretation of these results should be approached with care.[28] A null hypothesis that the average excess-dollar return is zero cannot be rejected.

In the previous section the model for spot commodity options was tested against a sample of 388 options available during 1973. Regression analysis indicates that the model provided biased, but useful, estimates of the market price. An attempt to exploit differences between model and market prices and to earn riskless arbitrage profits showed results insignificantly different from zero. Thus, a hypothesis of market efficiency could not be rejected.

Dynamics of Futures Prices

In addition to specifying the parametric form and dynamics of the spot price, the futures-spot process must also be specified. Futures contracts, which are defined in the following section, and commodity options written on futures contracts are both contingent upon futures price.

The futures price is the price agreed upon now for further delivery of the commodity. The date at which it is paid (by the buyer to the seller) is specified in the futures contract. The current conventions in futures markets will be described with the definition of futures contracts. Consistency both with the specification of the spot price and also with empirical observations are necessary in the dynamic description of futures prices.

Whether the futures price is equal to the expected spot price is unresolved issue in the literature. Cootner (1967) concluded that hedgers in futures markets (either long or short, whichever predominate) pay speculators a risk premium that is implicit in the futures price. Thus he claims the futures price should *not* equal the expected spot price. Miller (1973) in a capital-asset pricing-model application suggests that her evidence allows for no risk premium. Unfortunately, the key issue of the Cootner (1967) paper was ignored. If hedgers sometimes pay a premium to long speculators, and at other times pay a premium to short speculators, then the optimal holding strategy for a speculator will *not* be a buy-and-hold strategy (which is what Miller (1973) assumes implicitly by calculating average holding-period returns to a long position in futures contracts). Thus, the evidence of that study cannot be relied upon.

The futures price for T periods hence is denoted as $F(t)$ (the maturity notation T is omitted in most contexts). The futures price dynamics are assumed to follow the locally Brownian motion (the superscripts on μ and σ will be omitted when there is no chance for confusion):

$$dF = \mu(F,t)dt + \sigma(F,t)dz$$
$$\mu(F,t) \approx \mu^F(x,S,F,t)$$
$$\sigma(F,t) \approx \sigma^F(x,S,F,t) \tag{8.6}$$

The drift and instantaneous standard deviation are both suppressed functions of inventory and spot price as well as time and the future price. The dependence on inventory and spot price is suppressed, but not forgotten, especially in the empirical estimation.

Again, a broadly specified model (which can be simplified as the evidence dictates) is assumed. Thus, if no mean drift for the futures-price process is observed, $\mu(F,t)$ can be set to zero. Or, if the evidence dictates, a relative diffusion for futures prices can be assumed.

Valuation of Options on Futures Contracts

A futures contract is an unconditional promise to deliver a certain amount (one contract) of the commodity on the delivery date (T) for payment of a price F (known as the futures price for that delivery date). The price is to be paid *on the delivery date*. Thus, if $F(s)$ is the current futures price, then the value of a futures contract at time t, $s < t \leq T$ is:

$$Z(t) = (F(t) - F(s))B(t) \tag{8.7}$$

where $B(t) = e^{r(t-T)}$ is the value of a discount bond. Consistent with empirical evidence on default, the implicit discount bond is assumed to be riskless.

Two problems plague the evaluation of an option on this futures contract. First, an option on this futures contract written at a particular price $F(s)$ will be traded only when the future price again equals $F(s)$. The London Metal Exchange futures and options market closely conform to this particular theoretical construct. Second, most traded futures contracts (the International Commodity Clearing House in London and all American exchanges) required daily settlement by each side of the trade to mark to the current market price. That is, a loser must pay losses to the winner at the close of each day. At any time within the period from initiation to delivery, the actual-settlement-futures-contract value is a complicated function of the discounted disbursements from the settlement process. What starts out to be the simple evaluation of an American commodity option without payouts is actually a complex problem with daily payouts requiring a numerical solution.[29] An approximation to the complex solution is presented in the remainder of this section.

In what follows, assume that the future price sets the value of a pure futures contract to zero at initiation time s where $f = F(s)$ is the futures price at option initiation:

$$Z(s) = (F(s) - f)B(s) = 0.$$

The futures price $F(t)$ follows an absolute diffusion with instantaneous drift and variance that do not depend on the level of prices:

$$dF = \mu dt + \sigma dz.$$

Bt Itô's Lemma, the dynamics of the futures contract are:

$$dZ = \frac{\partial Z}{\partial F} dF + \frac{\partial Z}{\partial t} dt + \frac{1}{2} \frac{\partial^2 Z}{\partial F^2} (dF)^2 \equiv \mu_Z dt + \sigma_Z dz.$$

There are no intermediate payouts from the option or the futures contract, the maturity of the option and futures contract coincide and the exercise price for this option is zero. Once the premium is paid for this option, nothing else is due to complete this option contract! Upon delivery of the futures contract, the liability associated *with the futures contract* is due, but this is *not* part of the option contract.

Using arguments similar to those presented earlier in this chapter, the partial-differential equation for the option price $c(Z,t)$ including the terminal condition is:

$$\frac{1}{2} \sigma_Z^2 c_{ZZ} + rc_Z Z - rc + c_t = 0$$

$$c(Z(T),T) = Z(T)^{+}. \tag{8.8}$$

Performing a standard change of variables on the futures price $F = B(t)^{-1}Z + f$, the partial-differential equation for the value of the option $C(F,t)$ is:

$$\tfrac{1}{2}\sigma^{2}C_{FF} - rC + C_{t} = 0$$

$$C(F(T),T) = (F(T) - f)^{+}. \tag{8.9}$$

Using a technique due to Feller (1951), the solution for the value of an option on a pure futures contract is:[30]

$$C(F,t) = B(t)\{F(t)(N(Y_{1}) + N(Y_{2})) - F(s)(N(Y_{1}) - N(Y_{2}))\}$$
$$+ \sigma\sqrt{T-t}(n(Y_{1}) - n(Y_{2})) \tag{8.10}$$

$$\text{where } Y_{1} = \frac{(F(t) - F(s))B(t)}{\sigma\sqrt{T-t}}$$

$$Y_{2} = \frac{-(F(t) + F(s))B(t)}{\sigma\sqrt{T-t}}$$

$$\text{and } N(x) = \int_{-\infty}^{x} n(y)dy$$

$$n(y) = \frac{1}{\sqrt{2\pi}}\, e^{-y^{2}/2}.$$

Evidence on the Pricing of Commodity Options on Futures Contracts

Although the proposed commodity option-valuation equation does not conform exactly to the settlement convention on the International Commodities Clearing House, it is used as a close surrogate of the correct equation. Data on 155 options traded on seven contracts for three different commodities is presented for the period 12 January 1977 through 31 March 1977. This data represents approximately 1413 contracts of the various commodities. A description of the London commodity options appears in

Table 8–3
London Commodity Options on Soft-Commodity Futures Contracts

Commodity	Contract Size	Premium[a] and Basis[b] Quoted	Commissions[c]
Coffee	five metric tons	£ per metric tons	£ 32
Sugar	fifty metric tons	£ per metric tons	£ 36
Cocoa	ten metric tons	£ per metric tons	£ 32

[a]*Premium* is the price of the option.
[b]*Basis* is the exercise price for the option.
[c]One-half listed commission charged at origination, ½ charged at declaration (no declaration charge, if option abandoned).

table 8–3, the observation period is described in table 8–4, and the distribution of maturities in the sample is displayed in figure 8–3.

London commodity options are (almost) always written with the exercise price equal to the then current price, thus the contract trades initially at the money. Since the exercise price is not one of a small subset of predetermined prices, it is rare for a London option to trade in the secondary market. London options are effectively sold and held by the purchaser.

For each of the 155 option observations, the actual futures price and the maturity were used along with the other parameters to compute a model price for each option. London short-term interest rates for various maturities were obtained from the *Financial Times*. The variance was estimated for both absolute and relative diffusions using various periods of data and techniques.[31] Evidence on how these estimates affect the model option prices is presented later in this section.

The model prices were estimated using an absolute-diffusion option model with an adaptive-variance estimate. These model prices are compared to actual market prices in table 8–5 using simple regression techniques. Overall, the model price explained 84 percent of the variance in market price but this figure is deceptive for reasons that will become apparent shortly. The regression statistics for each of the three commodities and all seven contracts are presented in table 8–5. The intercepts, which are all expected to be zero, are significantly nonzero. The slopes for coffee and cocoa options are insignificantly different from one, but sugar options are mispriced by the model compared to current market price. The residuals for all of the regressions appear to be normal.

A similar regression utilizing prices of options divided by the exercise price is computed to look at the relative pricing ability of the model. Overall the relative model price only explains 34 percent of the variance in relative market price, but the slope is insignificantly different from one for the whole sample. The regression statistics for the relative pricing are given in table 8–6.

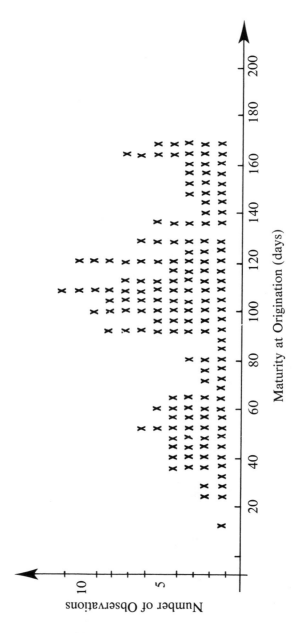

Figure 8–3. London Commodity Options: Distribution of Maturities

Table 8-4
London Commodity Options: Observation Period, 12 January 1977–31 March 1977

Contract	Observation Period	Number of Trading Days	Premium: Number of Observations Available	Volume[a] (Number of contracts) during Observation Period	Average Premium during Observation Period (per contract)	Expiration Date
March coffee	12 Jan 1977–20 Jan 1977	7	4	18	£1375	28 Feb 1977
May coffee	12 Jan 1977–25 Mar 1977	53	27	173	£1615	29 Apr 1977
July coffee	12 Jan 1977–31 Mar 1977	57	42	670	£2555	30 Jun 1977
May sugar	13 Jan 1977–22 Mar 1977	49	13	39	£ 430	1 Apr 1977
August sugar	13 Jan 1977–31 Mar 1977	56	38	410	£ 680	1 Jul 1977
May cocoa	17 Jan 1977–23 Mar 1977	47	16	47	£2280	29 Apr 1977
July cocoa	16 Feb 1977–31 Mar 1977	33	15	56	£2910	30 Jun 1977
			155			

[a]Volume reported is morning plus afternoon transactions where available. Actual volume exceeds this due to missing volume data in early part of period.

Table 8–5
London Commodity Options: Comparison of Market to Model Price and Residual Analysis
(market price) = $\alpha + \beta$*(model price)*

Analysis Variable	β	$H_0: \beta = 0$ t_β	α	t_α	R^2_{ADJ}	$\sigma_{(Residual)}$	$\hat{\sigma}(\beta)$	$H_0: \beta = 1$ t_β	Number of Observations	Studentized Range of Residuals
Overall	1.271	27.976	36	.550	.8354	364.211	.045	5.969	155	5.131
Coffee	.835	8.006	809	5.098	.4670	381.178	.104	1.581	73	3.979
Sugar	1.313	11.666	−205	−2.821	.7299	134.178	.113	2.779	51	5.264
Cocoa	.888	13.481	825	6.082	.8576	211.110	.066	−1.699	31	3.871
March coffee	6.964	4.912	−2584	−3.199	.8852	92.448	1.418	4.206	4	1.758
May coffee	−.236	−.507	1958	3.585	.0000	342.629	.047	−2.658	27	3.499
July coffee	.708	3.714	1084	3.228	.2378	389.965	.191	−1.531	42	3.409[a]
May sugar	1.831	4.864	−352	−2.119	.6538	157.290	.376	2.207	13	3.368
August sugar	1.622	11.184	−446	−4.363	.7705	107.292	.145	4.291	38	3.526
May cocoa	1.374	12.449	110	.629	.9112	98.610	.110	3.391	16	3.129
July cocoa	.959	7.640	600	1.942	.8038	256.945	.125	−.323	15	3.497

Note: Model uses absolute-diffusion-option model with adaptive-variance estimate.

[a]The probability that the estimated statistic (given the sample size) is from a normal distribution is less than .01. Since the errors in measurement of option value are not independent, the tests of significance are suspect. With data from the large transaction base, modifications will be made to perform the correct significance tests.

To check for major differences using absolute or relative-diffusion option-pricing models, the model prices for each diffusion and all variance-estimating techniques were computed. Given the relative homogeneity of the parameters, there was *no* essential difference based on the type of diffusion model used. Nor is a difference expected. If these options were not all at the money, the differences would be much larger.

The effect of various variance estimators and diffusion processes on the overall fit of the model versus the market is estimated and presented in table 8–7. The model fit as measured by R^2 is virtually identical for both processes and all variance techniques. The slope and intercept for the regressions utilizing the adaptive-variance estimate are demonstrably better than the others, with the intercept insignificantly different from zero and the slope nearer to one (although still significantly different than one).

To check the variance estimators another way, the implied standard deviations using an absolute-diffusion option model were calculated and compared to the various standard-deviation estimates. As table 8–8 shows, the adaptive estimates had the lowest mean square and mean absolute errors of the four variance techniques.

As with the spot-commodity options, an arbitrage portfolio was constructed consisting of the correct theoretical portions of the commodity option, futures contract, and riskless security. The results of this arbitrage portfolio are presented in table 8–9. Without including transaction costs, the initial average discrepancy between the market and model price was 436 pounds. The cumulative average hedging loss was 331 pounds, and the total return from the whole arbitrage operation was 104 pounds. While all of these estimates are statistically significant, none include any transaction costs. The inclusion of only the transaction cost of the initial purchase or sale of the option would make the whole arbitrage operation have profits insignificantly different from zero.

Further, to analyze the discrepancies of the model and point the way to improvement, the various market to model performance measures were compared to the starting date, maturity, variance estimate, and exercise prices in tables 8–10 through 8–13. Neither the starting date nor the maturity seems relative specially to the various performance measures. Although the initial guess of the model price is negatively related to the variance estimate, the cumulative hedging returns are positively related to the variance estimate. The total return from the option purchase and hedging operation is not significantly related to the variance estimate. The model performance measures seem to be minimally related to the exercise price.

Overall, the model seems to provide estimates of commodity-option prices on commodity futures contracts that are generally in line with those observed in the market. There does not appear to be significantly positive arbitrage opportunities in the London soft-commodity option market.

Table 8-6
London Commodity Options: Comparison of Market to Model Price—Relative to Exercise Price and Residual Analysis

[market price/exercise price] = $\alpha + \beta$[model price/exercise price]

Analysis Variable	$H_0: \beta = 0$		α	t_α	R^2_{ADJ}	$\sigma_{(Residual)}$	$\sigma(\beta)$	$H_0: \beta = 1$	Number of Observations	Studentized Range of Residuals
	β	t_β						t_β		
Overall	.825	9.010	.0359	4.324	.3424	.0269	.0916	1.910	155	4.443
Coffee	.600	4.173	.0692	5.448	.1857	.0245	.1438	−2.782	73	4.149
Sugar	1.267	10.697	−.0268	−2.343	.6940	.0206	.1184	2.255	51	5.171
Cocoa	.907	16.512	.0317	6.761	.9005	.0084	.0549	−1.694	31	4.049
March coffee	5.956	10.314	−.1501	−6.090	.9723	.0039	.5775	8.582	4	1.943
May coffee	.476	−1.071	.1343	4.289	.0056	.0203	.4443	−1.179	27	3.693
July coffee	−.625	−1.726	.1980	5.415	.0460	.0218	.3623	−4.485	42	4.036
May sugar	1.744	4.300	−.0486	−1.784	.5931	.0249	.0406	18.325	13	3.466
August sugar	1.502	9.458	−.0543	−3.255	.7051	.0175	.1502	3.342	38	3.269[a]
May cocoa	1.296	15.833	.0092	1.744	.9433	.0036	.0819	3.614	16	3.354
July cocoa	.946	9.697	.0256	2.549	.8685	.0104	.0976	−.055	15	3.504

Note: Model uses absolute-diffusion option model with adaptive-variance estimate.

[a]The probability that the estimated statistic (given the sample size) is from a normal distribution is less than .01. Since the errors in measurement of option value are not independent, the tests of significance are suspect. With data from the large transaction base, modifications will be made to perform the correct significance tests.

Table 8-7
London Commodity Options: Overall Comparison of Model to Market Price —Different Variance Estimators and Commodity Processes

(market price) = α + β(model price)

Diffusion Process	Variance Technique	β	$H_0: \beta = 0$ t_β	α	t_α	R^2_{ADJ}	$\sigma_{(Residual)}$	$\hat{\sigma}(\beta)$	$H_0: \beta = 1$ t_β
Absolute	All previous observations	2.257	25.387	−219.4	− 2.707	.8069	394.491	.0889	14.129
Absolute	100-day moving average	1.411	31.138	230.4	4.306	.8628	332.505	.0453	9.068
Absolute	30-day moving average	.781	25.624	598.5	11.409	.8098	391.536	.0305	− 7.200
Absolute	Adaptive	1.271	27.976	35.9	.550	.8354	364.212	.0454	5.966
Relative	All previous observations	2.268	25.103	−211.4	− 2.589	.8034	398.086	.0904	14.038
Relative	100-day moving average	1.419	31.057	233.5	4.36	.8622	333.258	.0457	9.174
Relative	30-day moving average	.788	25.692	597.5	11.412	.8106	390.702	.0307	− 6.93
Relative	Adaptive	1.279	27.934	37.2	.568	.8350	364.667	.0458	6.096

Note : 155 observations of price per contract in pounds.

Table 8–8
London Commodity Options: Direct Comparison of Implied Standard Deviation Estimates with a Priori Estimated Standard Deviations

Variance Technique	Mean Square Error	Mean Absolute Error
All previous observations	32.5681	4.86966
100-day moving average	21.3111	4.09137
30-day moving average	14.4184	3.06333
Adaptive	12.3335	2.82644

Summary and Conclusions

In this chapter, some introductory theoretical aspects of the pricing of commodity options on spot commodities and futures contracts are developed. A detailed discussion of the relevant inventory-carrying theory precedes the development of the models for spot and futures prices. The stochastic processes provided here determine the nature of the solutions for commodity-option prices.

Empirical evidence on the efficiency of the market is considered by comparing the theoretical model prices to the actual market prices, and by looking for riskless arbitrage profits. A sample of traded commodity options on London futures contracts (sugar, coffee, cocoa) is analyzed. Differences from market values are within the bounds of transaction costs. Another sample of options on spot commodities (silver) also demonstrates and confirms the general accuracy of the models previously proposed. Empirically, the option-pricing model provides estimates that are in agreement with the prices of traded options. A hypothesis of commodity option-market efficiency cannot be rejected.

Notes

1. The seminal piece of work on option pricing is Samuelson's (1965b) paper on rational warrant pricing. In that article, and Samuelson's and Merton's (1969) article, an equation for the warrant price is developed, based on relations among the stock, the warrant, and the riskless asset. This research has had several important extensions (Merton 1973; Black and Scholes 1972, 1973) in theory and empirical testing. For recent reviews of stock-option pricing, see Smith (1976) and Cox and Ross (1976b).

2. For example, metal dealers make option markets (primarily selling calls) and mortgage bankers buy puts (standbys) from packagers (and others).

Table 8-9
London Commodity Options: Descriptive Statistics of Market Price versus Model Price

	Mean	Standard Deviation	Minimum	Maximum	Skewness	Kurtosis	Studentized Range	Z^a
Market price/model price	1.272	.384	.599	2.84	.874	1.317[b]	5.81	8.790
Market price–model price (£)	385.4	403.0	−208.9	1214.9	.204	−1.236[b]	3.53[b]	11.868
|Market price−model price| (£)	435.6	347.7	.4	1214.9	.440	−1.086	3.49[b]	15.547
Cumulative hedging £ return	−331.2	645.7	−2227.9	1271.3	−.629	.508	5.42	−6.365
Total £ return	104.4	615.9	−1815.1	2169.7	−.428	.959	6.47	2.103
Final-day-hedge £ return	5.8	42.3	−197.1	371.6	4.936	44.451[b]	13.45[b]	1.702

Note: Model price for this comparison is calculated with variances modeled by an absolute diffusion estimated with an adaptive-filter technique.

[a]H_0: Mean = 0, except market price/model price H_0: Mean = 1; 155 observations.

[b]The probability that the estimated statistic (given the sample size = 155) is from a normal distribution is less than .01. Since the errors in measurement of option value are not independent, the tests of significance are suspect. With data from the large transaction base, modifications will be made to perform the correct significance tests.

Table 8-10

London Commodity Options: Performance of Model versus Market Price—Relationship with Starting Date

(performance measure) $= \alpha + \beta$*(starting date)*

Market-to-Model Performance Measure	β	t_β	α	t_α	R^2_{ADJ}	$\sigma_{(Residual)}$
Market price/model price	−.0064	−5.28	1.55	26.1	.149	.3551
Market price − model price ($£$)	−2.16	−1.58	478.2	7.1	.010	401.1
|Market price − model price| ($£$)	−1.34	−1.13	493.0	8.5	.002	347.4
Cumulative hedging $£$ return	3.08	1.41	−463.5	−4.3	.006	643.7
Total $£$ return	1.74	.83	29.55	.3	.000	616.5

Although no direct evidence exists, Mehl (1934) supports the contention that the trade (large holders) sells options to smaller traders. Throughout that study, Mehl contends (with very little empirical justification) that writers profited far more than did purchasers of privileges (options). (This contention is also popular in the stock-option literature.) The question of whether holders of inventories have a bias toward selling options is, as yet, unanswered.

3. Some demand is obvious to the extent that firms like Goldstein, Samuelson, Inc., grew from nothing to an estimated monthly premium volume of twenty-five million dollars in twenty months. To what extent this is due to fraudulent advertising and intense marketing is unknown. It is also difficult to infer demand from their growth, since there is evidence of serious underpricing of their commodity options.

Table 8-11

London Commodity Option: Performance of Model Versus Market Price—Relationship with Maturity

(performance measure) $= \alpha + \beta$*(maturity)*

Market-to-Model Performance Measure	β	t_β	α	t_α	R^2_{ADJ}	$\sigma_{(Residual)}$
Market price/model price	− .0006	− .82	1.34	16.0	.000	.3853
Market price − model price ($£$)	− .49	− .60	434.4	4.7	.000	403.8
|Market price − model price| ($£$)	− .66	− .93	500.8	6.7	.000	347.8
Cumulative hedging $£$ return	−1.05	− .81	−226.3	− 1.6	.000	646.5
Total $£$ return	−1.71	−1.377	274.5	2.1	.006	614.1

Table 8–12

London Commodity Options: Performance of Model Versus Market Price—Relationship with Variance Estimate

(performance measure = α + β(variance estimate)

Market-to-Model Performance Measure	β	t_β	α	t_α	R^2_{ADJ}	$\sigma_{(Residual)}$
Market price/model price	− .0018	− 8.83	1.49	42.2	.333	.3143
Market price − model price (£)	−1.44	−11.43	651.6	19.5	.457	297.0
|Market price − model price| (£)	−1.14	− 9.75	645.1	20.9	.379	273.9
Cumulative hedging £ return	1.31	5.13	−572.1	− 8.5	.141	598.4
Total £ return	.17	.65	73.0	1.1	.000	617.1

4. In the 1977 case of Lloyd, Carr, Inc., there is evidence of serious overpricing of commodity options. Since deceptive sales techniques have been alleged, it is difficult to infer demand, but annual sales volume when Lloyd, Carr, Inc., closed down was about fifty million dollars. Again, some demand for these options must have existed.

5. The issue of whether a risk premium is part of the price paid by the hedger in the futures case is a controversial topic with much academic research (see Cootner 1967; Johnson 1960; Schrock 1971; and Miller 1973). The payment of a premium for bearing risk is not directly at issue here.

However, it *is* possible to have one market (either option or futures) providing price insurance to hedgers at better rates, with lower transactions costs, or with increased flexibility in terms of hedging their supplies or needs.

Table 8–13

London Commodity Options: Performance of Model Versus Market Price—Relationship with Exercise Price

(performance measure) = α + β(exercise price)

Market-to-Model Performance Measure	β	t_β	α	t_α	R^2_{ADJ}	$\sigma_{(Residual)}$
Market price/model price	−.00002	4.99	.96	13.9	.135	.3580
Market price − model price (£)	.035	9.64	−150.5	− 2.5	.374	318.9
|Market price − model price| (£)	.028	8.43	12.4	.2	.313	288.3
Cumulative hedging £ return	.038	−5.69	249.5	2.2	.168	589.1
Total £ return	−.010	−1.47	262.9	2.23	.008	613.6

Essentially, this is an empirical question requiring investigation of the efficacy and cost of establishing various positions in each market.

6. One conjecture about the relationship between futures and options states that if there were no transaction costs, a futures contract could be made into a European-type option by placing an instantaneous buy and sell stop-loss order on the futures contract at the chosen exercise price.

Practically, completion of the instantaneous orders to buy and sell at the exercise price will *not* always be feasible due to possible jump discontinuities in price and maximum price fluctuations allowable in each day's trading (limits).

With continuous trading, assuming that no limit prices exist and price discontinuities did not occur, it seems that the conversion of the futures contract utilizing the trading scheme described above yields an option at zero premium. Perhaps then, the actual premiums observed (which are nonzero) imply something about the costs of establishing option and futures markets or the magnitude of risk premia in futures markets.

Unfortunately, even with the convenient assumption of continuous trading with diffusion-price, processes and no price limits, a portfolio policy of holding the futures contract only when its current price exceeds some exercise price is an anticipating function of current price. Since futures prices are random, no such portfolio policy can exist.

7. This theory was developed by Holbrook Working (1948, 1949), exposited by Brennan (1958) and Cootner (1964), and extended in Weymar (1968). An excellent summary of these concepts appears in Cootner (1967).

Cootner (1977) has extended the literature in this area by providing a theoretical justification for the supply-of-storage phenomenon.

8. Although convenience yield is generally thought to be evident only in soft commodities such as wheat and cocoa, Hoag (1971) demonstrates the effect for at least one precious metal—silver.

9. Exercise-price change is always present, because the exercise price is in nominal terms. The option contract is *not* protected against inflation. The issue is an index problem, since the value of the exercise price in terms of a basic bundle of commodities changes through time in a stochastic fashion. With short-term options the magnitude of the effect should not be large, but with perpetual options, this effect could predominate.

10. Merton (1973) demonstrates that the necessary call-option protection for a divident payout would be to increase the number of shares to be purchased for the exercise price by a percentage given by the dividend divided by the expayout price.

11. For short-maturity stock options, with known dividends, reducing the stock value by the present value of dividend payouts before the maturity of the option is a good approximation (Scholes 1973). Models developed by

Samuelson (1965b) and Samuelson and Merton (1969) consider the general case when returns on the option and its underlying stock differ. Cox (1975a) and Cox and Ross (1975a) consider the general case where payouts against the underlying return stream are possible.

12. The original work on option pricing by Bachelier (1900) utilized an absolute (arithmetic) diffusion. This process is criticized in contemporary literature as an unrealistic representation of stock prices due to a positive probability of negative prices. Since stock is a limited-liability asset, this can be an undesirable feature. An appropriate solution to the limited-liability problem adds a constraint that converts $S = 0$ to an absorbing or reflecting barrier depending upon the magnitude of bankruptcy costs.

In the case of commodities, *rational* economics will dictate that negative inventory will be an inaccessible (natural) boundary due to the price mechanism. Thus, an underlying absolute-diffusion process for inventory would be controlled by the problem to generate positive prices and have positive inventories held.

13. See Breiman (1968) for a description of locally Brownian processes.

14. In the following developments, subscripts will indicate partial derivatives with respect to the indicated variable; superscripts will designate which stochastic-process inventory (x), spot price (S), future price (F), payout stream (Q), or commodity option (c, C) is currently being considered; and exponents will be used exclusively in conjunction with square brackets where confusion may arise (for example, $[S]^{\beta/2}$).

15. See Itô and McKean (1974) or Gihman and Skorohod (1972) for a description of stochastic-differential equations, and the conditions under which Itô's Lemma is valid.

16. There is some empirical evidence of nonconstant variance for commodity prices (see Rocca 1969 and Mann and Heifner 1976). These studies ignore the inventory dependency and obtain results consistent with a general specification of $\mu(S,t)$ and $\sigma(S,t)$, but not with equation 8.2. Developments by Samuelson (1965b) and Miller (1973) assume that the variance is nonconstant. Evidence in Hoag (1978) supports a model consistent with equation 8.1, but *not* the relative diffusion 8.2.

17. It is interesting to note that Cootner's (1977) characterization of the spot price consists of a component that values the inventory through time at the discounted future price plus an option to sell the spot inventory at any intermediate time, if the price then seems reasonable compared to the discounted future price. This formulation is consistent with the specification of the spot-price dynamics as a locally Brownian motion.

18. The carrying-charge function $q(S,t)$ is assumed to be known with certainty. The estimation of the carrying-charge function from the current futures term structure is discussed in Hoag (1978).

19. The derivation of the option-pricing formula follows the heuristic technique used in previous literature (see Cox 1975a, Cox and Ross 1975). For a detailed proof of the formula including proof of the existence of the portfolio weights using stochastic-control theory see Hoag (1978).

20. The value of the riskless-portfolio weights given $\sigma_c = C_s \sigma(S,t)$ is $\alpha_s = -\alpha_c C_s S / C$ or $n_s = -n_c C_s$.

The option-pricing formula is strictly valid only for European options.

21. Merton (1973) solves the constant case for perpetual options and a relative diffusion. Ingersoll (1976) considers the case of price-proportional payouts for relative diffusions. Cox and Ross (1975) elegantly handle the linear (in-price) payout problem. Schwartz (1975) provides numerical solutions for stocks with discrete dividends using relative diffusions.

If the carrying charges $q(S,t)$ are a power function of the spot price with an exponent one more than the exponent of a constant elasticity of variable diffusion, an analytical solution (involving Bessel functions) can be derived.

22. Although other specifications are possible, the absorbing boundary at $S = 0$ is the simplest condition to impose. The numerical solution does not actually require any specification other than the terminal condition.

23. These options for 10,000 troy ounces of spot silver were bought and sold by Mocatta Metals. Data on exercise price, time to maturity, and premiums came from the *Mocatta Metals Daily Bulletin.*

24. Estimation of the spot price of silver is implicit in the estimate of the carrying-charge function from the current futures term structure (see Hoag 1978).

25. However, Samuelson (1965a) demonstrates that many possible *stationary* stochastic processes are consistent with observed returns on both stocks (with a mean drift) and commodities (with seasonals). This theoretical suggestion implies that the pattern of process-parameter variation over time should be subject to estimation.

26. The procedure and intermediate results are presented in detail in Hoag (1978).

27. The OLS regression equation was market price = 600 + 1.45 model price. OLS estimates of variances are inappropriate in this case since option prices are affected by the same underlying process and hence any errors would not be expected to be independent.

28. The distribution of the errors is nonnormal, and the errors are not independent. Thus, the conclusion should be interpreted carefully until further analysis on the larger data base is available.

29. For further valuation results on commodity options for the two types of futures contracts actually traded in London, see Hoag (1978).

30. A solution to the stock-option problem with an absolute diffusion

appears in Cox and Ross (1975). Black (1976) solves a similiar problem for a relative diffusion.

The solution 8.10 assumes (a second-order approximation) that

$$\sigma \left[\frac{1 - e^{2r(T-t)}}{2r} \right]^{\frac{1}{2}} \approx \sigma\sqrt{T - t}.$$

31. The techniques and evidence on which price process best fits the futures-price data is presented in Hoag (1978).

References

Bachelier, L.J. *Théorie de la Spéculations*. Paris: Gauthier-Villars, 1900. Reprinted in *The Random Character of Stock Market*. Edited by P.H. Cootner. Cambridge, Mass: MIT Press, 1964.

Black, F. "The Pricing of Commodity Contracts." *Journal of Financial Economics* (January/March) 1976.

Black, F., and Scholes, M. "The Pricing of Options and Corporate Liabilities." *Journal of Political Economy* (May/June) 1973.

_____. "The Valuation of Options Contracts and a Test of Market Efficiency." *Journal of Finance* (May) 1972.

Breiman, L. *Probability*. Menlo Park: Addison Wesley, 1968.

Brennan, M.J. "The Supply of Storage." *American Economic Review* (March) 1958.

Commodity Futures Trading Commission. "Recommended Policies on Commodity Option Transactions." 1976.

Cootner, P. "Asset Prices Under Uncertainty: II, Single Risky Asset, Perfectly Anticipated 'Harvests'." Mimeographed. Stanford University, 1977.

_____. "Speculation and Hedging." FRI Symposium on Price Effects of Speculation, 1967.

_____. *The Random Character of Stock Market Prices*. Cambridge, Mass.: MIT Press, 1964.

Cox, J. "The Valuation of Financial Claims." Mimeographed. University of Pennsylvania, (March) 1975a.

_____. "Notes on Option Pricing I: Constant Elasticity of Variance Diffusions." Mimeographed. Stanford University, (September) 1975b.

Cox, J., and Ross, S.A. "The Valuation of Options for Alternative Stochastic Processes." *Journal of Financial Economics* (January/ March) 1976a.

_____. "A Survey of Some New Results in Financial Option Pricing Theory." *Journal of Finance* (May) 1976b.

_____. "The Pricing of Options for Jump Processes." Mimeographed. University of Pennsylvania, 1975b.

_____. "The General Structure of Contingent Claim Pricing." Mimeographed. University of Pennsylvania, 1975a.

Feller, W. *An Introduction to Probability Theory and Its Applications* New York: John Wiley & Sons, 1951.

Gihman, I.I., and Skorohod, A.V. *Stochastic Differential Equations*. New York: Springer-Verlag, 1972.

Hoag, J.W. "The Pricing of Commodity Options: Theoretical and Empirical Research." Ph.D. dissertation, Stanford University, Graduate School of Business, 1978.

_____. "A Comparison of Interest Rates of Various Money Market Instruments and Term Structure Implied in Silver Futures Prices." Mimeographed. Stanford University, 1971.

Ingersoll, J. "A Theoretical and Empirical Investigation of the Dual Purpose Funds: An Applicaton of Contingent-Claims Analysis." *Journal of Financial Economics* (January/March) 1976.

Itô, K., and McKean, H.P., Jr. *Diffusion Processes and Their Sample Paths*. Berlin: Springer-Verlag, 1974.

Johnson, L. "The Theory of Hedging and Speculation in Commodity Futures." *Review of Economic Studies* (June) 1960.

Kruizenga, R.J. "Profit Return from Purchasing Puts and Calls." In Cootner, P. *The Random Character of Stock Market Prices*. Cambridge, Mass.: MIT Press, 1964.

Mann, J. S., and Heifner, R.G. "The Distribution of Short Run Commodity Price Movements." Economic Reporting Service, Technical bulletin no. 1536, March 1976.

Mehl, P. "Trading Privileges on the Chicago Board of Trade." USDA circular no. 323, 1934.

Merton, R.C. "Continuous Time Portfolio Theory and the Pricing of Contingent Claims." Mimeographed. University of Pittsburgh, 1976.

_____. "Theory of Rational Option Pricing." *Bell Journal of Economics and Management Science* 4 (1973).

Miller, Katherine D. "Futures Trading and Investor Returns: An Investigation of Commodity Market Risk Premiums." *Journal of Political Economy* 81 (November/December) 1973.

Rocca, L.H. "Time Series Analysis of Commodity Futures Prices." Ph.D. dissertation, University of California, Berkeley, 1969.

Ross, S.A. "Options and Efficiency." *Quarterly Journal of Economics* 90 (February) 1976.

Samuelson, P.A. "Stochastic Speculative Price." *Proceedings of the National Academy of Sciences* (February) 1971.

_____. "Proof that Properly Anticipated Prices Fluctuate Randomly." *Industrial Management Review* (Spring) 1965a.

_____. "Rational Theory of Warrant Pricing." *Industrial Management Review* (Spring) 1965b.

_____. "Intertemporal Price Speculation: A Prologue to the Theory of Speculation." *Weltwirtschaftliches Archiv* (December 1957).

Samuelson, P.A., and Merton R.C. "A Complete Model of Warrant Pricing that Maximizes Utility." *Industrial Management Review* (Winter) 1969.

Scholes, M. "The Valuation of CBOE Options, An Alternative to Stock Investment." Mimeographed. University of Chicago, 1973.

Schrock, N.W. "The Theory of Asset Choices, Simultaneous Holding of Short and Long Positions in the Futures Markets." *Journal of Political Economy* (March/April) 1971.

Schwartz, E. "Generalized Option Pricing Models: Numerical Solutions and the Pricing of a New Life Insurance Contract." Ph.D. dissertation, University of British Columbia, (September) 1975.

SEC v. Goldstein, Samuelson, Inc. "Complaint,Violation of Registration and Fraud Provisions of the Securities Acts of 1933 and 1934." (73–472–NML).

Smith, C.W. "Option Pricing: A Review." *Journal of Financial Economics* (January/March) 1976.

Stoll, H.R. "The Relationship Between Put and Call Option Prices." *Journal of Finance* (December) 1969.

Weymar, H. *The Dynamics of the World Cocoa Market*. Cambridge, Mass.: MIT Press, 1968.

Working, H. "The Theory of the Price of Storage." *American Economic Review* (December) 1949.

_____. "Theory of the Inverse Carrying Charge in Futures Markets." *Journal of Financial Economics* (February) 1948.

9

Options on Commodity Futures: Recent Experience in the London Market

Stephen Figlewski and
M. Desmond Fitzgerald

Futures contracts and options are closely related both in the instrument and in the manner in which they are traded. But while there are active markets for stock options and for commodity futures in the United States, regulatory approval has not yet been given for the trading of options on futures contracts. In London, on the other hand, a more complete market structure has existed for some time, with simultaneous trading in spot, futures, and options contracts for a number of commodities. This chapter analyzes the price behavior of London commodity options.

It will be worthwhile considering some institutional details about the London market for options on soft commodities. Such options have as their underlying asset a commodity futures contract. That is, if a call option is exercised, it is converted into a long position in the futures contract. The holder receives immediate payment of the exercise value of the option, less the margin required on the open futures position. The option maturity or expiration date is linked to the delivery date of the underlying commodity futures contract. For example, a call option for November cocoa would expire on the last trading day in October, approximately one month before the futures contract reached its delivery date. The precise option expiration dates corresponding to particular futures contracts vary between one soft commodity and another.

Options on soft commodities can be exercised prematurely; that is, they are *American options* in the conventional terminology. If a call option is exercised, creating a long position in the underlying futures contract, and is then closed by selling an identical futures contract, then there will be an immediate settlement of balances between the option buyer and the option seller. Of course, premature exercise is not necessary to lock in a realized profit, since this can be done by trading against the option; that is, selling the underlying future without exercising the option. Let us illustrate this in the case of cocoa. On January 10 an investor purchases a call option on May-delivery coffee with a striking price of 1,500 pounds per ton for a premium of

This research was conducted during 1981–1982 while Stephen Figlewski was a Batterymarch Fellow.

223

150 pounds per ton. By February 10, May coffee is trading at 2,000 pounds per ton. The option holder has a choice. He may exercise the option and close out his position and immediately realize 500 pounds per ton, or he can sell May-coffee futures at 2,000 pounds per ton. If there were no further price changes, he would eventually, at the option-expiration day, receive his 500 pounds per-ton profit. However, in this latter case, the option remains open and he retains the ability to do further trades between February 10 and the option-expiration date. For a floor member of the commodity exchange there would be no margin requirements on such a short futures position offset by an in-the-money commodity-option position.

Nevertheless, like an American put on a share of stock, in certain circumstances it will be optimal to exercise a call option on a futures contract prematurely. This occurs when the interest one could earn on the realizable intrinsic value of the option becomes greater than its remaining time value.

Generally London soft-commodity options are written at-the-money; that is, with the exercise price equal to the prevailing futures price at the time the option is written. There is no organized secondary market for these options. In general, they will be held by the purchaser until either they are exercised or they expire.

The following section describes the Black (1976) valuation model for options written on commodity futures contracts. A later section describes our data sources, followed by a section of the chapter in which we outline the empirical tests applied to London commodity option premiums and describe our test results. The final section presents our conclusions.

The Valuation of Commodity Options

As is well known, the Black and Scholes option-valuation methodology depends upon the insight that if a riskless-hedge portfolio can be set up consisting of the option plus an appropriate position in the underlying asset (whereby, for small movements in the underlying asset price, the change in the value of the option position exactly balances the change in the value of the asset position) then the return to such a portfolio must be the riskless rate of interest. For commodity options, such a riskless-hedge portfolio will consist of a position in the commodity option and an opposite position in the underlying futures contract. Black (1976) derives a variant of the standard Black and Scholes formula applicable to such options. This can be written:

$$C(S,X,T) = e^{-rT} SN(d_1) - XN(d_2)$$
$$d_1 = \frac{ln(S/X) + \sigma^2 T/2}{\sigma\sqrt{T}}$$

$$d_2 = d_1 - \sigma\sqrt{T} \tag{9.1}$$

where S equals the current price of the underlying commodity futures contract; X equals the exercise price; T equals the duration of the option; σ equals the volatility of the futures price; r equals the riskless interest rate; and $N(\ )$ equals the cumulative normal-distribution function.

If we compare this valuation model with the standard Black and Scholes formula, we note that an interest-rate factor has dropped out. This happens because it is assumed that the investment in a futures contract needed to create the riskless-hedge portfolio is zero because of the process of daily settlement of losses and gains to the futures contract. Moreover, the situation in London is even simpler since gains or losses on the options contract are offset against the futures contract before any margin calls are made. Thus as long as the hedge ratio is less than one, which is true by definition, a floor member of the exchange will never face margin calls on the futures side of his hedge portfolio.

However, the Black model only applies strictly to European commodity options, where premature exercise is not possible. As we have indicated earlier premature exercise of these options is sometimes desirable, although we have no statistics for the frequency of premature exercise. Using the Black model to value American options will give "fair" option premiums that are biased low. This should be borne in mind when considering the results discussed later in the chapter.

Another source of inaccuracy in the model price is the fact that it is based on the assumption that the price for the underlying futures contract follows a logarithmic diffusion process with a constant volatility. This process rules out discrete jumps in futures prices, and volatility that varies over time, both of which appear to be features of real-world futures-price movements.

Data and Test Methodology

The data analyzed in this chapter were provided by the International Commodities Clearing House in London, which acts as the central clearing house for all transactions on the London soft-commodity markets. All at-the-money option contracts traded on the soft-commodity exchanges have to be registered with and cleared through this organization. The data set consists of option premiums and related exercise prices for all recorded transactions in cocoa and sugar options for the period January 1980 through June 1981. These are transactions data; that is, the premiums represent true premiums that were actually paid to the option writers. The clearing house provided the data for each trading day in the form of an average premium for all the options traded that day and an average exercise price. Thus when we come to determine model prices, we are essentially considering the case of an investor purchasing a portfolio consisting of all the options traded on a particular day. This makes no essential difference to our valuation procedure. We also obtained the history of daily closing prices for the underlying futures from the clearing house for use in estimating price volatilities. As a measure of the riskless rate of interest, we used the relevant U.K. treasury bill rate. We used our data and the valuation formula 9.1 to estimate theoretical values for the commodity options for comparison with market prices. The one unobservable parameter in the formula is σ, the volatility of the futures price. In estimating model prices, we adopted three alternative measures of σ. These were a long-run estimate calculated from daily price changes in the year preceding the day on which an option was written; a short-run estimate calculated from daily price changes over the previous three months; and the actual volatility of the futures price during the lifetime of the option. The first two use only past-price data that would be available on the day the option was traded, while the third can be thought of as an ideal case; that is, assuming the true volatility were actually known. Thus we have four estimates of each option's value: the market price and three model prices conditional on different volatility estimates.

Because of the importance of duration on option value, we analyze options on each futures position separately. For example, *Sugar 1* refers to options written on the futures contract closest to expiration, *Sugar 2*, the next closest, and so on.

Empirical Results

We first examine the correlations between actual option premiums and the three different sets of model prices. These results are presented in table 9–1. The model prices using actual-volatility estimates are the least correlated with market prices. Moreover it is clear that correlations between model prices based on actual volatilities and prices generated using long-term and short-term historical volatilities are higher than those between market prices and actual-volatility model prices. This in turn suggests that implied variances in option premiums for London soft commodities are inferior predictors of future variances to variances derived from historical price data. This contrasts with the results of Chiras and Manaster (1978) for stock options. Finally, we may also conclude from table 9–1 that long-run variance estimates are better predictors of future variances than short-run estimates, as was observed in our earlier research (1981). Hence, we will utilize only the long-run variance estimates in our subsequent empirical tests.

The next step is to compare the model prices based on actual-volatility estimates and long-run historical-volatility estimates with the actual premiums at which option transactions were carried out. Tables 9–2 and 9–3 show average market prices and model prices for our two different variance estimates, together with mean absolute deviations and t-statistics for the hypothesis that the average prices are equal. Note that the number of observations for table 9–3 is generally smaller than for table 9–2. This is because actual lifetime volatilities, and hence table 9–3 model values, could only be calculated for futures contracts that expired during the sample period, while table 9–2 examines all options written during this period.

For sugar, in contrast to our previous results in Figlewski and Fitzgerald (1981), market prices are fairly close on average to those from the Black model. Only in the case of position-2 options is the difference between average model values and market values very significant, and, again in contrast to previous results, these premiums appear too low relative to model values, rather than too high. However, the mean absolute deviations show that while average values are close, there are fairly wide deviations on both sides.

It is worth mentioning at this point that patterns of overvaluation or undervaluation tend to persist through time, so that differences between model and market prices tend to be significantly autocorrelated. This implies that the t-statistics displayed in tables 9–2 and 9–3 tend to be biased upwards. Even with this bias, however, it does seem as if option premiums are significantly different from their fair-model values. All the cocoa options display market premiums well above their model values, and the degree of overvaluation appears to increase with increasing option duration. The options also seem overvalued when actual-volatility estimates are used in calculating model prices. Thus actual-transactions data confirm our previous conclusion that market premiums are not consistent with values derived from the Black valuation model.

We have already discussed various reasons why the Black model may not be a totally adequate model for valuing London commodity-option premiums, although it is hard to see how the relatively minor inaccuracies of the model could account for all of the discrepancies observed in tables 9–2 and 9–3. In any case, one does not require a totally accurate theoretical model to allow a test of option market efficiency. The appropriate test is whether the differences between model and market premiums constitute an information set upon which one can base a trading rule that produces abnormal risk-adjusted returns.

The procedure is to analyze the performance of hedge portfolios. Black and Scholes (1972) show that if one balances an option position against an opposite position in the underlying asset, one can create an approximately riskless hedge at each instant of time. The hedge ratio; that is, the quantity of the underlying asset to be sold against one unit of the option held long, is given by $e^{-rT}N(d_1)$, with terms defined as in equation 9.1. Of course, this

Table 9–1
Correlation of Market and Model Prices
Table 9–1a
Market Prices with Alternative-Model Prices

Option	Long-Run Variance Estimate	Short-Run Variance Estimate	Actual Variance
Sugar 1	0.626	0.665	0.621
Sugar 2	0.097	0.389	−0.189
Sugar 3	0.237	0.065	−0.114
Sugar 4	0.041	−0.005	0.056
Sugar 5	0.860	0.137	0.719
Cocoa 1	0.808	0.888	0.823
Cocoa 2	0.449	0.702	0.193
Cocoa 3	0.561	0.765	0.793
Cocoa 4	0.720	0.841	0.395
Cocoa 5	0.877	0.845	−0.505
Cocoa 6	0.871	0.910	—

value will change as a result of changes in the underlying asset price and the duration of the option contract. Technically the riskless nature of the hedge depends upon continuous rebalancing. In practice this is not possible—but if rebalancing is done only on a discrete basis then the return to the hedge portfolio becomes risky. We look at three rebalancing strategies: one where we rebalance every day as in Black and Scholes (1972), one where we rebalance every ten days, and finally a situation where we do not balance at

Table 9–2
Summary Statistics for Market and Model Prices Using Historical Volatility

	Position 1	Position 2	Position 3	Position 4	Position 5
Sugar					
Average market price	11.89	15.92	34.84	45.09	46.88
Average duration	1.1	3.7	7.1	9.9	13.8
Average model price	14.85	31.31	40.15	46.47	39.16
(*t*-statistic)	(2.65)	(13.82)	(4.57)	(0.97)	(8.94)
Mean absolute deviation	3.57	16.22	9.02	7.63	7.73
Number of observations	31	113	131	82	40
Cocoa					
Average market price	43.43	72.00	100.12	112.37	124.78
Average duration	2.1	3.8	8.1	11.6	14.6
Average model price	31.43	51.83	60.88	70.47	80.55
(*t*-statistic)	(1.38)	(4.94)	(19.84)	(23.84)	(27.62)
Mean absolute deviation	16.95	24.46	39.34	41.89	44.23
Number of observations	7	23	74	94	54

Table 9–1 b
Actual-Variance-Model Prices with Alternative-Model Prices

Actual Variance	Long-Run Variance Estimates	Short-Run Variance Estimates
Sugar 1	0.346	0.594
Sugar 2	0.890	0.539
Sugar 3	0.882	0.456
Sugar 4	0.980	0.532
Sugar 5	0.594	0.543
Cocoa 1	0.972	0.986
Cocoa 2	0.800	0.499
Cocoa 3	0.963	0.725
Cocoa 4	0.850	0.504
Cocoa 5	0.938	0.755

all over the life of the option. Boyle and Emanuel (1980) show that for discretely adjusted option hedges, conventional t-statistics used to test for the existence of significant excess returns are biased downwards because of serious skewness in the return distribution.

We examine two different alternative hedge-portfolio strategies. The first approach is to buy all the option contracts at market prices. The second is to

Table 9–3
Prices Using Actual Volatility

	Position 1	Position 2	Position 3	Position 4	Position 5
Sugar					
Average market price	14.46	15.56	28.85	48.47	39.70
Average duration	1.5	4.0	7.8	10.3	14.8
Average model price	19.10	46.72	48.68	52.75	46.54
(t-statistic)	(2.45)	(14.17)	(7.56)	(2.05)	(5.78)
Mean absolute deviation	4.78	31.80	21.43	9.20	7.14
Number of observations	14	66	49	38	21
Cocoa					
Average market price	71.67	71.95	100.12	125.61	138.83
Average duration	2.1	3.5	6.7	9.5	12.8
Average model price	36.30	51.57	66.04	81.18	93.76
(t-statistic)	(3.10)	(4.40)	(16.27)	(28.36)	(26.92)
Mean absolute deviation	35.36	24.73	34.12	44.44	45.07
Number of observations	3	21	37	37	29

Notes: Average duration is in months.
      t-statistics relate to the hypothesis that the average market and model prices are equal.

buy the options the model shows to be undervalued and sell the overvalued options at market prices. Of course, in different cases the portfolios chosen will be different according to the variance estimate used in constructing the model prices.

The intuitive rationale for these alternative investment strategies is fairly clear. A policy of buying all the options at the market prices in conjunction with a riskless hedge tests whether the options are systematically misvalued in the market. The second strategy tests whether the use of the valuation model can generate excess returns to trading in the commodity option market in the sample period.

Profits to the portfolios are defined as the return in pounds sterling in excess of the riskless rate of interest. We assume the investor is a floor member of the exchange so that he or she will not face margin calls on the futures contract side of the hedge portfolio as discussed earlier. Table 9–4 presents results for an investor buying all the options at market prices, either unhedged or in hedged portfolios, with the three rebalancing strategies. We immediately see that the strategy of buying all options at market prices and not hedging gives uniformly negative and significant returns. This is true for both cocoa, where market prices appeared to be overvalued relative to model values, and sugar, where, in general, option premiums appeared too low relative to model values. However, the profits consequently accruing to naked option writing are very risky, as evidenced by the standard deviations of the profits.

When we consider buying these options and putting them in a hedge portfolio, however, the picture changes considerably. Buying all sugar options at the market prices and hedging produces consistently positive returns that are generally significant. We can also observe that the effect of rebalancing goes in the expected direction. Moving from no rebalancing to ten-day rebalancing produces a substantial reduction in the standard deviation of profit, while all returns remain significantly positive. We note also that most of the risk reduction occurs in moving from no rebalancing to rebalancing every ten days. Moving to one-day rebalancing produces little additional risk reduction.

The results for hedging cocoa options also produces results consistent with the overvaluation observed in tables 9–2 and 9–3. For the portfolios where we rebalance, buying uniformly overvalued options produces consistent negative returns. We may also note that the positive returns recorded when we do not rebalance are a product of the consistent fall in cocoa-futures prices during our sample period; since futures prices fell, the short hedge in the futures contract made money while the option prices were bounded at zero.

In general, the results for these hedged portfolios confirm the message of the over- and undervaluation observed in tables 9–2 and 9–3, and suggest

Table 9-4
Mean Excess Return per Trade to Buying All Options

| | Unhedged | | Hedged | | | | | |
| | | | No Rebalancing | | Ten-Day Rebalancing | | One-Day Rebalancing | |
	Mean	Standard Deviation	Mean	Standard Deviation	Mean	Standard Deviation	Mean	Standard Deviation
Sugar 1	− 6.47 (3.11)	11.59	2.10 (1.63)	7.17	3.86 (2.94)	7.31	5.12 (3.14)	5.21
Sugar 2	− 12.18 (5.21)	23.38	31.34 (9.36)	33.47	22.31 (8.53)	26.16	23.17 (9.74)	23.79
Sugar 3	− 27.73 (7.33)	36.67	29.52 (9.28)	30.84	14.94 (8.24)	17.57	15.51 (8.91)	16.87
Sugar 4	− 46.60 (12.57)	26.99	4.73 (0.85)	40.52	8.98 (3.02)	21.67	10.04 (4.24)	17.26
Sugar 5	− 39.90 (6.74)	33.98	− 19.05 (3.89)	28.13	− 2.00 (0.84)	13.62	7.13 (3.64)	11.27
Cocoa 1	− 49.77 (2.85)	39.03	− 10.19 (0.80)	28.48	− 13.70 (1.43)	21.46	− 21.88 (1.82)	26.86
Cocoa 2	− 75.57 (8.64)	22.60	39.40 (4.17)	44.36	− 9.25 (7.20)	27.15	− 19.15 (3.97)	22.61
Cocoa 3	− 109.72 (43.71)	18.79	44.26 (5.63)	58.88	− 31.34 (11.08)	21.16	37.92 (15.93)	17.81
Cocoa 4	− 136.07 (89.42)	11.18	104.63 (12.02)	63.97	− 30.91 (14.56)	15.60	− 41.63 (26.71)	11.45
Cocoa 5	− 157.65 (82.01)	11.03	181.44 (26.49)	39.34	− 24.92 (11.67)	12.27	− 38.98 (19.93)	11.23

Note: t-statistics on the hypothesis that the mean return is zero are in parentheses.

there is potential for earning abnormal trading profits by using the differences between model and market prices.

Our final set of results analyzes the profitability of two strategies, both involving buying undervalued and selling overvalued options at market prices in a hedge-portfolio context. The first strategy is an operational strategy where we use long-run historical-volatility estimates to calculate model prices, for reasons we have discussed earlier, and where we rebalance the hedge portfolios every ten days. Ten-day rebalancing seems to achieve adequate risk reduction, while at the same time serving to keep monitoring and transactions costs to reasonble levels. We also give the results for what we term an ideal strategy: namely one where we use actual-volatility estimates to calculate model prices and rebalance the hedge portfolios every day. This strategy should give the maximum profits that could be achieved by a model-based trading rule, if the true volatility were known in advance.

For each set of portfolios table 9–5 gives the mean return, the t-statistics on the hypothesis that the mean return is zero, and appropriate loss statistics.

If we take the case of cocoa options first, in every case except for position-1 options, the excess returns to the operational strategy are positive and highly significant. Moreover, there is little evidence that using actual ex-post variances to estimate model prices results in a significant increase in profitability. More impressive than the actual profit figures are the loss statistics for the operational strategy for cocoa. Even for cocoa position 1 only 40 percent of trades show losses and the percentage drops to less than 10 percent for position 3 and actually to zero for position-4 options. The largest loss is always small relative to the average profit and to the net cash flow taken out of the position. As expected, the loss statistics improve further as we move from the operational to the ideal strategy.

The results for sugar options are very similar, though profit levels are not so high. Even so, mean profits are statistically significant for all options other than position-5 options, and the percentage of losses is never higher than 30 percent for the first four positions. Once again, moving from the operational strategy to the ideal strategy changes profits and loss statistics in the expected direction.

Overall these results present strong evidence that differences between market premiums and model prices derived from the Black model using historical-variance estimates constitute an information set that can be used to develop strategies of relatively low risk that earn substantial excess returns. This confirms the results from our earlier analysis of option data from 1977–1978. We note that this conclusion does not require that the Black model be a fully accurate valuation model for London commodity options. Moreover, transactions costs alone can not fully explain these results. The structure of commissions on the London soft-commodity exchanges is such that a floor

Table 9–5
Excess Returns to Strategies of Buying Undervalued and Selling Overvalued Options in a Hedged Portfolio

	Cocoa 1	Cocoa 2	Cocoa 3	Cocoa 4	Cocoa 5	Sugar 1	Sugar 2	Sugar 3	Sugar 4	Sugar 5
Operational Strategy										
Mean	13.70	16.54	31.34	30.91	24.92	3.05	22.31	14.76	10.69	2.00
(*t*-statistic)	(1.43)	(3.34)	(11.08)	(14.56)	(11.67)	(2.20)	(8.53)	(8.08)	(3.73)	(0.84)
Standard deviation	21.46	23.24	21.16	15.60	12.27	7.10	26.17	17.72	20.86	13.62
Average cost	−48.80	−66.10	−102.92	−124.59	−140.18	8.12	11.11	4.10	−13.29	−46.29
Percent of losses	40.0	27.3	8.93	0.0	6.1	25.8	14.0	19.2	26.42	42.4
Largest loss	−3.12	−20.12	−18.25	0.00	−2.73	−12.40	−7.16	−28.09	−62.30	−29.71
Ideal Strategy										
Mean	33.60	21.28	26.70	35.06	33.31	8.78	37.62	25.47	9.67	4.08
(*t*-statistic)	(2.01)	(5.35)	(12.35)	(19.15)	(17.54)	(6.50)	(14.74)	(9.46)	(3.99)	(3.01)
Standard deviation	28.97	18.30	13.15	11.14	10.23	5.05	20.74	18.84	14.93	6.20
Average cost	−71.67	−64.72	−100.15	−125.61	−138.83	11.61	12.59	15.50	9.91	26.37
Percent of Losses	0.0	14.3	2.7	0.0	0.0	7.1	0.0	2.0	10.5	23.81
Largest loss	0.00	−8.34	−2.12	0.00	0.00	−3.72	0.00	−0.71	−50.83	−2.41

Note: The *operational strategy* uses historical-volatility estimates and rebalances the hedge portfolio every ten trading days. The *ideal strategy* uses actual volatility over the option's life and rebalances daily. *t*-statistics related to the null hypothesis that the mean excess return to the strategy is zero.

member of the exchange can realize the profits outlined in table 9–5 net of transactions costs. While transactions costs could substantially diminish potential profits to these trading strategies for nonmembers of the exchange, this would not be case for full members.

The second explanation that might be put forward is that we have not tried to analyze the riskiness of these returns in terms of systematic and nonsystematic components. Hence we cannot say that these returns really constitute abnormal risk-adjusted returns in a capital-asset-pricing-model sense. While we freely confess we have not carried out such a test, which is a task for future research, the numbers represented in table 9–5 are so large that this explanation seems unlikely.

Conclusions

We are basically left with two main conclusions. First it does not appear as if the simple Black model is fully appropriate for valuing these London commodity options. This is to be expected since it is based on very specific assumptions about the stochastic process followed by futures prices and does not take into account the possibility of premature exercise. More work clearly needs to be done on establishing complete models for commodity option valuation.

Even so, we find the abnormal returns and loss percentages for our hedge portfolios purchased at market prices hard to reconcile with the view that divergences between model prices and market prices are due simply to an inadequate model. Nor does the existence of transactions costs seem likely to be a full explanation, since all the profits shown can be earned by exchange members net of transaction costs. (The fixed cost of buying and maintaining a membership remains, however.) The evidence we have found points to the conclusion that there is at present little model-based trading in this market and that option premiums are being determined by the interplay of supply and demand from writers and buyers who view options primarily as trading instruments. In that case, option prices will reflect traders' speculative forecasts of the evolution of the price for the underlying futures contract, rather than being set in a manner consistent with theoretical contingent-claims valuation models.

It is worth noting that early tests of the Black Scholes model in the U.S. stock market; for example, Black and Scholes (1973) and Galai (1977), also showed statistically significant deviations of market from model prices and excess returns to hedged portfolios. These appeared to be much smaller in percentage terms than what we have found for commodity options, but this may be due to the fact that the required equity investment in a hedged option-stock portfolio is much larger than for an option-futures portfolio. It is not clear how different the "mispricing" of the options themselves is in the London Market than it was for U.S. stocks before use of the options-pricing model became widespread.

References

Black, F. "The Pricing of Commodity Contracts." *Journal of Financial Economics* 3 (1976): 167–179.

Black, F., and Scholes, M. "The Valuation of Option Contracts and a Test of Market Efficiency" *Journal of Finance* 27 (1972): 399–417.

Boyle, P., and Emanuel, D. "Discretely Adjusted Option Hedges." *Journal of Financial Economics* 8 (1980): 259–282.

Chiras, D.P., and Manaster, S. "The Information Content of Option Prices and a Test of Market Efficiency." *Journal of Financial Economics* 6 213–234.

Figlewski, S., and Fitzgerald, M.D. "The Pricing Behaviour of London Commodity Options" Chicago Board of Trade International Research Seminar Series, 1981.

Galai, D. "Tests of Market Efficiency of the Chicago Board Options Exchange." *Journal of Business* 50 (1977): 165–197.

List of Contributors

Edward C. Blomeyer, Louisiana State University

Richard A. Brealey, London Business School

Michael J. Brennan, University of British Columbia

Edwin T. Burton, Smith Barney, Harris Upham & Company

John C. Cox, Stanford University

Stephen Figlewski, New York University

M. Desmond Fitzgerald, The City University of London

Dan Galai, Hebrew University and University of California, Los Angeles

James W. Hoag, University of California, Berkeley

Stewart D. Hodges, London Business School

Robert Jarrow, Cornell University

Robert C. Klemkosky, Indiana University

Mark Rubinstein, University of California, Berkeley

Andrew Rudd, Barr Rosenberg Associates

Eduardo S. Schwartz, University of British Columbia

Michael J.P. Selby, London Business School

About the Editor

Menachem Brenner is a senior lecturer at the Jerusalem School of Business, Hebrew University, and a visiting professor at the Graduate School of Business Administration, New York University. He received the B.A. at the Hebrew University and the Ph.D. at Cornell University. He has served as visiting professor at the University of California, Berkeley, and at the University of Bergamo. He also has served as a research associate at the Bank of Israel. He is the author or coauthor of numerous articles. His current research interests include empirical investigations of the option-pricing theory, inflation and asset life, and dividends and taxes.